Life Of The Amir Dost Mohammed Khan, Of Kabul V1: With His Political Proceedings Towards The English, Russian, And Persian Governments

Mohan Lal

LIFE

OF THE

AMIR DOST MOHAMMED KHAN,

OF

KABUL:

WITH HIS POLITICAL PROCEEDINGS TOWARDS THE

ENGLISH, RUSSIAN, AND PERSIAN GOVERNMENTS,

INCLUDING THE

VICTORY AND DISASTERS OF THE BRITISH ARMY

IN

AFGHANISTAN.

BY MOHAN LAL, Esq.,

KNIGHT OF THE PERSIAN ORDER OF THE LION AND SUN ; LATELY ATTACHED TO THE
MISSION IN KABUL.

IN TWO VOLUMES.

VOL. I.

LONDON:

LONGMAN, BROWN, GREEN, AND LONGMANS,

PATERNOSTER-ROW.

———

1846.

MOHAN LÁL, K.L.S.

HER MOST GRACIOUS MAJESTY QUEEN VICTORIA.

DEDICATION

TO

HER MOST GRACIOUS MAJESTY QUEEN VICTORIA,

SOVEREIGN OF

GREAT BRITAIN AND OF THE INDIAN EMPIRE,

AND TO HER ROYAL CONSORT,

HIS ROYAL HIGHNESS THE PRINCE ALBERT.

SINCE the creation of the world it has been the custom and rule of the devoted loyal servants of every ancient and modern Government, that either on receiving marks of distinction, or the honour of being presented to their lawful Sovereign, they submit some present showing their homage and attachment to the Throne. This usage of submissive devotion has not been limited to human beings, but it has been adopted ever by other species of God's creatures, and has met with the approbation of the greatest in the world. If we trace back as far as three thousand years, we find, from tradition as well as from historical anecdotes, one of the most striking instances in an insignificant creature of God, namely, a small ant having secured a grain of rice in its forceps, crept some distance, and having gained an access into the presence of the wise and great Solomon, laid it under his feet, who accepted the said present ! !

My fortunes have been bright, and I may say enviable, even in this land, by having the honour of being presented to your Majesty and to your Royal Highness, and also invited to your palace. The conversation which I had the good fortune to have with your Royal Highness, mingled with your detailed and minute knowledge of all the sad events of Afghanistan, did not only cause sensations of surprise in me, but was a source of proud gratification as showing that the conduct and zeal of public servants abroad, whether English or foreigner, are justly noticed and appreciated by so dignified a personage as your Royal Highness. Taking all the preceding points into consideration, I am utterly at a loss how to show my heartfelt gratitude, and in what manner to lay my unfeigned homage and devoted attachment at the feet of your gracious Majesty and your Royal Highness but by dedicating this work—the unworthy endeavours of my feeble pen in a foreign language.

If the honour so to dedicate this book is conferred upon me, it will at once show to the subjects of your Majesty's Indian Empire, that your Majesty knows how to appreciate their fidelity and devotion, and will lead them to the lofty consideration and appreciation of their present English Sovereign in a more dignified manner than they or their predecessors had ever enjoyed.

For my own humble part, I shall say no more; but conclude this dedication by adding that, while I live I shall consider myself the proudest and happiest servant by promoting the honour and interest of your mighty Government, and with heart shall ever pray, that as long as the oceans are filled with water, and the heavens decorated with sun and moon, the gracious shadow of your Majesty and his Royal Highness the Prince Albert may never be diminished from the heads of your British and Indian subjects, and both the kingdoms of England and India may never be deprived of the protection of your royal descendants.

MOHAN LAL, *Kashmirian.*

(*In the Service of the Honourable East India Company.*)

4, *George Street, Manchester Square,*
London, 20th *June,* 1846.

PREFACE.

THE kind reception which my late publication, 'Travels in the Panjab and Afghanistan,' has met with from the public, deserves my hearty thanks. The greater part of my Travels having been published some years ago, had in some measure lost the interest of novelty; but the flattering mention made of them in the last edition of the valuable work of the Honourable Mountstuart Elphinstone,* a most

* " Mohan Lal, a (Kashmirian) gentleman of Delhi, accompanied Sir Alexander Burnes to Bokhara, and came back by Mashad and Hirat, has also published his travels. They appeared in English at Calcutta, and would have been invaluable if they had not been preceded by the works already mentioned. Even now they contain much new matter, and from the spirit of inquiry and observation as well as the command of a foreign language which they display, reflect high credit on the author and on the English Institution (now the College) at Delhi, where he received his education."—ELPHINSTONE's *Kabul*, 1838.

talented and respected authority of this country, induced me to reprint them, with some additional information on the Commerce of the marts on the Indus.

Neither in the preceding publication nor in this, do I for a moment pretend to boast of the value of its information, eloquence, or style. On the contrary, I am fearfully conscious of abundant errors both in grammar, idiom, and, above all, of repetitions; but when I tell the public that I am a stranger to the customs, manners, and in great measure to the language of the English, and that I have written the MSS. and published these two volumes in a short space of time, without the assistance of a friend, as I had expected, I feel assured that I shall be excused on account of these great deficiencies. Whatever portion of the MSS. of these volumes (excepting about one hundred pages in the beginning) I was able to write every day, went to press immediately in the same way; and this will plainly account for errors and repetitions.

Besides the great expense incurred by the publishers in bringing out my late Travels, and these volumes, I beg to state, that about 300*l.* has been disbursed by me in employing a copyist, paper, and some of the portraits; a fact which will exonerate me from the imputation of having published them merely with the view of benefiting myself by their sale.

Whilst in Afghanistan I had prepared the ' Life of Dost Mohammed Khan,' both in English and Persian; and the information on which the MS. was prepared was supplied to me by his own courtiers and relations: but unfortunately all the MSS. were plundered during the insurrection of Kabul, and delivered to Mohammed Akbar Khan, who refused to give them back to me on any account. Afterwards it was out of my power to collect such satisfactory accounts as would place the circumstances of the Amir's life in a chronological series; and I therefore fear that these volumes will on many occasions be open to censure for misplacing the occurrences and the subjects contained in them.

The anecdotes inserted in the work, and especially in reference to the adventures and morals of the Amir Dost Mohammed Khan, &c., were generally communicated to me by the people with whom he associated. Not knowing what would be agreeable to the "English mind," and anxious as I was to avoid anything unpleasant of every kind, particularly when the Dedication was approved of by Her Majesty, and returned to me with only one correction, I wrote to the publishers and printers to erase such lines from the manuscripts as they might think not consistent with the rules of this country. To this, I am told, they kindly attended.

The Dedication to Her Majesty, and, I may say, the whole of the work, is written after the Persian style. Purity of idiom and eloquence in composition, which are at the command of the natives of this civilized land, are not to be expected from a foreigner of a limited education, like myself. The generosity of the impartial community at large will, on these considerations, forgive me for the blunders of every description which may disfigure the pages of these unworthy volumes.

The observations which I have made on our policy in Afghanistan, the reasons of sending an expedition, its means of success, and the cause of the disasters, are entirely the repetition of what I had despatched to the Government of India, in 1842, and which received the favourable notice of the Earl of

Ellenborough, then Governor-General of India. His Lordship writes to the Secret Committee at home in the following flattering manner.*

" In the letter from the intelligent Mohan Lal, which forms one of the enclosures of this letter, your Honourable Committee will be put in possession of the manner in which the King Shah Shuja-ul-Mulk was, on the 5th April, treacherously murdered by a son of Navab Mohammed Zaman Khan.

" Your Honourable Committee will peruse with deep interest the observations on the causes of the late insurrection at Kabul.

" Your Honourable Committee will find amongst the enclosures No. 24, an interesting paper by Mohan Lal, on the causes of the Afghan insurrection, and on the events which succeeded the outbreak at Kabul in November last.

(Signed) " ELLENBOROUGH."

The opinions so favourably expressed by this high

* 'Parliamentary Blue Book of Afghanistan,' pages 262, 264, 341.—I have left out many words, and omitted several other names, to make this extract as short as possible.

and talented personage then holding the reins of the empire of India, will, I am sure, be a sufficient ground for me to request the public to throw a glance on the contents of these volumes, and to grant forgiveness for the errors.

MOHAN LAL, *Kashmirian.*

30th June, 1846.

4, *George Street,*
Manchester Square, London.

CONTENTS OF VOL. I.

CHAPTER III.

CHAPTER IV.

CHAPTER V.

CHAPTER X.

CHAPTER XI.

CHAPTER XII.

ILLUSTRATIONS OF VOL. I.

LIFE

OF THE

AMIR DOST MOHAMMED KHAN,

OF

KABUL.

CHAPTER I.

Sons of Abdal—Honourable Mountstuart Elphinstone, late Captain Arthur Conolly, and Sir Alexander Burnes—Predecessors of Dost Mohammed Khan—Origin of the Afghans—Sons of Rahimdad—Dost's Father becomes Chief—Promoted—Goes to punish the Momand Chief—Gets a title—Goes to fight the Osbeks—Places Zaman on the throne—Salary of Dost's father —Dost strikes coin so as to honour the name of his father— Envy of Vafadar Khan against Sarfraz Khan—Names of the Chiefs murdered with Sarfraz Khan—Folly of Vafadar Khan —Miracle of Dost's uncle.

ABDAL was the first and founder of the Abdali tribe. He left three sons, namely, Fofal, Barak, and Alako. If I were to mention the names and lineal descent of the offspring of Fofal and Alako, it would lengthen

B

this book too much. The very valuable account of
the kingdom of Kabul, by the Honourable Mountstuart Elphinstone, contains a correct and minute
description of their descendants, as well as botanical,
mineral, and animal information concerning that territory. In short, this interesting work has been a
guide to many, and is as useful to travellers in Afghanistan as the mariner's compass is to voyagers on
the seas. This honourable gentleman has made an
everlasting impression on the minds of the people of
Central Asia of his most amiable, kind, and noble
disposition. It is a source of great pride to the travellers of Europe or British India to hear his name
even into the remotest parts of Afghanistan with
respect and tone of affection from the lips of those
who are in general unaware of the names of the distinguished men of their own country. His generosity
has gained for him the immortal name of " Hatim
Tai,"* and his talents as a statesman the high appellation of " Socrates."† I can without any hesitation
say that it was the name of " Ulfrishteen " (Elphinstone) which was the passport for the " army of the

* Famous for unlimited bounties in the old Persian histories.
† Celebrated minister and adviser of Alexander the Great.

Indus" to march through Afghanistan without any
opposition.   The valuable books of the late Captain
Arthur Conolly and of Sir Alexander Burnes give
us descriptions which also add to our knowledge of
this celebrated and far-extended tribe.   My object
is to write about the early life, rise, and government
of Dost Mohammed Khan, mentioning the names of
his immediate predecessors, the sons of Barak, and
not the sons of Fofal and of Alako.

Haji Jamal Khan, grandfather of Dost Mohammed Khan, was son of Usaf, son of Yaru, son of
Mohammed, son of Ȯmar Khan, son of Khizar
Khan, son of Ismail, son of Nek, son of Daru, son
of Saifal, son of Barak, the second son of Abdal.
Tradition says that through successive generations
Abdal descended from the Israelitish household; but
to speak the truth, the origin of the Afghans is so
obscure, that no one, even among the oldest and
most clever of the tribe, can give satisfactory information on this point.   Some of the Afghans, recognising their descent from the children of Israel, feel
ashamed of their being related by blood to the Jews,
upon whom they look as infidels.   Concerning the
obscurity of the true descent of the Afghans, if curi-

osity induces any one to desire to know more on that difficult subject, I can safely refer to and justly quote from the highly esteemed book by the Honourable Mountstuart Elphinstone. "After this cursory notice of the facts relating to the Afghans which are ascertained by authentic history, we may now examine what they say of themselves. The account they give of their own origin is worthy of attention, and has already attracted the notice of an eminent Orientalist. They maintain that they are descended from Afghan, the son of Irmia, or Berkia, son of Saul, king of Israel, and all their histories of their nation begin with relating the transactions of the Jews from Abraham down to the captivity. Their narrative of those transactions appears to agree with that of the other Mohammedans; and though interspersed with some wild fables, does not essentially differ from the Scripture. After the captivity (they allege that) part of the children of Afghan withdrew to the mountains of Ghore, and part to the neighbourhood of Mecca, in Arabia.

"So far this account is destitute of probability. It is known that ten of the twelve tribes remained in the East after the return of their brethren to

Judea, and the supposition that the Afghans are
their descendants explains easily the disappearance
of the one people and the appearance of the other.
The rest of the story is confirmed by the fact that
the Jews were very numerous in Arabia at the time
of Mohammed, and the principal division of them
bore the appellation of Khyber, which is still a district in Afghanistan, if not of an Afghan tribe. The
theory is plausible, and may be true; but when
closely examined, it will appear to rest on a vague
tradition alone; and even that tradition is clouded
with many inconsistencies and contradictions.

" The Afghan historians proceed to relate that the
children of Israel, both in Ghore and in Arabia,
preserved their knowledge of the unity of God and
the purity of their religious belief, and that on the
appearance of the last and greatest of the prophets
(Mohammed) the Afghans of Ghore listened to the
invitation of their Arabian brethren, the chief of
whom was Khauled (or Caled), son of Waleed, so
famous for his conquest of Syria, and marched to
the aid of the true faith, under the command of
Kyse, afterwards surnamed Abdoolresheed. The
Arabian historians, on the contrary, bring the descent

of Khauled from a well known tribe of their own
nation, omit the name of Kyse on their list of the
prophets, companions, or allies,* and are entirely
silent on the subject of the Afghan succours. Even
the Afghan historians, although they describe their
countrymen as a numerous people during their Arabian campaign, and though it appears from a sarcasm
attributed by those historians to the Prophet (who
declared Pushtoo to be the language of hell), that
they already spoke their national and peculiar tongue,
yet do not scruple in another place to derive the
whole nation from the loins of the very Kyse who
commanded during the period of the above-mentioned transactions.

" If any other argument were required to disprove
this part of the history, it is furnished by the Afghan
historians themselves, who state that Saul was the
forty-fifth in descent from Abraham, and Kyse the
thirty-seventh from Saul. The first of these gene-
alogies is utterly inconsistent with those of the Sacred Writings, and the second allows only thirty-
seven generations for a period of sixteen hundred

* Ansaur, " Assisters."

years.* If to these facts we add that Saul had no son named either Irmia or Berkia, and that if the existence of his grandson Afghan be admitted, no trace of that patriarch's name remains among his descendants; and if we consider the easy faith with which all rude nations receive accounts favourable to their own antiquity, I fear we must class the descent of the Afghans from the Jews with that of the Romans and the British from the Trojans, and that of the Irish from the Milesians or Bramins." †

* This number is from the Taureekhee Sher Shaubee. The Taureekhee-Morussa give a much greater number, but then it introduces forty-five generations between Abraham and Jacob.

† This subject is briefly discussed by Sir William Jones, in a note on a translation by Mr. Vansittart (*Asiatic Researches*, vol. ii., Art. 4). That elegant scholar is inclined to believe this supposed descent, which he strengthens by four reasons. His first argument is drawn from the resemblance of the name of Hazaureh to Arsareth, the country whither the Jews are said by Esdras to have retired; but this reasoning, which was never very satisfactory, is destroyed by the fact that the Hazaurehs are a nation who have but recently occupied and given their name to a part of Afghanistan. The second argument is built on the traditions examined in the text, and on the assertion of the Persian historians, probably derived from those traditions, and at no time very deserving of faith. The third is founded on the Jewish names of the Afghans; but those they probably have derived from the Arabs, like all other Mohammedan nations. Their ancient names have no resemblance to those of the Jews.

It must be borne in mind that the Honourable Mountstuart Elphinstone's mission terminated at

The last argument is founded on a supposed resemblance between the Pushtoo and Chaldaic languages, of which the reader will hereafter be enabled to judge. Many points of resemblance between the manners of the Afghans and those of the Jews might be adduced, but such a similarity is usual between nations in the same stage of. society; and if it were admitted as a proof of identity, the Tartars and the Arabs, the Germans and the Russians, might be proved the same.

It is also maintained by more than one European writer, that the Afghans are a Caucasian tribe, and particularly that they are descended from the Armenians. In the extent sometimes allowed to the name of Caucasus, the Afghans still inhabit that celebrated mountain; but if it be meant that they ever lived to the west of the Caspian Sea, the assertion appears to be unsupported by proof. Their Armenian descent is utterly unknown to themselves, though constantly in the mouths of the Armenians; and the story told by the latter people of the Afghans having become Mussulmans to avoid the long fasts prescribed by their own church, is too inconsistent with history to deserve a moment's consideration. I may add, that I have compared a short Armenian vocabulary with the Pushtoo, and could perceive no resemblance between the languages; and I once read a good deal of a Pushtoo vocabulary to a well-informed Armenian, who, though he strenuously asserted the descent of the Afghans from his countrymen, yet owned that he could not discover a word common to their language and his own. I have not had the same advantage with the language of other Caucasian tribes, but I compared about two hundred and fifty Georgian words with the corresponding ones in Pushtoo, and nothing could be more different; and I know no ground for connecting the Afghans with

Peshavar, and that he was never himself in Kabul. But the information given in his account of that

the Western Caucasus, except the assertion of a German traveller, whose name I forget, that he saw Afghans there during the last century, which proves too much.

Ferishta mentions that Kyse, the son of Haushem, and Huneef, the son of Kyse, were two of the earliest Arab commanders in Khorassaun (Briggs, Ferishta, vol. i., p. 3). He also states that Khauled, son of Abdoollah, being afraid to return to Arabia, settled in the hills of Solimaun, and gave his daughter to a converted Afghan chief (p. 5). It was probably from these facts that the names of Kyse and Khauled were suggested to the Afghan author, who first thought of ennobling his nation by connecting it with that of the Prophet.

I may here notice, that none of the ancient Afghan names bear the slightest resemblance to those of the Arabs or the Jews. The progenitors of four great divisions of the nation were Serrabun, Ghoorghoosht, Betnee, and Kurleh or Kuranee. The tribes immediately sprung from these are Abdal, Ghilzie, Khukhye, Cauker, &c. &c., and it is not till more recent subdivisions that we find Euzofzyes, Mahommedzyes, Solimaun Khail, and other Arabic and Hebrew derivatives. Professor Dorn, of Kharkov, who has translated a history of the Afghans, and has added many learned notes, discusses severally the theories that have been maintained of the descent of the Afghans: first, from the Copts; second, the Jews; third, the Georgians; fourth, the Toolks; fifth, the Moguls; sixth, the Armenians; and mentions more cursorily the opinions that they are descended from the Indo-Scythians, Medians, Sogdians, Persians, and Indians: on considering all which he comes to the rational conclusion that they cannot be traced to any tribe or country beyond their present seats and the adjoining mountains. 1838.

kingdom, as well as its immediate neighbourhood and more distant dominions, is so correct, and everything is described in such a manner, that all readers would at once think the honourable gentleman had himself been in the capital, had traversed the whole country, and examined all its wonders personally. Above all, his sojourn in Peshavar, while negotiating with the late Shah Shuja, his constant communication, directly and indirectly, with the people of all ranks, and his civil and liberal manners towards every one, created a most wonderful and noble reversion of respect for the generosity, truth, and justice of the British nation in the hearts of the inhabitants of that part of Asia, and on this account all European travellers have been well treated, and many of the Afghan chiefs offered their homage to Lord Keane when advancing upon Cabul. This high-minded gentleman describes the Barakzais, the tribe of Dost Mohammed Khan, as follows:—" The next clan to the Populzye, which it far exceeds in numbers, is the Baurekzyes. This great clan inhabits the country south of Candahar, the valley of Urghessaun, the banks of the Helmud, and the dry plains which that river divides. Those near Can-

HON. MOUNT STUART ELPHINSTONE.

dahar, and many of those in Urghessaun and on the Helmud, are led by the fertility of their soil to agriculture, and the industry of others has even produced caureezes and cultivation in the midst of the desert, but the greater part of the tribe is composed of shepherds. They are a spirited and warlike clan, and as Fatah Khan is now their chief, they make a much more conspicuous figure than any other tribe among the Afghans. At present the grand vizier and almost all the great officers of state are Baurekzyes, and they owe their elevation to the courage and attachment of their clan.

" Their numbers are not less than thirty thousand families."

Let us return to Haji Jamal Khan, son of Usaf. In the reign of Ahmad Shah Durrani, Haji Jamal Khan, the grandfather of Dost Mohammed, became a noble of great influence; and when Taimur Shah ascended the throne of Afghanistan, he died, and left four sons, namely: Rahimdad Khan, Payandah Khan, Harun Khan, and Bahadar Khan. His Majesty made the first of these chief of the Barakzai tribe, in the room of his father Haji Jamal. But he possessed a mean disposition, which induced all the tribe to stand against him; and they complained to the king that the chief, Rahimdad Khan, having a bad temper, does not invite his equals and followers to his table, and never dines in the company of the nobles, but alone in the house. Such conduct is disgraceful to the name of their chief, and therefore they are not willing to render him homage.

His Majesty accepted the appeal of the tribe, dismissed Rahimdad Khan from the chiefship, and appointed him keeper of the Government papers. He left eight sons, Abdul Khan, Abdulmajid, Abdul Kabir, Abdul Salem, Abdulhakim, Abdulhamid, Abdullah, and Abdul vahid Khan.

On the dismissal or death of Rahimdad Khan, Taimur Shah nominated Payandah Khan, the father of Dost Mohammed, as chief of the Barakzai tribe. His civil and liberal conduct towards the people made him popular. His fidelity and attachment to the state rendered him the favourite of the king.

Meanwhile Sardar Madad Khan set out to punish the obstinacy of Azad Khan, the governor of Kashmir; and Payandah Khan, the father of Dost Mohammed, embraced this favourable opportunity of distinguishing himself, and accompanied the Sardar on his expedition. He fought bravely with the governor, who was routed and subjugated. When the Sardar returned from Kashmir to Kabul, and waited upon the king, he mentioned the services of Payandah Khan with the highest praise. Having had previously a good opinion of this individual, and hearing now of his brilliant achievements at Kashmir, his Majesty ordered him to proceed to Shal and Quetta, and to collect the revenue of those districts. He performed this duty to the advantage of the state, and satisfaction of the populace. On this occasion every one spoke highly of the talents of Payandah Khan.

These successive and good services of Payandah Khan wrought upon the heart of the king, who not only rewarded him by adding the Ghilzai division to his flag, but also allowed him to stand near the throne, and thus his promotion was advancing continually.

In the meantime Prince Abbas, son of Taimur Shah, rebelled against his father, and Arsalan Khan Momand became his adherent. His Majesty ordered Payandah Khan to quell this disturbance. He

marched at the head of an army, and on reaching
Lalpurah he rode his horse through the river without
fear of being drowned. His followers imitated the
heroic conduct of their leader, and found themselves
on the other side of the river without any loss.
Arsalan Khan, having no power of opposing him,
was obliged to fly. Payandah Khan, after gaining
the victory, returned to the presence of the Shah.

The Shah, agreeably to the advice of Payandah
Khan, went off for Peshavar; and he also accompanied the royal camp. On reaching the city,
Arsalan Khan was summoned to appear, and was
put to death in the court. The rebellious son,
Prince Abbas, threw himself on the mercy of his
father, the Shah, and after obtaining pardon for his
misdemeanour, came back to Kabul with the king.
His Majesty was so much pleased with the valuable services rendered by Payandah Khan that he
honoured him with the title of Sarfraz (Lofty)
Khan.

After some time the peace of the western frontier
of Kabul was disturbed by the Ozbek tribe. This
disturbance frightened the king to such a degree
that he had determined to quit the capital and

escape to Herat. On hearing of such a cowardly purpose in his Majesty, the father of Dost Mohammed Khan, who was entitled Sarfraz Khan, with his usual resolution and fidelity, persuaded the Shah to remain on the throne, and himself marched towards Balkh. In the exercise of his sagacity and sound wisdom, he made peace with the Ozbek chief, and returned to Kabul without having occasion to use his sword. The favour of the king increased daily towards him, but unfortunately his Majesty expired after a short interval.

On the death of Taimur Shah some of the Durranis were anxious to place Prince Abbas on the throne, and others wished that Mahmud should succeed him. In short, every chief was puzzled to determine on whose head the crown should be placed. Sarfraz Khan, however, gave the sceptre of the realm into the hands of Prince Zaman, afterwards called Shah Zaman. His Majesty therefore loved him as dearly as his own life, and daily bestowed upon him fresh marks of royal distinction.

The continued services of Sarfraz Khan made Shah Zaman so much attached to him that in addition to the command of the Barakzai tribe, and the

division of the Ghilzais, his Majesty attached part
of the Qizalbash force to his detachment, and appointed for him an annual salary of about eighty
thousand rupees.   How pleasing it would have been
if Sarfraz Khan had lived to see the divine favour
shown in behalf of his son Dost Mohammed Khan,
who ascended the throne of the late Kabul kings,
and employed many people equal in rank with his
father! Nay, also his old uncles, the brothers of
Sarfraz Khan, as Jabbar Khan, Mohammed Zaman
Khan, and Usman Khan, acknowledged their young
nephew as their superior, and received from him a
higher salary than Sarfraz Khan got from the old
king of Kabul.

As soon as Dost Mohammed Khan gained distinction, and became chief of Kabul, he stamped the
following verse on the coin, and this honoured and
gave permanence to the name of his affectionate
father :—

> " Simo tila be shams o qamar medahad naved."
> " Vaq te ravaj Sikhai Payandah Khan rasid."

> " Silver and gold give the happy tidings to sun and moon that
> the time has arrived for the currency of Payandah Khan's coin."

It would certainly be wonderful if Sarfraz Khan

could hear with his own ears that his enterprising son Dost Mohammed had become as celebrated as one of the kings, and that the ambassadors of the British, the Russian, the Persian, and the Turkistan governments waited in his court. It happens seldom in this sad and changing world that parents are alive to derive pleasure from the prosperity of their promising sons; and if they ever happen to be alive, still when the child has gained dignity, it is to be regretted that he seldom pleases them entirely by performing his filial duties according to their expectation.

When Vafadar Khan became the minister of Shah Zaman, he gained the highest favour of his Majesty by the use of his sweet words and intrigues in the court. Afterwards by his hypocrisy and false accusations he induced the king to treat all the nobles with contempt, and to look upon them with distrust; and prevailed on his Majesty to make him prime minister of the kingdom. When he was sure that Shah Zaman had become disgusted with his deceit with regard to the chiefs, he represented to the king that Sarfraz Khan was intriguing with Shah Shuja,

c

with the view to dethrone his Majesty, and make
Shah Shuja sovereign of Afghanistan. He added
the names of some other chiefs as his adherents in
this act of disloyalty. Shah Zaman, who was afterwards blind of both eyes, seemed blind of sense at
this time, for as soon as he heard the false accusations of Vafadar Khan, he sent for Sarfraz Khan
and put him to death without making any investigation into the facts or circumstances of the alleged
treason. The envious conduct of Vafadar Khan did
not cease upon accomplishing the murder of Dost
Mohammed Khan's father, Sarfraz Khan. This
was followed by that of other chiefs also, namely:
of Mohammed Azim Khan Alakozai, of Qamruddin
Khan, of Amin-ul-mulk babri, of Hazar Khan Ghilzai, of Amir Arsalan Khan, of Jafar Khan Javan
Sher, of Zaman Khan Rekabashi, &c., who all fell
victims to the envy of Vafadar Khan.

After the unjust massacre of the above named
nobles, there remained not a talented and qualified
man who could manage the affairs of the realm, and
govern to the satisfaction of the people of all ranks.
In short, the behaviour of the minister, Vafadar, was

offensive to all. He oppressed the subjects, and he
paid the forces in soap and red colours, instead of
money; he made also many deductions in their pay,
which at length caused every one to be thirsty for
his blood, and at length this was shed most igno-
miniously.

When Sarfraz Khan was murdered, Harun Khan
acted as governor of the district of Girashk for him.
The latter died, and left two sons, namely, Shah
Savar Khan and Amardin Khan. His brother,
Bahadar Khan, was a man of much piety, and
shunned all worldly affairs. He was day and night
engaged in prayers. The ladies of the household of
Sarfraz Khan mentioned that when he was in deep
contemplation of the Almighty God, a heavy gold
chain was generally coming out from his mouth and
going into it again. He was said to be a stranger
to the stratagems of the Afghans, and a lover of
God. His son, Mohammed Rahim Khan, entitled
Amin-ul-mulk, was also known to abhor the tyrannical
habits of the Afghans, and by his amiable disposition
had added honour to the good name of his father.
He married a lady of Kashmir, whose virtues, love

of her husband, and good conduct in the days of adversity, are worthy of my notice. I will mention them more fully in the proper place, and especially concerning her being forced to marry Dost Mohammed Khan when she was a widow.

CHAPTER II.

Brothers of Dost Mohammed Khan—Dost's early training—
Shah Zaman—Dost becomes the confidential agent of Fatah
Khan—Defeat of Shah Shuja—Youth of Dost Mohammed
Khan—He returns to Kabul—His sister married to Shah
Shuja—Fatah Khan's treaty with Mukhtar and with Qaisar—
Intrepidity of Dost—He and Fatah leave Qandhar—They
rebel from Shah Shuja—Are compelled to return to Qandhar—
Fatah Khan is confined, and Dost escapes—Dost besieges
Qandhar—Fatah is released—Dost and Fatah join Kam Ran—
Dost gains a victory—Fights with Shuja—Makes peace, and
allies himself with Shuja—Dost and his brother desert the
camp—Shuja gains a victory—Measures of Dost—His bravery
—He defeats his enemy—Shah Mahmud becomes king, Fatah
Khan vizir, and Dost is dignified—Mirza Ali Khan—Mo-
hammed Azim Khan—Dost is made Sardar—Expedition to
Kashmir—Rebellion in Kabul—Suppressed—War with the
Sikhs.

WHEN the Sarfraz Khan was murdered he left twenty-
one sons and several daughters. If I did not mention that they had different mothers, it might puzzle
the reader to consider that so many children were
born from one mother. The celebrated Vazir Fatah
Khan, afterwards entitled Shah Dost by Mahmud
Shah, was the eldest son of Sarfraz Khan. He, Tai-

mur Quli Khan, and Mohammed Azim Khan were
brothers from one mother, who belonged to the Nus-
rat Khail clan.   Then Navabs Asad Khan, Samad
Khan, and Turrahbaz Khan were born from the
Barakzai mother.   The seventh son of the Sarfraz
Khan was Ata Mohammed Khan, who was the real
brother of Yar Mohammed Khan, of Sultan Mohammed Khan, of Said Mohammed Khan, and of
Pir Mohammed Khan.   Their mother was from the
Alakozai family.   Purdil Khan, who was the twelfth
son of the Sarfraz Khan, was brother to Sherdil, to
Kohindil, and to Mehardil Khan.   These descended
from their mother of the Idu Khail clan of the Hu-
tak Ghilzai.   The well known Navab Jabbar Khan
is said to be the seventeenth son of the Sarfraz, and
is the only one from his mother, of whom mention
is made in the book of Mr. Vigne.*   The reputation

* " The Nawab Jubar Khan well deserves the name of the
Feringis friend, was then about fifty-five years old, to judge from
his appearance, standing about five feet nine, with a corpulent
person, dark aquiline features, and somewhat of a Jewish look,
having a very good tempered expression. His mother was a
slave girl in the Zunana of Poyundu Khan; his father gave her
in marriage to a water-carrier, but still continued his attentions
to her. By the custom of these countries a servant marrying a
slave becomes also a slave. When the Nawab was born the

of her character stands now high. Jumma Khan was born from an Afghan slave girl. Aslam Khan's mother was also a slave of the tribe of Kafar Siahposh. The hero of my tale, Dost Mohammed Khan, was the twentieth, and his younger brother, Amir Mohammed Khan, was the twenty-first son of the Sarfraz Khan; their mother being from the Siah Mansur family, a branch of the Persian tribe, which was looked upon with disgrace and contempt, by the others, the Afghan wives of the Sarfraz Khan.

I must safely say that the mother of Dost Mohammed was the favourite wife of Sarfraz Khan. She accompanied him in the various campaigns, and would not allow him to rise early and march long after sunrise. For this she was blessed by the troops and camp followers, who did not like to start earlier in cold.

When the Sarfraz was no more, Fatah Khan, with the sons of his own uncles, namely, Abdul Sa-

waterman took the child to Poyundu Khan, and told him that he knew more about the child than he himself did. For many years the Nawab was running about the Bala Hissar of Kabul, and was called the waterman's son. Mohamed Azim Khan took notice of him, owned him as his brother, and procured him an appointment as governor of Dhera Ghaze Khan."

PEDIGREE OF DOST MOHAMMED.

Dost Mohammed Khan ⚭ Mohammed Afzal Khan and his brother, Mohammed Akram Khan. Mohammed Akbar Khan. Ghulam Haidar, Mohammed Amir Khan. Sherjan Khan.

{ There are five or six other younger brothers, and so many sisters. }

Amir Mohammed Khan ⚭ Sham Shurdin Khan.

Islam Khan.

Ata Mohammed Khan, Yar Mohammed Khan, Sultan Mohammed Khan, Sayd Mohammed Khan, Pir Mohammed Khan. — Peshawar chiefs.

Fatah Khan. Taimur Quli Khan. Mohammed Azim Khan.

Novab Asad Khan ⚭ Novab Mohammed Zaman Khan. Turrahbaz Khan. Navab Samad Khan ⚭ Sardar Mohammed Usman Khan.

Purdil Khan, Sherdil Khan, Kohindil Khan, Rahamdil Khan, Mehardil Khan — Candhar chiefs.

Jabbar Khan Navab.

Jumma Khan.

SIAH MANSUR, Persian. — SIAH POSH, slave girl. — ALAKO-ZAI. — NUSRA KHAIL. — PAYANDAH KHAN had eight wives: — BARAK-ZAI. — IDU KHAIL. — Kohis-tani slave girl. — Afghan slave girl.

Bahadar Khan.
Harun Khan.
Rahimdad —— Haji Jamal, grandfather of Dost Mohammed Khan.

Usaf.

Yaru.

Mohammed.

Omar Khan.

Khizar Khan.

Ismail.

Nek.

Daru Nika.

Saifal.

Barak.

Fofal. —— Alako.

ABDAL.

Tradition says that the eighteenth descendant of Israel was Abdal.

lam, Abdul Vahid, Mohammed Rahim Khan Amin-
ul-mulk, and two other confidential men, made their
escape through one of the bulwarks of the city of
Qandhar to Girishk, and took up their abode in the
fort named Sadat. After a short stay in that place,
he went through Sistan to Persia, and joined Mahmud Shah in Kirman, whither he had fled through
fear of Zaman Shah. These were the days in which
the descendants and family of Payandah Khan suffered most miserably. They were begging from
morning till night for pieces of bread. Many were
prisoners, and others had taken shelter in the mausoleum of the late Ahmad Shah, with the view of
gaining food which was daily distributed for charity's
sake. No doubt my hero was included in the company and shared their miseries.

Abdul Majid Khan, son of the uncle of Dost
Mohammed Khan, asserting his claim, after the Afghan custom, to inherit the widow of the nearest
relation, forced the widowed mother of the latter to
marry him. His brother Abdulamin Khan married
the sister of Dost Mohammed Khan in the same
forcible manner. While these unfortunate events
were taking place in the family of the Sarfraz Khan,

Dost Mahommed Khan, with his younger brother
Amir Mohammed Khan, lived four years in one of
the forts of Maruf, which belonged to the new husband of his mother, called Abdulmajid Khan. At
this time he was from seven to eight years of
age.

Meanwhile Fatah Khan returned with Mahmud
Shah from Persia, and encamped in the village of
Amirbaldan, situated in the vicinity of Sistan. In
this place he met with Mirakhor, who was one of
the chiefs of Shah Zaman, and governor of Qandhar.
The Mirakhor, without gaining any information of
the strength of Fatah Khan's force, was overawed by
the reputation of his rival's celebrated bravery, and
was compelled to flee, leaving his tents and camp
equipage in possession of Mahmud Shah. Now the
stars of the descendants of the Sarfraz began to
shine.

Fatah Khan, with Mahmud Shah, marched from
Sistan and came to Girashk with pleasant spirits.
Here he sent for his servant, named Mohammed,
and gave his young brothers, Dost Mohammed and
Amir Mohammed, into his charge, with injunctions
to take very great care of them, and especially of

the former. He also fixed a handsome income for
the maintenance of his enterprising brother.

After doing good offices for the improvement of
Dost Mohammed Khan, Fatah Khan, and Shah,
Mahmud marched against Qandhar and laid siege
to the city. While the siege and skirmishes were
going on, Yayha Khan Barakzai fled from the town
and joined Fatah Khan. The latter, after forty-two
days' blockading, made numerous ladders and took
Qandhar by escalade. Immediately after this he
confined the Prince Haidar in the palace along with
Yar Mohammed Khan, &c. &c., the chiefs of Shah
Zaman's party. Fatah Khan asked Mahmud Shah
to put Abdulrahim Khan Sadozai and his father to
death, and to publish that the deed was done by the
Durrani chiefs. By fabricating this story, Fatah
Khan was anxious to excite the suspicion of Shah
Zaman against the Durranis, and to form an attachment to himself and to Shah Mahmud. Any one
who was reported to have a little wealth became a
prey to Fatah Khan's extortion. He, as well as
Mahmud Shah, hoarded up a great deal of money
by oppressing the merchants and cultivators, who
provided them with all supplies for the war. When

fully prepared, they moved from Qandhar with arms towards Kabul to meet Shah Zaman.

At this time Dost Mohammed Khan had reached the twelfth year of his age. He obtained a situation under his brother Fatah, and attended upon him as "abdar," water-bearer, on every occasion. After some time he got an additional service, that of having the charge of preparing the smoking-pipe for Fatah Khan.

When Shah Zaman had intelligence of the movement of Mahmud Shah and Fatah Khan in the direction of Kabul, he left all the heavy and royal baggage in charge of Shah Shuja, and marched himself lightly equipped to oppose the enemy. On arriving at Mokar he inspected his army, and he found it consisted of nearly forty thousand foot and horsemen. Ahmad Khan Nurzai, who had one thousand horse under his command, was appointed to form the advance guard of the army. This commander made rapid intrigues with Fatah Khan, deserted Shah Zaman, and offered his services to Mahmud Shah. When this news reached Shah Zaman, he thought that all his chiefs and forces had become disgusted with him through the ill behaviour

of his minister, Vafadar Khan,* and, instead of
fighting for him, they would probably seize and deliver him up to the enemy. Already overcome by
this fear, he was himself routed without a moment's
opposition. On escaping from before Mahmud Shah's
camp, his Majesty was informed that the inhabitants
of Kabul had placed themselves on the road to this
city, with the intention to plunder his Majesty.
With this fearful view he took a different route to
go down to Jalalabad, and thence to Peshavar. For
the purpose of passing the night he stopped in the
fort of Ashaq, who, having learned the deplorable
flight and condition of the Shah, lost no time in receiving the person of his Majesty, and by express
conveyed a report of the same to Mahmud Shah and
Fatah Khan. They immediately dispatched Navab
Asad Khan with directions to bring Shah Zaman

* Mohammed Osman Khan, the son of this unwise Vafadar
Khan, was entitled Nazamuddaulah by the influence of the late
Sir William Macnaghten and Sir Alexander Burnes, and was
made minister of the late Shah Shuja in Kabul. This person
imitated his father, and suggested such imprudent measures to
the newly arrived functionary as caused disturbances, the loss of
thousands of lives, honour, and also of Afghanistan. For particulars of the character of Vafadar Khan, see Major Hugh's
' Campaign in Afghanistan,' p. 378-9.

and his minister both as prisoners. He reached the fort of Ashaq, and brought the captives from thence to Jagdalak. Here he blinded Shah Zaman, and Vafadar Khan was put to death along with his brother in the Bala Hissar of Kabul.

Much has been said and known about the celebrated diamond of Kohi Nur (mountain of light), wherefore on this subject I add nothing more than that Shah Zaman, before he was taken captive, concealed it in the wall of the tower where he lived in the fort of Ashaq. He did not point out the place of its concealment to Shah Mahmud, but to his brother, Shah Shuja. When the latter ascended the throne he took out the precious diamond, and when his evil stars predominated he was deprived of it by force by Ranjit Singh.* This Lion of the Panjab, Naunelal Singh ("Hotspur"), and poor Sher Singh, tied that diamond on their arms on happy occasions. When the latter was murdered, and anarchy took deep root in Lahaur, Rajah Hira Singh, the late minister of Maharajah Dalip Singh, got possession of the diamond, and sent it to his father's stronghold in the Jammu Hills, where, no doubt, the

* Died in 1839.

present rajah, Golab Singh, has it in his possession. Rajah Hira Singh had also murdered Missar Beli Ram, the keeper of it, for fear of his saying that it has been received and sent by him to Golab Singh. Now if any inquiry be made with regard to this valuable gem, the Rajah will say he cannot find it, because it was in the charge of Beli Ram, who is now no more.

When the reign of Shah Zaman was at an end, Fatah Khan placed Mahmud Shah on the throne of Kabul, and admitted Dost Mohammed Khan into all the secrets of each party. This promising young man was in attendance upon him at all times, and never went to sleep till Fatah was gone to his bed. He stood before him all the day with his hands closed, a token of respect among the Afghans. It was not an unusual occurrence, that when Fatah Khan was in his sleeping-room, Dost Mohammed Khan stood watching his safety.

After some time had passed, Shah Shuja prepared an army to proceed against Mahmud Shah and Fatah Khan at Kabul, and to revenge the outrage done by them to his brother Shah Zaman. On hearing this, Fatah Khan and Prince Kam Ran, son

of Mahmud Shah, quitted Kabul to check him.
Near the village of Ishpan the armies fought with
each other. In the beginning of the battle the warriors of Fatah Khan became dispirited, but at length
Shah Shuja was routed and overcome. Whatever
royal property and treasures were left to him by the
late kings fell into the hands of the followers of
Fatah Khan, and many of them were very much
enriched. Shah Shuja fled, and the Vazir Fatah
Khan, flushed with success, went down to Peshavar
for the purpose of collecting the revenue of that
place. At this time Mahmud Shah had very little
force in Kabul, which induced Abdulrahim Khan
Ghilzai to make the Logar people his partizans, and
to rebel against his Majesty. He set out for Kabul,
and the king, being alarmed, released Mukhtar-ud-
daulah, Ahmad Khan Nurzai, and Akram Khan
Ghilzai from custody, and sent them to oppose the
refractory chief. These chiefs collected about three
thousand men, while the enemy was at the head of
twenty thousand horse and foot. A hard fight
ensued between the Ghilzai rebels and the Durranis
of the king, who lost Taj Mohammed Khan, Akram Khan Ghilzai, and Sher Mohammed Khan, who

had much influence in the kingdom. Finally the
Durranis were victorious: and the rebels, after losing
numerous followers, retired to their native villages.
The heads of the dead were cut off and brought by
the Durranis into the presence of Mahmud Shah.
He ordered them to be heaped up outside the palace,
on the cliff known by the name of "Tapaikhaki-
balkh."

In the mean time Shahabuddin Tokhi, finding that
the city of Qandhar was without troops, collected
a large body of forces, and proceeded to take it.
Abdul Majid Khan Barakzai, Saidal Khan Alakozai, and Salah Mohammed Khan Ghilzai, quitted
the city to oppose the Tokhi chief on the road. The
armies fought on "Puli Sangi," where two hundred
Durranis and one thousand Ghilzais were killed. It
was curious that the army of the king, fighting
against rebels at two different places and far from
each other, gained two victories in one day and at
the same hour.

The Vazir Fatah Khan, in the beginning of spring,
appointed Abdul Vahid Khan as governor of Peshavar, and Khojah Mohammed Khan Fofalzai was
left with him. Prince Kam Ran and the Vazir Fatah

D

Khan returned to Kabul and dispatched Mukhtar-
ud-daulah and Ahmad Khan Nurzai to strengthen
the city of Qandhar. They were also directed by
the above-mentioned chief to destroy all the Ghilzai
forts which were situated on and in the vicinity of
their march. They did the same, and after settling
the disturbances of the southern kingdom, they come
back to Kabul.

While peace was thus being established on the
southern side, a fresh rebellion broke out in the
East. "Fatah Khan Babakarzai" took up his residence in the house of the priests of "Ozbin," and
besought them to take up his cause. They assembled
a large body of plunderers, and with the aid of Jabbar Khail and Ahmadzai tribe, which in all amounted
to about forty thousand men, they came with the
above-mentioned rebel, and made breastworks near
"Munar Chakri" to fight with the king's forces.
The Vazir Fatah Khan moved with an army to
punish this refractory multitude, which, after a little
fighting, was defeated and dispersed. The Vazir cut
off nearly one hundred heads of the rebels and
brought them into the city. After this he went to
collect the revenues of the country of Bannu, and on

his way back was surprised by the arrival of the news that Prince Qaisar of Herat, being unable to wage war with the prince Haji Firoz, had fled, and had sought refuge and aid from the king of Persia; and that after passing some time in that country, he had marched to seize on the city of Qandhar. On this he immediately joined Prince Kam Ran at Qandhar, and marched to check the progress of Qaisar. They met and fought with each other at Kokran, in which place Akram Khan Ghilzai was killed on the part of Kam Ran, and Prince Qaisar was taken prisoner and carried to Kabul.

While Fatah Khan was engaged in suppressing the aforesaid disorders in the kingdom, the enterprising Dost Mohammed Khan was with him. His heroic conduct and persevering energy of mind were very pleasing in the eyes of the Vazir, and were the subject of jealousy of his older and younger brothers. His age at this time was fourteen years. As his intrepidity was the topic of the warrior's conversation, his beauty also rendered him a favourite with the people in those days.

After that time the Vazir Fatah Khan, along with Dost Mohammed Khan, directed his course back to

Kabul. This afforded a favourable opportunity for Shah Shuja at Peshavar, who, finding that the territory of Qandhar was left without forces, proceeded through the Vazir's country to take it if possible. Akram Khan Barakzai, Mohammed Ali Khan, and Mir Akbar were then with his Majesty. No sooner had Fatah Khan and Dost Mohammed Khan heard of the movement of Shah Shuja towards Qandhar, than they set out to assist Prince Kam Ran against his Majesty. When they reached that place they confined Ghafur Khan Barakzai, Saidel Khan Alakozai, and Khojah Mohammed Khan Badozai, believing that they were likely to go over to Shah Shuja. This intelligence alarmed Mukhtar-uddaulah, who thought that the daily increasing power of Fatah Khan would some day ruin him; and to prevent this evil he excited the Mirvaiz, Khojah Khanji and Sayad Ashraf to take his part.

The seditious Mirvaiz assembled the inhabitants (Sunnis) of Kabul, and on religious pretence excited their animosity against the Kuzilbashes (Shias). He added that Mahmud Shah and Fatah Khan, contrary to their own religion, are protectors of the Shias, the annihilation of which tribe is incumbent

on the Sunnis' faith. As the greater part of the
Qizilbash force was advancing with Fatah Khan
and Dost Mohammed Khan towards Qandhar, the
Mirvaiz, finding their part of the town weakened in
its defence, he ordered the Kabul, Kohistan, and
Ghilzai people to make a sudden attack on it; and
one of the divisions of the Qizilbash fort, occupied
by the Khafis, was plundered, and Shah Mahmud
besieged in Bala Hissar. At last his Majesty was
taken prisoner, and Shah Shuja planted on the
throne.

As soon as Fatah Khan was informed of his
master's dethronement, he quitted Qandhar immediately with Dost Mohammed Khan, to fight with
Shah Shuja in Kabul. About four miles from the
city a battle took place between Shah Shuja and
Fatah Khan, in which the latter was beaten, and
compelled to join Prince Kam Ran at Qandhar.
Shah Shuja being victorious returned to Kabul.

As Navab Asad Khan, uncle of Dost, was a prisoner in the Bala Hisar of Kabul, Mukhtar-ud-
daulah supplicated his Majesty to release him, and
allow him to be his guest. The Shah complied with
his request, and Mukhtar-ud-daulah did every honour

to Asad Khan. The Nawab being desirous to destroy all feelings of animosity between the Sadozai
and Barakzai family, wished to make matrimonial
connexions among them; consequently the sister of
Dost Mohammed Khan was married to Shah Shuja.
After this his Majesty requested Navab Asad Khan,
Gul Mohammed Khan, the brother of Mukhtar-ud-
daulah and Dost Mohammed Khan, to go to the Vazir
Fatah Khan at Qandhar, and after assuring him of
every attention and respect on the part of the king
to induce him to relinquish all designs of supporting
Mahmud Shah, and to attach himself to Shah Shuja.
The latter also made an oath to restore him to the
rank and privileges of his late father the Sarfraz
Khan, and to treat him with all due consideration.
The aforesaid chiefs went down to Qandhar, and
delivered the messages of the king to Fatah Khan,
who was pleased with this unexpected condescension
in Shah Shuja, and immediately marched for Kabul. Prince Kam Ran was broken-hearted at this
unhappy turn of affairs, and was obliged to take
refuge in Hirat.

When the intelligence of Fatah Khan's departure
from Qandhar reached Mukhtar-ud-daulah at Kabul,

he went down to meet him at Ghazni, and conducted him to the presence of the king. Fatah Khan did not receive the favours of his Majesty as stipulated, nor was the Ghilzai division of the army placed under his charge. He was nearly two months in the house of Mukhtar-ud-daulah, who treated him with distinction and civility. In the meantime Akram Khan advised Shah Shuja to proceed to Peshavar, and there to put Fatah Khan and Mukhtar-ud-daulah into custody, and so to save himself from all fear of injury from them. One of the men who was aware of this secret went and said to Mukhtar-ud-daulah that Akram Khan and Shah Shuja had contrived to ruin them. Mukhtar-ud-daulah was lost in wonder at such ungrateful contrivances of Shuja, whom he had shortly before made king, after dethroning Mahmud Shah. He said to himself, that if he were to rebel openly just now, to prevent the ill designs of his antagonist, it would bring a load of disgrace to his own long-earned reputation. He therefore advanced seventy thousand rupees secretly to Fatah Khan, and told him to wait in Kabul on the excuse of procuring a marching equipage, while he himself would go with Shuja to Peshavar. He added also,

that when Fatah Khan should receive the news of
the Shah's arrival in Tezin, he should immediately
commence proceedings as a foe to the king, and
should cause the release of the chiefs, namely: Baqar
Khan, Ibrahim Khan, Mirza Abul Qasim Khan,
and Mardan Khan, and convey them to Shah Zadah Qaisar at Qandhar. These chiefs were the
friends of Shah Mahmud, and therefore had been
put into confinement by Shah Shuja. While
Mukhtar and Fatah Khan were planning these proceedings against Shah Shuja, they entered into an
agreement with each other, that the friends and
enemies of the one should be friends and enemies of
the other, and both should join when an antagonist
appeared against either of them.

No sooner had Shah Shuja reached Tezin on his
way to Jalalabad than he heard of the hostile views
of Mukhtar and Fatah Khan. Immediately he
issued orders that a strong cavalry force should
return to Kabul, and bring the captive nobles of
Shah Mahmud to his presence, along with the guard
already with them. Before this cavalry had reached
Kabul the brave Fatah Khan took all the chiefs out
of custody, and conducted them to Qandhar, through

Lahogard.* Shah Zadah Qaisar was ruling in Qandhar at that time, and Ahmad Khan Nurzai was his minister. Fatah Khan, after long marches, reached the "Edgah" gate of Qandhar at midnight, and bribed the guard to report his arrival secretly to Agha Idrak, then confidential eunuch of the Shah Zadah. When he heard this he instantly waited upon Qaisar, and mentioned the arrival of Fatah Khan, with this message, "If the Shah Zadah had any intention of becoming a king, this seemed a good opportunity, and he (Fatah Khan) would place him on the throne; otherwise he should send him a quiet and plain answer."

As soon as Qaisar received the overtures of Fatah Khan he came at midnight to meet him at the gate, without being noticed by any one. Fatah Khan said to the prince, that if his royal highness would deliver to him Ahmad Khan Nurzai, and take an oath that he would be gratefully attached to him for ever, he would either shed all his own blood on his behalf, or would make him king of Afghanistan. Otherwise he would go to Hirat, and offer the same assistance to Prince Kam Ran.

* Commonly called Logar.

Shah Zahah Qaisar accepted the good advice of
Fatah Khan, and both wrote an agreement on a leaf
of the Qoran, under their respective seals, binding
themselves to each other with perpetual attachment.
When this was settled, Fatah Khan conducted the
prince to his palace in the city, and ordered his two
thousand horsemen to dismount and proceed under
the command of Dost Mohammed Khan, to sur-
round the house, and seize the person of Ahmad
Khan Nurzai, by taking the "Char Suq" road.
The hero Dost Mohammed Khan succeeded in
opening the door of Ahmad Khan's house, and
seized him while in bed. After this he tied his
hands and feet, and imprisoned him in the house of
Shah Zadah Qaisar.

In the morning the courtiers as well as the citizens did not see Ahmad Khan passing to "Darbar"
as usual, and were astonished to perceive that in his
place Fatah Khan and Dost Mohammed Khan had
attended the court of Shah Zadah; and no one
knew what had become of the unfortunate Ahmad
Khan. This sudden change of the nobility created
the utmost terror among the Afghan chiefs, and
curiosity among the citizens. The latter proceeded

to see the prisoner in the palace, to satisfy their curiosity; and the former persuaded Qaisar to put Fatah Khan in confinement. On this his royal highness, being forgetful of his solemn oath, made an artifice to seize Fatah Khan, and with this view asked him to give him a private entertainment in the garden, where he secretly made arrangements with the chiefs to shackle him immediately.

However, this fraud of the ungrateful Qaisar came to the knowledge of Fatah Khan, who begged Qaisar to allow him leisure of two days to prepare the articles of the entertainment, while he meant to manage his own defence. At this crisis he found no remedy but to appoint the brave Dost Moham-med Khan superintendent of the feast, and com-mandant of his personal guard. Consequently, he (Dost) decorated a most beautiful apartment to receive the prince, and being himself armed cap-a-pie, as well as at the head of five hundred good fighting soldiers, stood in the presence of his royal highness, and by his alert manners showed him that he was watching the safety of his brother the Vazir.

When the prince, as well as the Durrani nobility,

observed that their designs of catching Fatah Khan
were frustrated by the vigilance of Dost Mohammed
Khan, they pretended that the object of the meeting
was to obtain the rescue of Ahmad Khan Nurzai.
For this they also offered a present of one lakh of
rupees to the prince and to the Vazir, on the part of
the captive. They also married his daughter to the
prince that day. This arrangement caused his release, and his reappointment to the situation of the
lieutenant-governor of Qandhar.

Meanwhile Fatah Khan, with Dost Mohammed,
Ata Mohammed, and Khowajah Mohammed Khan,
proceeded to attack Kabul. When he reached
Kaleti Ghilzai he was deserted by Ata Mohammed
Khan, and other Nurzai chiefs, who went back and
joined Ahmad Khan at Qandhar. Fatah Khan,
relying on the intrepidity of Dost Mohammed Khan,
cared very little for the faithless conduct of the
deserters, and with his heroic brother continued his
march towards Kabul. When he arrived at the
village named Top, the news of the movement of
Shah Shuja from Peshavar, as well as his arrival at
Qilai Qazi to oppose him, spread in the camp of the
Barakzai chiefs. On this, about midnight, Faizullah

Khan Fofalzai, along with five hundred horsemen, left Fatah and Dost, and joined Shah Shuja.

This desertion caused great consternation in the camp of Fatah Khan, whom Dost wisely advised to retrace his steps to Candhar. Before they reached Kalat they were informed that Prince Kam Ran was in possession of Qandhar, and that Ahmad Khan, the lieutenant-governor, without firing a shot, had stolen his way to his native fort in the adjacent country. As soon as Fatah and Dost heard this they sent Shah Zadah Qaisar in charge of Khowajah Mohammed to Dehlah, and themselves with the rest of their brothers waited upon Prince Kam Ran at Qandhar. They passed about two months in great distress with him, and at last begged him to advance them some money to distribute among their followers. The prince, notwithstanding that he had a great deal of wealth, swore that he had none to give them.

Fatah and Dost took immediate steps to intrigue with their former master, Prince Qaisar, against Prince Kam Ran, whom they, when every thing was in their own favour, turned out of the city; and they then invited the former to take his place. In these times of agitation Dost failed also in the respect which was due to the royal household, and omitted no opportunity to plunder and rob the royal ladies. After the Shah Zadah Qaisar, with the assistance of Fatah Khan and Dost Mohammed Khan, had seized the government of Qandhar, his royal highness dispatched Mohammed Ali Khan, and Mir Akbar, to Shah Shuja and Mukhtar-ud-daulah, and proposed that if he would allow him the possession of Qandhar, Shikarpur, and their dependencies, he would destroy Kam Ran, with Haji Firozuddin. He also suggested that if his Majesty suspected the attachment of his royal highness, and the fidelity of Fatah Khan and of Dost Mohammed Khan, he would immediately send their brother Mohammed Azim Khan as a hostage to the Shah.

Shah Shuja-ul-Mulk did not accept the offers of Shah Zadah, but continued his march to Qandhar. When the royal camp was near a village called "Chishmah Shadi," Dost Mohammed and Fatah Khan fled from the city to Frah, and the Shah Zadah, in company with Khowajah Mohammed Khan, proceeded to take shelter in "Dehlah." This intelligence disappointed his Majesty, who set out by express to get the Shah Zadah if possible. Mukhtar-ud-daulah secretly conveyed the news to the Shah Zadah, who quitted "Dehlah," to secure himself in some distant and out of the way place.

On this Shah Shuja entered the city of Qandhar, and offered the most kind and honourable treatment to Dost Mohammed and Fatah Khan, who immediately waited upon him. Four days afterwards Shah Zaman and Mukhtar-ud-daulah went and brought Shah Zadah Qaisar with Khowajah Mohammed Khan into the presence of his Majesty, who pardoned them for their past misdeeds and restored the government of Qandhar to them. Shah Shuja, in company with Dost Mohammed and Fatah Khan, proceeded to Sindh, where he received the usual tribute from the Meers, and bent his course by the Derajat and Peshavar to Kabul.

Meanwhile the Mir Alam Khan was deprived of the governorship of Derah Ghazi Khan, and Ata Mohammed Khan Nurzai was placed by Shah Shuja in that important situation. This alarmed Dost Mohammed and Fatah Khan to such an extent, that they found no safety for their persons but in flying towards Hirat. The Mir Alam also fled at the

head of some good and brave cavalry, and gained
employment under Shah Zadah Qaisar in Qandhar.
In Hirat Dost Mohammed and Fatah Khan did all
in their power to induce Shah Zadah Haji Firoz to
attack Qandhar and Kabul, but he did not comply
with their request. He said he had not ambition to
rule the kingdom of Afghanistan, and was well
satisfied with the present possession of Hirat.

The refusal of Shah Zadah Haji Firoz broke the
hearts of Dost Mohammed and Fatah Khan, and
even compelled them to return to Shah Zadah Qaisar at Qandhar. Here Khowajah Mohammed Khan
Fofalzai, with the friendly assistance of the Mir
Alam Khan Nurzai, began to insult Dost Mohammed and Fatah Khan with dispute about equality,
and intrigued with Shah Zaman, who at this time
was living with his son Shah Zadah Qaisar in Qandhar, to put them both in confinement.

With this view Shah Zaman begged the confiden-
tial servants of Shah Zadah Qaisar, who were the
Mir Alam Khan Nurzai and Shah Navaz Khan
Achakzai, to call upon Dost Mohammed and Fatah
Khan, and state on the part of his Majesty that they
should give him a grand entertainment. The quick-

sighted Dost Mohammed Khan discovered the real
object of the pretended familiarity and base affection
of Shah Zaman, and both brothers apparently showed
themselves highly honoured by such favour of Shah
Zaman.   They made preparations for three different
entertainments; one on their own part, the second
from Navab Asad Khan, and the third from Mohammed Azim Khan.

Upon the one hand Fatah Khan was preparing
everything pompously to receive Shah Zaman in the
beautiful garden of Maranjan, as if he were not
aware of the conspiracy, and on the other, the active
Dost Mohammed was secretly engaged in adding to
the number of his body guard, and kept a piercing
eye on all sides to secure the safety of his brother,
Fatah Khan, and of himself, in case the conspirators
should dare to injure them.   His celerity and readiness to meet any blow showed Shah Zaman and
Shah Zadah Qaisar the impossibility of making them
the victims of the conspiracy, and therefore to remove every suspicion from the minds of Dost Mohammed and Fatah Khan, the Shah conferred the
dress of honour on them.   Thus the watchfulness of
the hero of my tale frustrated the designs of the

E

conspirators, who in great despair made all possible
schemes to gain their mean object during the day,
but availed nothing.

At last Shah Zaman and Shah Zadah Qaisar left
the entertainment, and on returning to the palace
gave orders that no chief should enter the court-yard
accompanied by more than five attendants. During
twenty days Fatah Khan managed to take about
one hundred men with him, when he was waiting
upon Shah Zadah, and thus secured his safety for
such a period. At length, the Shah Zadah concealed
some of his strong men in his garden, when he gave
orders that his nobles should wait to pay their respects. This was done, and suddenly the Mir Alam
Khan, the nephew of the Sardar Ahmad Khan, surnamed Saifuddaulah, lifted up Fatah Khan and
threw him down on the ground, which broke two of
his teeth, and immediately they made him a prisoner. After this the friends of Fatah Khan, namely,
Navab Asad Khan, Mirza Mohammed Raza, and
Agha Mehndi, were similarly treated; but the brave
Dost Mohammed was fortunately aware of the impending danger, and lost no time, but called his followers, who amounted to about five hundred men.

It was not in the power of Shah Zadah to catch Dost Mohammed Khan, when thus protected.

It was impossible for a man like Dost Mohammed Khan to see his brother, Fatah Khan, suffering in custody without using his utmost energy to obtain the freedom of the dear captive. At the head of his followers he made a bold rush into the outer gate of the palace, but on reaching the door of the residence of the Shah Zadah, where Fatah Khan was confined, he was disappointed to observe that it was shut, and not only strongly defended, but all the walls and towers filled with matchlock men. They all at once fired at him, and he, having no means to ascend the walls, relinquished the attack. However, he besieged the palace; on which the Shah Zadah ordered Khowajah Mohammed Khan and the other chiefs to shut the gates of the city, and thus cut off the means of escape from Dost Mohammed Khan when thus reduced in the number of his adherents. One of the friends of Mohammed Azim Khan secretly sent this news to the Dost, and added also that the chiefs, with five hundred men each, had been ordered to take charge of the different gates and towers of the city against him.

On receiving this unpleasant intelligence, which might make to tremble almost the bravest leader, the hero Dost, with his usual perseverance and presence of mind, assembled his brothers and the heads of his small handful of men, with whom he held a council of war. He stated, " that the captivity of his elder brother, Fatah Khan, is of course painful to every one of the present party, and most heart-rending it is to leave him lingering in the hands of the enemy; but as the Shah Zadah has made every preparation either to destroy or to seize this small party, if his royal highness succeeds in either of his plans, we shall not only be sufferers, but shall also lose the hope of securing the liberty of Fatah Khan for ever. Consequently, we must draw our swords, and with energetic determination killing our opposers on the road, force our way through the gates, and go down to Girishk." The party accepted this advice as the best, and gladly followed him who gave it so wisely. On approaching the gate, Dost Mohammed killed some men of the guard stationed to impede his progress; and thus opening the gate made his escape to his stronghold in Girishk. On this, Shah Zaman advised his son, Shah Zadah Qaisar, to

cut off the head of Fatah Khan in return for his
being the instrument in blinding his Majesty and
forcing him from the throne; but the Shah Zadah
lent more attentive ears to the advice of Mukhtar-
ud-daulah and Mohammed Khan, than to that of his
father, and thus saved the life of his prisoner.

At this time a large caravan from Persia passed
through Hirat for Qandhar, and had scarcely reached
the vicinity of Girishk, when Dost Mohammed Khan
with Mohammed Azim Khan placed himself in its
way. When the store of booty was near and in his
view, he galloped forward and deprived all the merchants of their goods and cash. He paid no attention to the heart-rending shrieks and complaints of
the traders; and being in possession of about four
lakhs of rupees, he raised troops, proceeded at the
head of them, and laid siege to Qandhar. During
nearly three months he surrounded the city so closely
that all communication with the garrison was stopped,
and the supplies of grain and ammunition were
nearly consumed. While Dost Mohammed Khan
was daily reducing the Shah Zadah to a dangerous
perplexity by a regular and protracted siege, Mukhtar-ud-daulah was also not less active in favour of

Fatah Khan. Shah Zadah Qaisar had much regard for Mukhtar, who sent him a petition begging him to release Fatah Khan, "otherwise his brother, the brave Dost, will destroy the city of Qandhar, and I shall be able to secure no respect for the royal family when captured." He also asked Shah Shuja to write to Shah Zadah to the same effect. The Shah instructed the Shah Zadah that, on releasing Fatah Khan, he was to ask him to send Mohammed Azim Khan, with the Gholam Khanah (Persian troops), to remain as hostages with his Majesty, the Shah Zadah considering this a most lucky opportunity to please Shah Shuja by obeying his orders, and much more so to get rid of the Dost's siege, gave an immediate acquiescence to the request of his Majesty, and set Fatah Khan free, who also sent the demanded hostages to Shuja.

After some time Shah Shuja dispatched Mohammed Azim and Ata Mohammed Khan on special service to Multan, and on their return from that quarter they passed through Deratjat and Peshavar on their way to Qandhar. As soon as they arrived at that place, Dost Mohammed and Fatah Khan rebelled from Shah Shuja and Shah Zadah Qaisar,

and declared themselves willing to support Shah
Zadah Kam Ran against them. When his Majesty
heard this sad news he immediately wrote to Shah
Zadah Qaisar to proceed with four thousand horsemen and attack the rebels. Dost Mohammed and
Fatah Khan, having been informed of the hostile
steps of Qaisar, solicited Shah Zadah Haji Firoz of
Hirat to lend them aid. To this his royal highness
agreed, and dispatched Shah Zadah Milak Qaisar at
the head of three thousand cavalry to their assistance. It was in the plain near the fort of Azim
Khan where the allied forces under the Dost engaged with those of Shah Zadah Qaisar. After a
fight, in which about two thousand men were killed
and wounded on both sides, the hero of my tale,
Dost Mohammed Khan, and his brother, Fatah
Khan, were victorious, and the army of Shah Zadah
routed.

When the intelligence of the defeat of Shah Zadah reached the Imperial court of Shah Shuja, he
proceeded quickly in person to defend the city of
Qandhar. On this, Fatah Khan and the Mir Alam
Khan made preparations to oppose the progress of
his Majesty. Since there was no other person so

qualified as Dost Mohammed Khan, both in conducting political affairs and in the energetic duties
of a field-marshal, the whole party unanimously
elected the lion of my subject to undertake that important post.

The field-marshal, Dost Mohammed, with his accustomed alacrity and perseverance, led his troops
to oppose Shah Shuja, whom he met near Qarah-
bagh, or rather in Obeh.   A battle ensued, and both
parties fought desperately, when the Sardar Ahmad
Khan Nurzai became the medium of a negotiation
between the Shah and Dost Mohammed Khan.
War was changed into peace, on which Dost Mohammed returned to Girishk, and Shah Shuja, after
replacing Shah Zadah Qaisar in the government of
Qandhar, moved back to Kabul with Mukhtar-ud-
daulah.

It was not long after the arrival of Shah Shuja in
Kabul that his Majesty was surrounded with new
difficulties, and thought to have recourse to the services of the brave Dost Mohammed and of Fatah
Khan.   The affairs of the capital took a most fright-
ful aspect.   The prime minister, Mukhtar-ud-daulah,
in junction with the celebrated hypocrite, the Mir

Vaiz, the priest of Kabul, rebelled against his royal master, with the view to recognise Shah Zadah Qaisar, governor of Qandhar, as sovereign of Afghanistan. When this cheerless information reached the ears of his Majesty, he immediately sent a deputation consisting of the Durrani nobles of the realm, namely, the Sardar Madad Khan Is-haqzai, Ahmad Khan Nurzai, some members of the royal family, and holy descendant of the Prophet the Sadats, as well as other " Aq Saqal," silver-bearded people of respectability, to Dost Mohammed and Fatah Khan in Girishk.

The deputation of the Shah, after engaging and pledging themselves for the personal safety and good treatment of Dost Mohammed and of Fatah Khan, conducted them to Qandhar. As soon as this report spread in the country, Mukhtar-ud-daulah and the Mir Vaiz, as well as their followers, relinquished all their rebellious designs for the time. Shah Shuja felt very anxious to secure the closer alliance of Dost Mohammed and of Fatah Khan, and therefore he himself met them in Qandhar. His Majesty gave them every assurance of his favour and attachment, and delivered to them a sealed engagement written

on the holy leaf of the "Qoran," and at the same
time conferred the title of "Sardar i Sardaran"
(chief of chiefs) upon Fatah Khan: he also gave a
most valuable dress of honour, along with a superior
horse with gold trappings, to Dost, and one lakh of
rupees for their expenses.

After Shah Shuja had succeeded in obtaining the
good will and services of Dost and Fatah Khan, he
proceeded to raise tribute from the Meers of Sindh;
but the Sindhians made preparations to fight with
the Shah.   On this the nobles of the court, namely,
Akram Khan, &c. &c., petitioned the Shah to make
peace on getting five lakhs of rupees from them;
while the hero Dost Mohammed and Fatah Khan,
relying on their intrepidity and sagacity, begged the
Shah not to lend an ear to the proposals of Akram,
but to leave the whole affair to their arrangement.
They also added that, without using arms and sacri-
ficing lives, they would get from the Meers and fill
the royal coffers with thirty lakhs of rupees.   However, Akram foolishly prevailed on his Majesty to
follow his counsel; and going secretly to the Meers
at night, brought only five lakhs of rupees, and made
an arrangement with them.

This proceeding of Akram Khan, which was nothing but a tissue of folly and crooked understanding, not only showed the weakness of the Shah's powers to the Sindhians and caused a loss of twenty-five lakhs of rupees to the royal treasury, but it also excited the extreme displeasure of Dost Mohammed and Fatah Khan. They deeply lamented the damage sustained by the ill counsel of Akram Khan, and became exceedingly wrathful, that the Shah, instead of paying attention to their advantageous advice, followed that of their inferior and fool.

Dost Mohammed and Fatah Khan were so much disgusted with the above-mentioned proceedings, that they left Haidarabad and came up to Shikarpur. Hither the Shah followed them and apologized to them. He swore that nothing of the kind should happen in future, and that all the affairs of his government, whether internal or external, should be adjusted by their guidance. As nature had cultivated noble and independent notions in the head and heart of Dost, he therefore could not be estranged by ill usage of this kind, but was determined to oblige and serve the Shah evidently and openly, and agreed to fight with Shah Zadah Qaisar,

Mukhtar-ud-daulah, and Mir Vaiz, who had again assumed the character of enemies to the Shah.

In the mean time the news of the movements of Shah Zadah Qaisar and Mukhtar-ud-daulah towards Peshavar was brought to Shah Shuja, who proceeded with Dost and Fatah Khan to Derah Ghazai Khan, with the intention to strike a blow on the party of Shah Zadah Qaisar at Peshavar. Before the march commenced, the watchful Dost Mohammed directed his and Fatah Khan's family to steal their way to Qandhar, and the Navab Asad Khan was appointed to take charge of them; and he at the same time said that he would soon join them with Fatah Khan.

It should be recollected here that Mukhtar-ud-daulah was always on friendly terms with Fatah Khan and with Dost. He now, being the chief instrument of recognising Shah Zadah Qaisar, against whom Shah Shuja was proceeding, wrote secretly to Dost and to Fatah, that if they still adhere to the bonds of friendship and their oath with him, they are to desert Shah Shuja immediately, and kindle the flame of insurrection in the dominion of his Majesty in Qandhar, which no doubt would agitate and ruin the measures of the Shah beyond remedy. While

Shah Shuja was about six miles from Derah, Dost
Mohammed and Fatah Khan deserted the royal
camp and took their route towards Qandhar. The
report of the desertion of Dost Mohammed and
Fatah Khan thunderstruck Shuja, who, however,
relying much more on the protection of God than on
the assistance of the deserters, continued his march
to Peshavar.

It was near the village of Tahkal, in the suburbs
of Peshavar, where the force of Shah Shuja fought
with that of Shah Zadan Qaisar. After a severe
conflict Mukhtar-ud-daulah fell in the field, and his
brother Haji Mir Ahmad and Khowajah Mohammed
Khan also followed him. The victory was on the
side of Shah Shuja, who at once set out for Kabul
and put to death the fanatic ringleader the Mir Vaiz,
priest of that city. As soon as his Majesty got rid
of the said priest he started to punish Dost Mohammed and Fatah Khan at Qandhar, who had
deserted him at Derah.

When Dost Mohammed and Fatah were informed
of the hostile movements of Shah Shuja, they raised
a large army, and under the royal shadow of Shah
Mahmud and of Shah Zadah Kam Ran, set out to

oppose Shah Shuja. Dost Mohammed volunteered to
be the head of the advanced guard, and was accompanied by his step-brother Purdil Khan, and also by
Nur Mohammed Khan, the brother of Khowajah
Mohammed Khan, who was slain in the late battle
of Tahkal, in Peshavar. The very moment he had
reached Kalat i Ghilzai, Nur Mohammed Khan went
over to Shah Shuja, and Ata Mohammed Khan
Nurzai and Yahya Khan Bamzai, who were commanders of large bodies of troops, fled towards Dehlah and Murghab.

At the time these sad desertions took place, and
the leader of the advanced guard remained alone,
Shuja would not have hesitated a moment to seize
and destroy him (Dost Mohammed) by surprise, but
he knew his brave heart and wise head, and therefore
avoided a skirmish with him. It is said by the
people that at this crisis Dost Mohammed was afraid
of Shah Shuja, because he was deserted and alone,
and the Shah was afraid of the talents and heroism
of Dost, lest he might cause dissension among his
followers. These fears, entertained on both sides,
prevented an immediate contest, and afforded a
favourable opportunity to Dost Mohammed Khan

to retrace his steps and join his brother Fatah
Khan.

On the approach of Shuja's army, Mahmud Shah,
being aided only by Fatah Khan and Dost Mohammed, found himself too weak to fight with Shah Shuja,
and therefore in this low spirit he fled to Girishk.

After some time Dost Mohammed and Fatah
Khan left Girishk and went to Sabzvar, where they
remained for three months.   During their sojourn in
this place they were informed that Shah Shuja had
left Qandhar for Kabul, and appointed Shah Zadah
Yunas, with Azam Khan Nasakhchibashi and the
Mir Alam Khan, governor of the former city.

Meanwhile Dost Mohammed and Fatah Khan
heard that two large caravans were to pass near
Khashrod, one from Qandhar to Persia, and the other
from the latter country to the former.   On this they
placed themselves on the road of the caravans, and
the very moment they encountered with them every
article fell into the possession of these noble highway-
men.   They gained plenty of money by this plunder
from the merchants.   Immediately after this they
raised an army and prepared themselves to attack
Qandhar.

Dost Mohammed and Fatah Khan met no opposition on the line of their march to Qandhar, which place they fortunately took with little trouble. The governor of this place fled, and joined his master Shah Shuja in Derajat; and Mir Alam Khan, the lieutenant-governor, being a relative of Pir Mohammed Khan Alakozai, threw himself on the protection of Shah Mahmud, who was again made nominal king by Dost and Fatah. After arranging the government affairs of Qandhar, Dost Mohammed and Fatah Khan proceeded to take Kabul, under favour of the name of Shah Mahmud. They succeeded in gaining possession of this capital, and sent Mohammed Azim Khan towards Peshavar to oppose Shah Shuja.

While Mohammed Azim Khan was encamped at Balabagh to intercept the progress of Shah Shuja, Dost Mohammed and Fatah Khan were strengthening themselves and weakening their adversaries in Kabul. Among them was the Mir Alam Khan, whom they confined and treated with barbarous cruelty. Shah Shuja, at the head of twenty-five thousand men, proceeded from Peshavar to Kabul. When the royal army reached Jalalabad, Mohammed Azim Khan, finding himself unable to oppose his Majesty, left the highway and took shelter in the different skirts of the Sufaid Koh.

No sooner had the above-mentioned intelligence reached Dost Mohammed and Fatah Khan than they marched down to Surkhab to bring Mahmud Shah with them. These three enterprising men had no more than three thousand soldiers, and knew the strength of the army they were going to fight with; but Dost Mohammed's bravery, mingled with policy, was always depended upon, and generally productive of the results of victory. On their arrival in the vicinity of the Lukhi of Surkhab, they thought that if the Durrani chiefs should cause the release of the Mir Alam Khan, he would probably succeed in joining Shah Shuja, and desertions might take place among the followers on both sides. To prevent this anticipated misfortune, Dost Mohammed and Fatah Khan murdered the poor prisoner.

Now Dost Mohammed and Fatah Khan held a council of war with their subordinate chiefs in the presence of Shah Mahmud, and stated that it was most contrary to the rules of policy and of war to appear in the open field with a small force of three thousand before a monarch or enemy of twenty-five

F

thousand well mounted cavalry and well equipped
infantry. The only thing they think now advisable
to preserve warlike fame and gain honour is to avoid
a general action, and then with determined spirit to
attack the enemy by surprise. They also proposed that,
until the enemy were perfectly routed, they should
not divide themselves into small bodies, and commence to plunder their respective antagonists, as was
usual with the Afghans, because this would cause
great confusion among them, and probably the
enemy would get the benefit of it. They also added
that, though the enemy exceeded them in power and
number of men, none of them ought to be disheartened and go over to him, believing that the
victory would always attend his army, because such
conduct would not only cause a disgraceful name for
the man himself who should do so, but would also
dishearten the rest of their followers.

These counsels of Dost Mohammed Khan were
applauded by Mahmud Shah, Fatah Khan, and the
chiefs, on which they left everything of peace and
war to his sound and wise management. He remained all day concealed in the bushes or "lukhi,"
and about evening he marched with all his forces.

He made a long march under cover of the darkness of night, and about five in the morning he attacked the Sardar Madad Khan, Azam Khan, and Ghafur Khan, who commanded ten thousand foot and horse, and had been sent as an advanced brigade. Persons who were present in the field of battle told me that it was out of the power of any man's tongue to describe the matchless alacrity, prowess, and steadiness of Dost Mohammed Khan in this grand battle. In one moment he was seen making a havoc in the lines of the enemy, and then, forcing his way back, he was observed to encourage his followers to fight; and another time he was perceived to restore order among the undisciplined soldiers. Madad Khan and Azam Khan, commanding the opposite forces, now felt the narrowness of their situation, and at the same time were panic-struck to see that Dost Mohammed was causing great slaughter in their army, which was already much reduced in number and in power. At length Dost Mohammed Khan routed and dispersed the enemy, who suffered exceedingly both in men and in baggage.

When the report of the defeat of the strong royal force under Madad Khan, &c. &c., by a small body.

of troops under the personal command of Dost Mohammed Khan reached the camp of Shah Shuja, it
not only incensed his Majesty, but alarmed him
much, and made him proceed in person to check the
progress of Dost Mohammed Khan. Shah Shuja
had still fifteen thousand good soldiers under the
command of the celebrated Akram Khan, who made
the King believe that Shah Mahmud's forces were
only three thousand men, and that they would not
stand before him; and also that Dost Mohammed
would soon lose the name of victorious, which he lately
obtained in consequence of the ill management of Madad Khan.   It appears that Akram Khan was either
jealous, or had foolish brains to suppose that he could
beat an army headed by Dost Mohammed Khan,
who was never once known to leave a field of battle
without gaining the victory, except some foresighted
policy had induced him to do so. However, Shah
Shuja made all necessary arrangements for waging
war with Mahmud Shah and Fatah Khan, evidently
proud of the superiority of his army, yet in heart
extremely fearful of the energies of Dost Mohammed
Khan.   I heard from several credible people in
Afghanistan that at this time of the war Shah Shuja

said confidentially to his minister, that while Dost
Mohammed is not captured, the victory is not to be
expected; and while he is alive the crown will not
be on his (Shuja's) head.* The forces on both
sides were arrayed in the field, those of Shah Shuja
commanded by the Sardar Akram Khan, and those
of Shah Mahmud were guided by the personal and
heroic directions of Dost Mohammed Khan. A
battle ensued, and after a severe conflict the Sardar
Akram Khan was killed, with many hundreds of
Shuja's army. Some say that the deceased was cut
down by Dost himself; and others add that he had
received a ball from some of his own followers. The
fall of such a high nobleman in the field, with so
many hundred followers, produced an alarming feeling in the forces of Shuja. His Majesty was also
himself frightened, and at last compelled to flee.
All the rest of his followers also dispersed.

Shah Mahmud and Fatah Khan, happy in their
success, and proud of the victory gained by their
brave adherent Dost Mohammed Khan, returned to
Kabul, and Mahmud was placed on the throne and
acknowledged as King of Afghanistan. Fatah Khan,

* This appears to be a wonderful and true prophecy.

the elder brother of Dost Mohammed Khan, was appointed prime minister of the Shah, and he gave the charge of various important situations to his brothers. Since the qualifications for conducting war, unshaken courage and persevering generalship, as well as the talents for administering the affairs of the realm, prudent foresight and sound policy, were shining on the forehead of Dost Mohammed Khan, Mahmud Shah and the Vizir considered his presence with themselves of much value, and consequently he was selected as next person to the Vazir, but in reality he was first in everything.

The Vazir desired Mohammed Azim Khan to go with Shah Zadah Kam Ran, and take Peshavar, and he (Azim) therefore sent Jabbar Khan, with his secretary, Mirza Ali Khan, to collect the revenue of Derah Ghazi Khan. As the secretary possessed high talents for arranging the affairs of government, he was summoned by Mohammed Azim Khan, who desired him to take charge of every thing under him. Being a native of the civilized part of Persia, and a deep politician, his conduct and kind disposition obtained the praise of almost every man in the country. His credit and word were so much respected by the wealthy merchants that he was able to raise six lakhs of rupees in one day, which had never formerly been done by any one. He had full information of almost every thing in Afghanistan, and gained the highest favour of Mohammed Azim Khan, for whom he collected a great deal of wealth, and also caused every body to look upon him as the first noble in Afghanistan. This, however, excited great hatred against himself, especially that of Dost Mohammed and the rest of his brothers. They secretly said to the Vazir Fatah Khan that the intention of Mirza Ali Khan is to strengthen the power of his immediate master, Mohammed Azim Khan, to make you and every one of your brothers dependent upon him; and that the time is not distant when we may all be reduced to bondage under him. On this the Vazir Fatah Khan sent for Mirza Ali Khan, and requested him to get three lakhs of rupees for him from his master, as he intended to go to Kashmir. The Mirza delivered the message to Mohammed Azim, but got no satisfactory reply. He told him the same again, and even went so far in his conversation with Mohammed Azim Khan as to say that if he would not

give the demanded sum quickly to the Vazir, he
would bring himself into much difficulty. He then
agreed to pay the sum next day.

Mirza Ali passed a very happy hour, thinking
that his success in gaining the money from his
master Mohammed Azim Khan would secure the
good will of the Vazir Fatah Khan, and of Dost
Mohammed Khan; but unluckily the Vizir had a
wine party that night, and was a little intoxicated.
Now the enemies of Mirza availed themselves of
such a favourable opportunity of speaking against
him to the Vazir; and added, that the Mirza would
shortly induce Mahommed Azim Khan to stand up
in opposition to the Vazir, because he had hoarded
up an immense sum of money, and gained the
attachment of every man for his master: adding,
that if he were immediately put to death, then
Mohammed Azim Khan, having no ill adviser like
him, would never dare to offend the Vazir.

The Vazir was alarmed at this fabricated report of the enemies of Mirza Ali Khan, and as he
was a little intoxicated he resolved at once to put an
end to the life of the poor Mirza. Considering that
no one could perpetrate the deed immediately but

Dost Mohammed Khan, he therefore sent for him, and said privately to him, that without fearing Mohammed Azim Khan, he was to go quickly and kill Mirza Ali Khan his secretary.

On receiving the orders of the Vazir, Dost Mohammed armed himself cap-a-pie, and taking six men with him went and remained waiting on the road between the house of Mohammed Azim Khan and the Mirza. It was about midnight when the Mirza passed by Dost Mohammed Khan, whom he saw, and said, "What has brought your highness here at this late hour? I hope all is good." He also added, that Dost Mohammed should freely command his services if he could be of any use to him. He replied to the Mirza, that he had got a secret communication for him, and would tell him if he moved aside from the servants. He stopped his horse, whereupon Dost Mohammed, holding the mane of his horse with his left hand, and taking his dagger in the right, asked the Mirza to bend his head to hear him. While Dost Mohammed pretended to tell him something of his own invention, and found that the Mirza was hearing him without any suspicion, he stabbed him between the shoulders, and throwing him off his horse cut him in many places. This was the commencement of the murders which Dost Mahommed Khan afterwards frequently committed.

When Mohammed Azim Khan was informed of the murder of his beloved and useful secretary, Mirza Ali Khan, by the hands of Dost Mohammed Khan, there were no bounds to his grief and anger against the perpetrator of this shocking deed. That very moment he ordered his followers to get ready for fight, and he came out of his house with them. Dost Mohammed immediately joined the Vazir, and told him that Mirza Ali was no more, and that his master was preparing to revenge himself upon him for the assassination. While he was speaking with the Vazir, information arrived that Mohammed Azim Khan was going to report to Mahmud Shah the unlawful conduct of the murderer, and beg him to co-operate in punishing the conspirators.

On this the Vazir Fatah Khan sent Mohammed Rahim, Ata-ullah Khan, and Shah Ghazi Dilavar, with the holy Qoran in their hands, begging Mohammed Azim Khan to pardon him and Dost for the past, and added to him, that if the Vazir was destroyed the result would be nothing short of the downfall of the whole family, as the good and ill fortune of Mohammed Azim Khan were closely connected with those of the Vazir, Dost Mohammed, and the rest of the brothers. He (Mohammed Azim), for the sake of the respect due to the Qoran, went back to his house, without going and reporting the case to Mahmud Shah, and remained quiet, though vexed.

After the lapse of three or four days the Vazir Fatah Khan, by the advice of the politic Dost Mohammed, went in person to apologise to Mohammed Azim Khan for the murder of his secretary Mirza Ali Khan; Dost Mohammed also accompanied him. They both pretended to express sorrow for the loss of his Mirza; they consoled him, and apologised to him exceedingly. Afterwards they all proceeded together to the palace, and stated before Mahmud Shah, that they were all one-hearted brethren, and that the past accident was all forgotten.

From time to time the Vazir Fatah Khan treated Dost Mohammed Khan with much consideration, and had a high opinion of his bravery, enterprising character, and experience, from which he had gained

numerous advantages.   He accordingly used his
influence in the court, and at last succeeded in
inducing Mahmud Shah to confer the title of Sardar,
or chief, upon Dost Mohammed Khan, and to give
him much more influence in the affairs of government.   Now the Sardar of my tale became the
object of more jealousy among his brothers.   Every
one of them feared and suspected him; and they, as
well as the other chiefs, feeling alarmed, began to
say among themselves, that it was not unlikely the
Sardar Dost Mohammed Khan would soon send
them also to join Mirza Ali Khan.

In short, the Sardar Dost Mohammed Khan
established his plans so firmly, and grew so much in
power, that he never acted on the advice of any
individual, but managed affairs by his own mature
deliberation.   This established the affection and
confidence of the Vazir in him much more than
before, and his influence increased more and more
daily.   The Sardar was always present in the night
parties of the Vazir, and bore a golden cup per-
manently in his hands.   He filled it with water and
sometimes with wine, as the Vazir requested, and
gave it to him to drink.

It is said that when the Vazir was a little tipsy at these wine parties, he generally gave a hint to the Sardar Dost Mohammed Khan to enter his room (whence his beloved wife, named Bhagi, was witnessing the pleasures of the party) to prepare his bed. While the Sardar was engaged in performing this duty, his graceful, youthful, and comely person, had desperately won the love and heart of the above-mentioned lady. It was out of her power to keep her feelings secret any longer from the beloved object—the Sardar Dost Mohammed Khan, the pleasure of whose society she enjoyed till the Vazir, her noble husband, entered the apartment. It is not known whether the Vazir was aware of this fire of love between his wife and the Sardar, which was every day gaining strength. On many occasions the Vazir allowed him to remain in his private room to enjoy the advantages of his society and conversation. It must be remembered that neither Shah Mahmud nor his Vazir Fatah Khan could boast of their good morals. There was no limit to their most dissipated practices. Sardar Dost Mohammed Khan was undoubtedly a beautiful lad, and therefore a real favourite of the Vazir, who allowed generally his beautiful brother to remain in his palace, and thus gain the royal favours and power.

When the Vazir Fatah Khan received the required sum from Mohammed Azim Khan, he made the necessary arrangements for undertaking an expedition against the Governor of Kashmir, named Ata Mohammed Khan Bamzai, son of the late Mukhtar-ud-daulah. Before the army of the Vazir, under the immediate command of the sardar Dost Mohammed Khan, reached the suburbs of Kashmir, the said Governor sent overtures, and agreed to pay the tribute of three lakhs of rupees annually to the Kabul government; which promise was gladly accepted by the Vazir and the Sardar. Hence they sent their agents to receive the stipulated sum, and bent their course towards Multan.

Immediately after their departure the agents of the Vazir Fatah Khan, and of the Sardar Dost Mahommed Khan, were driven out of Kashmir by Ata Mohammed Khan, the governor of that place; and with all haste they joined their masters in the country of Multan. On their arrival they reported to the Vazir and to the Sardar that the said governor had treated them with disgrace, and refused

to pay the tribute.   On this the Vazir and the
Sardar retraced their steps by the Esakhail route, and
purposed to weaken the power of the refractory
governor by besieging and reducing the fort of
Atak.

In the mean time the unfortunate news came from
Kabul that the Sayad Ashraf and Sayad Ata, the
great fanatics, had placed Shah Zadah Abbas on the
throne, and intended to excite their Sunni followers
to attack the Persians.   This not only frustrated all
the plans of the Vazir Fatah Khan, and of the
Sardar Dost Mohammed Khan, but created great
confusion amid the Persian division of their army,
—the foundation of their power.   They came and
stated to the Vazir and to the Sardar, that if they
were not allowed immediately to return to Kabul
for the purpose of protecting their fellow Persians
against the intended attack of the Sunnis, their
wives and children, now in Kabul, would be massacred, or made slaves by the bigoted enemies of
their creed.   The generals assured the Persians of
their protection, and begged them to stay one month
longer in their camp, to reduce the turbulent Governor of Kashmir; but they were so uneasy about

their families, that against the wish of their masters they struck their tents and took the road to
Kabul.

The departure of the Persian division of the army
of the Vazir Fatah Khan and of the Sardar Dost
Mohammed Khan weakened their power so much,
that they had no remedy but to cross the Atak and
follow them to Peshavar. Here a council of war
was held between the wise Sardar and the Vazir;
and it was resolved that the latter, with his nominal
king Mahmud Shah, should remain in Peshavar,
and that the former, along with Mohammed Azim
Khan, and the head of the returning division of the
Persians, should proceed to Kabul, whither the
Vazir and Mahmud Shah should soon follow them.
After speedy and double marches every day the
Sardar Dost Mohammed Khan and his Persian
party reached Kabul; and for ten days a hard fight
continued between him and the rebels, headed by
Shah Zadah, afterwards called Shah Abbas. In
this battle the victory was won by the Sardar, and
Shah Abbas was made prisoner. The principal fac-
tious chiefs, as Sayad Ashraf, with his tumultuous
friends of Kohistan, were ordered by the Sardar to

be executed. The other fanatic rebel Sayad Ata was laid down on his breast on the ground, and then an elephant was made to trample on him, which crushed him to death. Such was the end of Sayad Ata, a descendant of the Prophet!!

The Vazir Fatah Khan, and Mahmud Shah, on their return, found that every thing was quiet in Kabul, and that the wicked men had been annihilated by the Sardar Dost Mohammed and Mohammed Azim Khan. They all passed about one year in the arduous duty of restoring order, peace, and security, in the administration of the government. The reform and improvement in the revenue and mercantile matters introduced by the sagacious Sardar filled the empty chests of the government with money. The money coined in the temporary reign of the unfortunate Shah Abbas had much mixture of copper in it, and very little silver. To this the Sardar paid particular attention, and melting the whole of the bad coin, ordered that purer silver should be obtained and be struck into new coin of proper value.

No sooner had the affairs of the government improved, and the state treasury was a little filled,

G

than the Vazir Fatah Khan and the Sardar Dost
Mohammed Khan made preparations for an expedition against Kashmir, but it is said that the Vazir
was not so quick as usual, and appeared very slow
in his preparations for an immediate departure.
This was at once observed by the sharp eyes of the
Sardar, who addressed the following speech to the
Vazir in open " darbar" or court. "It appears to
me that the victory gained last year, the annihilation of the seditious chiefs, the confinement of Shah
Zadah Abbas, the repossession of Kabul, and the
elevation of our King Shah Mahmud to the throne
of his forefathers, by the use of the sword, and by
the wisdom of the members of our family, have
been a sufficient source of gratification to those who
are attached to our fortunes and to his Majesty
Shah Mahmud. Not only this, but the citizens,
fearless of the attacks of the lawless followers of the
late rebel Sayad Ashraf of Kohistan, sleep comfort-
ably: reform and improvement have been successfully introduced into the agitated affairs of government, may our King Shah Mahmud, and my noble
brother the present Vazir, as well as the rest of
chiefs, including myself, enjoy the fruit of our hard

earned authority; but I regret to say that the luxurious habits of the king, and of my noble brother
the Vazir, and the carelessness of the other chiefs,
bid fair to cause that the present condition of the
country be not a lasting one; and that the enjoyments of my superiors be not durable; and in this
respect the most blind and foolish policy appears to
prevail. One cause for every one of the above-mentioned individuals falling into luxurious indolence
appears to be, that they forget the seditious conduct
of Ata Mohammed Khan, governor of the rich
valley of Kashmir, without the possession of which
region no king of Afghanistan has been, or ever
will be, able to maintain a large army and the royal
dignity." The noble hearers, as well as the Vazir,
made no opposition to the speech of the Sardar, but
every one cried aloud the words "Bisyar Khub"
(well done) with cheers. The Sardar added, "Notwithstanding the peace and pleasure which every
one seems to enjoy, and that to imitate them there
is an open field for me also, yet the rules of sound
and foresighted diplomacy, which are always wander-
ing in my heart and brain, have not allowed me to
rest a moment, and I shall never be easy until some

mature steps are taken to punish the hostile obstinacy of Ata Mohammed Khan, the governor of
Kashmir, who turned the government agent, as well
as that of my noble brother the Vazir, with disgrace
out of the valley; and refused to pay the stipulated
sum of tribute. It is not possible to defray the
general expenses of the movements of an army under
my noble brother the Vazir, to check the restless
spirit of the discontented chiefs, unless the country
of Kashmir be ceded to us." This speech of the
Sardar Dost Mohammed Khan did not only cause
the cheers of the assembly, but excited all the chiefs,
and his noble brother the Vazir, to set out immediately for Kashmir.

On this a great number of horses were distributed
among the chiefs, and the state treasury was opened
to pay the troops, who went off with the Vazir Fatah
Khan and the Sardar Dost Mohammed Khan for
Kashmir. When they reached Atak, and were in
the western part of the Panjab, they entered into an
offensive and defensive alliance with the lion of this
state, the late Maharajah Ranjit Singh. His Majesty
the Maharajah assisted them with a large Sikh force
to chastise the governor of Kashmir, named Ata

Mohammed Khan. The governor was busy making the necessary preparations to defend himself. When all negotiations failed, both armies were ordered to get ready for fighting the next morning. The Sardar Dost Mohammed Khan led the Kabul army with steadiness and order, and suddenly engaged with the enemy. A great action took place between the two Afghan chiefs, and after a great loss of men on both sides, the lion of Kabul was successful, and Ata Mohammed Khan, the governor, with his brother Gholam Mohammed, were totally routed and made prisoners.

After the rich and celebrated valley of Kashmir came thus into the possession of the Vazir Fatah Khan and of the Sardar Dost Mohammed Khan, they dismissed the Sikh general to return with his army to the Maharajah, and gave him some friendly presents for his Highness. As some intrigues were in existence between the prisoners and the Sikh general, he therefore begged the Vazir and the Sardar to have them released, and allow them to proceed with him to Lahore. The Sardar thoroughly disapproved, and gave his reasons for so doing. He also pointed out to the Vazir the harm which would

undoubtedly follow if the prisoners were delivered
over to the Sikh government; nevertheless the
general succeeded in inducing the Vazir to allow
Gholam Mohammed Khan to go with him, and to
keep his brother, the late governor, still by him as
a prisoner. This extremely annoyed the Sardar,
who, in a tone of displeasure, said to his noble brother
the Vazir, " Allow me to prophesy the calamity
which the release of Gholam Mohammed Khan will
bring upon our heads, and remorse to you for your
unwise policy," &c. &c.

The day was not far distant when the symptoms
of the misfortunes which the Sardar Dost Mohammed
Khan had predicted, began to appear, on the very
arrival of Gholam Mohammed Khan in the court of
Ranjit Singh. He insisted upon his third brother
Jahandad Khan, the commandar of Atak, selling
that fort to the Sikh government; and his brother
did so on receiving one lakh of rupees for it. The
occupation of that important fort by the Sikh garrison provided the Maharajah with the key of the
conquest not only of Kashmir after a short time, but
of many other Afghan places on the western bank of
the Indus. Now the Vazir repented of his folly in

liberating Gholam Mohammed Khan, and giving him
to the Sikh chief, which he had done utterly against
the advice of Dost Mohammed Khan.

The Vazir Fatah Khan felt himself in a very com-
plicated situation, and was lost in speculations how
to repair his mistake, and put his affairs on a better
footing. He appointed Mohammed Azim Khan
governor of Kashmir, and himself, with the Sardar
Dost Mohammed Khan, quitted that valley for Atak.
Here they resolved to attack the Sikh garrison. On
this the Lion of Panjab dispatched an army of thirty
thousand men, under the command of Divan Moh-
kam Chand, Bhai Ram Singh, Dal Singh, and
Ghaus Kham, with directions to destroy the Afghan
force. This large army encamped on the bank
Nilab branch of the Indus, and engaged in action
with the Vazir and the Sardar. The latter was the
hero of the field, and his exploits of that day were
highly applauded by the Sikh generals. At last the
Sikh army succeeded in depriving the Afghans of
the place whence they were provided with water.

It was about midday that the sun grew hotter, and
the weather exceedingly warm, whilst both armies
were annihilating their respective antagonists. The

thirst, in consequence of the scarcity of water, was sadly felt in the army of the Vazir and of the Sardar, on which the former begged the latter hero to take command of the Qizilbash or Persian cavalry, and at once rush into the main column of the Sikh army. On this occasion the Sardar and his Qizilbash fought so desperately that the Sikh heroes gave them the title of gallants of the first class, and the ornamental title of celebrated and matchless champions (Rustam and Afra si ab*) of the old days. The Sardar rushed into the main line of the enemy, captured some of their guns, and forced them to leave their ground and retreat; but unfortunately some of the Afghans, overpowered by thirst, made such a disorderly attack on the other division of the Sikh army, that they were repulsed with loss: and thus the Kabul army, under the Vazir and the Sardar, after gaining once victory and guns, was routed, and compelled to fall back upon Peshavar, and from thence they marched to Kabul. Here the news arrived that Shah Shuja, with the Shah Zadah Haidar, had collected a large force, and having fought with the Navab Jabbar Khan, the governor of Derah Ghazi Khan, were

* Fabulous warriors of Shah Namah.

defeated. Though this intelligence was acceptable to them, yet it excited the jealousy of the Navab's brothers, the Vazir and the Sardar, who proceeded to supplant him. On their arrival at Derah they said to the Navab that, with regard to the sum of three lakhs of rupees, the balance of the revenues of Derah, he was squandering all this to satisfy his vanity and idle pleasures; and that, therefore, they must dismiss the Navab, having done which they returned with Mahmud Shah to Kabul.

CHAPTER III.

Brothers envy Dost Mohammed Khan—He chastises the Kohistanis—Expedition against Hirat—Murder of the Vazir Fatah
Khan—The Sardar takes up arms—Besieges the Bala Hisar—
Takes Kabul, and makes Sultan Ali king, and himself minister—
His intrigues—Murder of Shah Sultan Ali—Mohammed Azim
Khan—The Sardar procures money from the Sindhians—He
deserts—Takes Ghazni—Fights with Azim Khan—Corre-
sponds with Ranjit Singh—Sikh force at Peshavar—Dost's
treachery towards Azim Khan—Death of Azim Khan.

ALTHOUGH the Sardar Dost Mohammed Khan received kindness and honour from his principal brothers, as the Vazir Fatah Khan, &c., yet being born
from a mother of a different creed, and not of a high
Afghan family, he was looked upon with contempt
by the other brothers, who boasted that they were
descended from pure and noble parents. On several
occasions the jealousy of the brothers threw him into
all the distresses of poverty. His dependants and
horses have often passed nights and days without a
piece of bread for the human being or a blade of
grass for the horses.

In spite of this cheerless state of life, Dost Mohammed Khan never departed from the perseverance of his mind, combined as it was with all the external appearances of sincerity, and real internal hypocrisy. He was trying to gain ascendancy by all means possible, and therefore in return for all the animosity of his jealous brothers his behaviour towards them was at all times civil and obliging. This sometimes made them exceedingly ashamed of their own conduct, and at the same time astonished at his superior wisdom and management. His sweet words were supported by flattery, and he showed himself regardless of that respect which his own age was entitled to receive from his younger brothers, who were prosperous while himself was poor; and by these means he had created and organised such sound schemes for his own success that none could dare to hope to annihilate him. I have heard with my own ears from the Sardar Dost Mohammed Khan, that he had gone without food for three or four days successively, and several nights, after taking only a morsel of dry bread or a handful of half-fried grain—that in the mean time he had often laid himself down on the bare ground, making the stone his pillow; and also, having no means to maintain servants, he had many times saddled his own horse. While his heart was wounded with these painful wants, his conversation was always refreshed by a lively wit and a smiling countenance, leaving behind an impression of admiration on the hearts of the chiefs under his brothers.

The Sardar Dost Mohammed Khan was excessively fond of drinking, and carried it to an extreme excess. It is said that he has emptied several dozens of bottles in one night, and did not cease from drinking until he was quite intoxicated, and could not drink a drop more. He has often become senseless with drinking, and has on that account kept himself confined in bed during many days. He has been often seen in a state of stupidity on horseback, and having no turban, but a skull-cap on his head.

It has been stated by the early companions of the Sardar Dost Mohammed Khan, and confirmed by his own mouth, that he had and still has an extraordinary taste for music. When pleased with drinking wine, he has often sung ballads, and played upon the " Rabab," a kind of fiddle. His intimate friend and supporter was Gholam Khan Populzai; and both

these persons were considered in Afghanistan the
first players on the " Rabab." The fort of Nanchi
was the favourite seat where Dost Mohammed Khan
formed his pleasure parties, and these were generally
composed of Gholam Khan Populzai, Mirza Abdul
Sami, and Agha Mohammed. The former, being
richer than the Sardar, assisted him frequently in
pecuniary matters, and clothed and fed him on many
occasions. Gradually he gained rather more influence, yet was in the habit of drinking.

It was on the evening of a beautiful day in the
spring, that the eldest son of the Sardar Dost Mohammed Khan, named Mohammed Afzal Khan,
drank wine with his younger brother, Mohammed
Akhbar Khan, and both of them met him drunk.
He was incensed at their conduct, and determined
to punish them. He seized and bruised them severely; and at last taking them up to the roof, threw
them down on stony ground, by which he had nearly
endangered their existence. On this his favourite
wife, the mother of Mohammed Akhbar Khan, who
is wiser than the other wives of the Sardar, was informed of the dangerous state of her son. She went
to her husband and stated that he himself is desirous

of drinking, while he punishes the sons, and persuades them to the contrary; and that this is not just, as the wise of former days have said that a son cannot well inherit the property unless he follows the example of his father, and that consequently they imitated him in drinking. Hearing these words from the lips of his favourite, the Sardar felt ashamed, and then swore not to drink wine any more.

At the time Mahmud Shah returned from Derahjat, the chiefs of Kohistan, especially the head men and priests of Istalif, made an open rebellion. The Vazir Fatah Khan formed an expedition against them, but was obliged to fall back unsuccessful, having spoiled their cultivation and gardens. This made the rebels suffer the risk of starvation, and they made a resolution and agreed with each other to revenge the loss by destroying the residence of the Vazir in Kabul, and ruining his garden by ploughing over the young plants with a plough drawn by asses, which they did immediately the Vazir quitted the capital to punish some other distant refractory chiefs.

The Shah Mahmud and the Vazir Fatah Khan did all in their power to induce the Kohistanis to come into allegiance by bribes, titles, and rewards; but all this was useless: and when any threatening preparations were made against them they ascended the mountains. This disorderly state of things continued for some time, when the Sardar Dost Mohammed Khan volunteered to undertake the government of Kohistan and to punish the ringleaders. The Shah and the Vazir gladly accepted the offer, and made him governor of that turbulent district. He left Kabul with his followers, and encamped at Nanchi the first day. Here he passed the night with his Qizilbash friends in drinking, singing, and dancing, and also committed some other idle acts unworthy of his dignity. Navab Asad Khan having heard of it, advised the Sardar not to do any base act of the kind hereafter, as it will fix an everlasting stigma on his character. To this he replied, that though he was guilty of folly, yet the charge is not so bad as the mean and covetous oppression of the Navab himself. The latter requested him to explain what he meant; on which the Sardar reminded him that on a certain time he saw at the court of the Navab that a woman complained against her husband. He was summoned, and proved clearly that he had been always partial to his wife, and had never given her any reason for dissatisfaction. After a long investigation, the Navab discovered that the old husband being careless of the rules of society, disgusted his wife. Here the Sardar stated that the Navab Asad Khan decided that both were guilty, and therefore commanded them to pay three hundred rupees as a fine to him, besides suffering a long imprisonment. When this was asserted by the Sardar as a sample of the justice distributed by the Navab with regard to the wife and her husband, he caused the whole assembly to laugh at the farce of his adviser, the Navab, who thenceforward ceased to interfere with the Sardar.

Next day, the Sardar Dost Mohammed Khan entered the valley of Kohistan, where he succeeded in seizing numerous robbers, whom he immediately executed. Also by his sweet and hypocritical words, as well as by all possible sacred oaths, he induced the various rebel chiefs to wait upon him, and then lost no time in murdering them. On his arrival at Charkar, the Sardar took up his quarters in the fort of Faiz Khan. He induced Aslam Khan and Saqi Khan by a solemn agreement to join him in Charkar with other chiefs; and they relied on his oaths and

paid him their respects. In order to banish all suspicion of his evil intentions towards them, he married the daughter of Baqa Khan, one of the chiefs,
and thus, after gaining their confidence, put the
father of the new bride to death. This assumed
garb of sincerity was, however, merely a mask; and
while the chiefs were dining with him, the Sardar
made a signal to cut off their heads. There was
still one of his greatest foes alive, whom the Sardar
wished to destroy, and while he was in existence the
Sardar considered that the tranquillity would exist
neither in Kohistan nor in Kabul, where the people
of the Sunni sect always raise tumult by his aid.
He sent deputation after deputation with solemn de-
clarations written on the Qoran, and assured Khojah
Khanji of his highest regard and respect towards
him. He addressed him as a father, and stated that
his intention was to give charge of the government
of Kohistan to him, and himself go back to Kabul.
All these flattering but false oaths produced no effect
upon the cautious Khojah. Hereupon the Sardar
Dost Mohammed Khan adopted a most novel measure to get hold of him at the sacrifice of another
man. Khojah Khanji, like other chiefs of Kohistan,

H

had many enemies, and one of the strongest was
with Dost Mohammed Khan. He put him to the
sword, and thus boasted the sincerity of his good
wish towards the Khojah, as proved by destroying
his enemy. This vile deed was perpetrated at Ba-
yan, where he begged the Khojah to honour him
with his company, to settle past differences at the
place of the murder of his antagonist. Induced at
length, and blinded by his destiny, he came with a
large number of followers. No one of course was
better able than the Sardar Dost Mohammed Khan
to restore confidence by his sweet language, in the
Khojah, whom he addressed on every occasion as his
venerable father. In the evening the Sardar led his
guest inside of the fort, on the pretence that he might
survey the valuable property of his enemy, whom the
Sardar just destroyed in order to ensnare the Khojah.
As soon as he was within, the gates of the castle
were shut in the face of his followers, and the Sardar
praised the gun of the Khojah, and desired him to
show it to him. Immediately after this he ordered
his Qizilbash companions to assassinate the Khojah,
whom he at the same time called his father! and his
head was thrown over the walls amid the large retinue

of this unfortunate victim. At this sad occurrence
his followers determined to attack the fort, and fired
for a considerable part of the night; but in the morning they all dispersed, leaving the Sardar Dost Mohammed Khan to enjoy the triumph of his wilful
murders. This was not the end of his dexterity in
such deeds, for he massacred in one day eight of
the chiefs at Charkar, and Sayad Ashrat of Opiyan,
men of great influence and reverence, shared the
same fate. When he had no more blood to shed, he
engaged himself in arranging matters for collecting
the revenues and distributing justice. In two months
he completed these affairs and returned to Kabul.

While the Sardar Dost Mohammed Khan was employed in Kohistan, he was accompanied by Jai
Singh, a Sikh chieftain, with whom he had become
acquainted, when the latter was on a mission to Peshavar. Shah Mahmud and the Vazir Fatah Khan
finding that the affairs in Kohistan were all satisfactorily settled by the Sardar Dost Mohammed Khan,
they appointed a governor in Kabul, and themselves
started for Peshavar. Hence they dispatched the
Navab Asad Khan to Sardar Mohammed Azim
Khan in Kashmir, demanding the sum of twenty

lakhs of rupees, the arrears of the revenue of that valley. He delayed the payment of the sum, by which he hastened the departure of the army of the Shah to Kashmir. Mohammed Azim Khan, having heard of the hostile movements of his brothers under his Majesty, assembled all the chiefs with their forces, strengthened the fort of Muzaffarabad with a strong garrison, and afterwards encamped on the road between the two hills to check the progress of his enemy. The Sardar Dost Mohammed Khan was called upon to lead the attacking army. He found that the road was narrow, and closely occupied by Azim Khan, and that an attempt to force through would cause a great slaughter of his men. On mature deliberation he commands his followers to dismount from their horses and follow him to fight on foot in ascending the hills, and thus compel Azim Khan to fall back on Kashmir. The Sardar forced the garrison of Muzaffarabad to surrender, on which the enemy strongly occupied all the heights of the mountains which closely commanded the route of the Sardar's force. Here the Shah and the Vazir, as well as Dost Mohammed Khan, found themselves placed in a difficult position, and without any prospect of gaining a victory. Nevertheless the perfidy of the latter did more good to their cause than the swords of his party. He wrote letters to some of the chiefs in the camp of Azim Khan, stating that he had received all their letters, and laid them under the feet of Shah and of the Vazir. He added that these have appreciated their good will, and believe that they will fulfil their promised resolution by imprisoning and bringing the disloyal chief (Azim) into the presence of his Majesty early next day, while all in the camp are engaged in attending to their morning prayers. The cunning Sardar directed the bearer of the letters to pass by such a road and company on guard, so that he might be detected, and his letters and himself taken to Mohammed Khan. It was done accordingly, and caused in him the utmost alarm. He began to suspect that all his retinue were bribed, and that he would no doubt be delivered as a prisoner to the Sardar. In the mean time he continued his talk of fighting to the last, and yet on the other hand he secretly opened a negotiation with his foes. While this was going on, the winter and snow caused a great loss on both sides, and a treaty of peace was concluded on condition of receiving pro-

visions for two weeks, and a sum of thirteen lakhs of
rupees. Azim Khan came in person to the Sardar
Dost Mohammed Khan, and there having tied a
sword to his neck and the Holy Qoran on his head,*
he accompanied the Sardar thence to the royal camp.
The Vazir Fatah Khan, with the consent of his royal
master, pardoned Azim Khan, embraced and kissed
him as his brother. Such was the fruitful result of
the Sardar's perfidious letters!

The army of Mahmud Shah returned to Kabul,
and after passing the few months of the winter there,
intended to go to Qandhar. The intelligence of the
Sikhs having been attacked by Mohammed Azim
Khan in Kashmir, and of their having been routed
by him with great loss, inspired a joyful and fresh
enthusiasm in the Vazir Fatah Khan and the Sardar
Dost Mohammed Khan, and they prepared an expedition for defending Hirat against the Persians. On
reaching Qandhar they received information that
their nephew Abdul Vahid Khan, at the head of the
Hirat army, had been defeated by the Persian prince
Hasan Ali Mirza at Ghoryan, and probably taken
prisoner.

* A sign of confessing to be guilty, and imploring pardon.

This news alarmed the Vazir Fatah Khan, who, leaving Mahmud Shah at Qandhar, set out with great haste to stop the Persians before they might come upon Hirat, and the Sardar Dost Mohammed Khan of course was with him. Mahmud Shah was not well disposed towards Haji Firozuddin, the prince and ruler of Hirat, in consequence of his not assisting him when routed by Shah Shuja, and thus gave secret encouragement to the Vazir for the purpose of punishing the Shah Zadah Firoz, who was his own brother. All the Afghans and other chiefs of Khorasan became attached to them by the liberality of the Vazir and the flattering tongue of the Sardar. A battle ensued; it was fought bravely, and the Vazir was slightly wounded by the Persian army or by his own adherents; but of this the certainty is not known. This wound, however, caused the Vazir to abandon the field of action, where Dost Mohammed Khan had distinguished himself to an amazing degree.

Shah Zadah Haji Firozuddin treated the Vazir Fatah Khan with marked distinction, and commanded all his chiefs to pay their respects every morning to the Vazir before they come to his Royal

Highness; but this generous feeling of the Shah
Zadah made no favourable impression upon his guest.
He directed the active Dost Mohammed Khan to
enter the city of Hirat, under the pretence of being
invited, and to place his Kohistan followers in small
parties for the night, in the different houses of relations and friends. The Vazir added, that when the
chiefs of the Haji should come to see him next day
out of the city, he should make them prisoners, and
Dost Mohammed Khan was to shut the gates of the
city, and take possession of the palace " Arg " with
the prince. He entered the city, as was arranged,
with his retinue, and after the sun rose and the Shah
Zadah's courtiers had gone out to Fatah Khan, as
usual, the Sardar Dost Mohammed Khan massacred
the palace-guard and seized the person of the Shah
Zadah Firoz. Afterwards he commenced to plunder
and to gain possession of all the jewels, gold, and
treasure of the captive prince, and even went so
far as to despoil the inmates of the household; and
committed an unparalleled deed by taking off the
jewelled band which fastened the trowsers of the
wife of the Prince Malik Qasim, the son of the
captive, and treated her rudely in other ways. The

pillaged lady was the sister of Kam Ran, to whom she sent her profaned robe; and the Shah Zadah, or her brother, resolved and swore to revenge the injury. Fatah Khan was informed of the immense booty which the Sardar had taken, and also his improper conduct towards the royal lady; and the Vazir planned to take the plundered property from the Sardar Dost Mohammed Khan, and to chastise him for his deeds in the Palace. The Sardar having heard of this made his way through the mountains to join his brother Mohammed Azim Khan, the governor of Kashmir. He was there put under restraint by the direction of the Vazir, who was preparing again to wage war with the Persians.

The Shah Zadah Kam Ran reached Hirat, internally determined to have revenge, and yet externally he appeared very civil to the Vazir Fatah Khan. He advised him to procrastinate his second expedition against the Persians, and that it would be better to give rest to his army. In the mean time he laid a plot for the ruin of the Vazir; and many other Durrani chiefs, who had been reduced to subordination by the Vazir, and were jealous of his increasing power, joined him in planning the destruc-

tion of the Vazir. He was seized by Kam Ran at
the consent of his father Mahmud Shah, and blinded
by Ata Mohammed Khan Bamzai. His brothers
contrived their escape from Hirat, excepting Purdil
Khan, who was also released on the condition of his
continuing loyal and obedient to the prince. No
tragedy of modern days can be compared with that
barbarous one that ended the life of the Vazir. He
was conducted blind, and pinioned, into the presence
of Mahmud Shah, whom he had elevated to the
throne. The Shah asked him to write to his rebellious brothers to submit, to which he replied with
fortitude, that he was a poor blind prisoner, and had
no influence over his brothers. Mahmud Shah was
incensed at his obstinacy, and ordered him to be put to
the sword, and the Vazir was cruelly and deliberately
butchered by the courtiers, cutting him limb from
limb, and joint from joint, as was reported, after his
nose, ears, fingers, and lips, had been chopped off.
His fortitude was so extraordinary that he neither
showed a sign of the pain he suffered, nor asked the
perpetrators to diminish their cruelties, and his head
was at last sliced from his lacerated body. Such was
the shocking result of the misconduct of his brother

the Sardar Dost Mohammed Khan towards the royal female in Hirat. However, the end of the Vazir Fatah Khan was the end of the Sadozai realm, and an omen for the accession of the new dynasty of the Barakzais, or his brothers in Afghanistan.

Mohammed Azim Khan wrote from Kashmir to Shah Shuja, and assured him of the united aid of his brothers, as well as of the Sardar Dost Mohammed Khan, against Shah Mahmud, who had ordered his brother the Vazir to be murdered. Shuja was joined by Nawab Mohammed Zaman Khan, and after defeating Samandar Khan, he took possession of Derah Ghazi Khan. The Sardar received the sum of three lakhs of rupees from his brother Azim Khan in Kashmir, and assembled a moderate force to join his brothers Yar, Sultan, and Pir Mohammed Khan in Peshavar, and these elevated and acknowledged the Prince Ayub, king of Afghanistan. The Sardar also made secret engagements with the Prince Sultan Ali, and secured his consent to make him sovereign if necessary. Mahmud Shah was frightened to death by the threatening news that the Barakzai had resolved to supplant him in the throne. In the mean time Ranjit Singh caused an alarm towards Atak,

which forced the brothers of the Vazir to leave
Peshavar and take shelter in Lalpurah. Hence the
Sardar Dost Mohammed Khan sent a few beautiful
horses, with some other presents, to the Lion of
Panjab; and as soon as he returned towards his
capital, the Sardar, with his brothers Yar Mohammed
Khan, &c., came through the Khaibar upon Peshavar,
and compelled Jahandad Khan, the Bamzai, to flee
to the country of the Yusafzais.

On this Ata Mohammed Khan, the Bamzai, relation of Jahandad Khan, induced Mahmud Shah and
Kam Ran to send Prince Jahangir, the son of the
latter, with him, and to subdue all the Barakzai
rebels, as he called Sardar Dost Mohammed Khan,
the brother of the murdered Vazir. He succeeded
in his proposals to the king, and came to Kabul with
the prince. Immediately the Sardar wrote an offensive and defensive treaty on the margin of the Holy
Qoran, and in an important article thereof he and
his brothers bound themselves by a solemn oath to
divide the kingdom for ever between themselves and
Ata Mohammed Khan, if he agreed to lend no
assistance whatever either to Shah Shuja, to Kam
Ran, or to any other Sadozai. The Sardar dis-

patched this treaty in charge of a confidential adherent, and Ata Mohammed Khan, knowing that
neither Shah Shuja nor Mahmud Shah, with Kam
Ran, could shine in the presence of the brighter
talents of the Sardar, he accepted the offers made in
the treaty. He sent a secret letter to the Sardar
Dost Mohammed Khan with a verbal token to make
it more sincere, and which was in these words:
"When the late Vazir Fatah Khan left you with
Prince Kam Ran a long time ago in Qandhar, the
friendship between us (Dost and Ata Mohammed)
was strengthened by a solemn oath." If this was
true, the Sardar Dost Mohammed Khan was to
march for Kabul with easiness of mind, and at
Khovajah Rivash he will meet and confer with the
Sardar himself. At the arrival of such a flatter-
ing communication from Ata Mohammed Khan
Bamzai, the Sardar made arrangements to leave
Ayub Shah at Peshavar, and taking with him Shah
Zadah Sultan Ali and Ismail, he set out for Kabul.
The Sardar was well aware that the former Shah
Zadah was the master of three or four lakhs of
rupees, and he therefore renewed his promise and
oaths of putting the crown of Kabul on his head, and

gave hopes of the same nature secretly to the latter Shah Zadah.

After uninterrupted and rapid marches the Sardar Dost Mohammed Khan reached Butkhak with the Shah Zadahs,—and the Prince Jahangir ordered Ata Mohammed Khan, the Bamzai (who had already entered into intrigues with the Sardar), and Baqar Khan, to meet the Sardar with arms, and to shut themselves within the citadel of the Bala Hisar in Kabul, with a considerable store of provisions, with the view to be besieged by the enemy to resist till relieved by Mahmud Shah and Kam Ran his father. Ata Mohammed Khan pitched his tent near the village of Bibi Mahru,* and the Sardar Dost Mohammed Khan, with Navab Samad Yar and Pir Mohammed Khan, moved and encamped at Khova-jah Rivash, as previously appointed, and about ten o'clock at night Hafizji, the son of Mir Vaiz, and Mulla Hidayat Ullah, effected a clandestine inter-view between the Sardar and Ata Mohammed, the head of the Jahangir's army. The treaty which had been formerly contracted through their respective

---

* Where the British troops under Brigadier Shelton were defeated at the outbreak in Kabul in 1841.

deputations, was now solemnly renewed personally.
This treaty was resealed by the Sardar, Yar Mohammed, and by Navab Samad Khan, to Ata Mohammed Khan, who was to desert Jahangir, and
allow the Sardar to attack the Bala Hisar. Ata
Mohammed Khan desired that Pir Mohammed Khan
should add his name and seal to this agreement,
being one of the brothers of the same family as the
Sardar Dost Mohammed Khan. As the object of
the Sardar was to destroy Ata Mohammed Khan,
after he had obtained his end, he therefore thought
proper not to include Pir Mohammed Khan in the
treaty, for the purpose of employing him against his
meditated future enemy, with whom he was now
contracting terms of friendship. With this view the
Sardar stated repeatedly to Ata Mohammed Khan
that Pir Mohammed Khan was young and not fit to
be trusted with such important secrets, and that there
was no need of his appearing to be a party in the
treaty; but that he will, no doubt, follow the example
of his brothers respecting the articles of the agreement. Ata Mohammed Khan outwardly harangued
his followers, that if they relax in their exertions in

promoting the cause of their royal masters, Shah Mahmud, Shah Zadah Kam Ran, or Shah Zadah Jahangir, and fail to punish the Barakzai rebels (Sardar Dost Mohammed Khan, &c.), the wrath of the Almighty God will fall upon them and curse them if they betray his cause. He continued his treacherous harangues for a few days, while secretly he exchanged a great many oaths of perpetual friendship with the Sardar Dost Mohammed Khan, and was thus betraying his own sovereign. It was agreed that they were to have a second interview with each other in the " Burj i Vazir," and ratify the agreements with much more satisfactory and solemn swearings and ceremonies. Ata Mohammed came accordingly, and as soon as he entered the door of the " Burj i Vazir " the Sardar Dost Mohammed Khan induced his brother Pir Mohammed (whom he had purposely kept out of the treaty), to throw down his newly and solemnly made friend, Ata Mohammed Khan, on the ground, and to pluck out his eyes; and he accordingly perpetrated this foul deed. The deprivation of sight drove away all ambitious thoughts from the head of the blind chief, who, while governor of Kashmir, had inflicted similar injuries on numerous persons, and had also taken a prominent part in blinding the late Fatah Khan.

The Sardar Dost Mohammed Khan, relieved from a powerful enemy, or an intriguing friend, resolved to besiege the Bala Hisar. Shah Zadah Jahangir was treacherously advised by some of his adherents (with whom Dost Mohammed Khan was intriguing) to evacuate the lower citadel, and to close himself, with his retinue, in the upper one; and the empty part of the Bala Hisar was instantly possessed by the enemy. A battle ensued, and Dost Mohammed Khan formed a mine and blew up part of the gate of the other citadel. Shah Zadah Jahangir then found himself in a dangerous situation, and being accompanied by his confidential friends, he stole his escape towards Ghazni.

Now, after such an extraordinary display of talent and perseverance of mind, after such intrigues and murders, and this surprising run of good luck, the Sardar Dost Mohammed Khan found himself master of Kabul;—but the peace of his mind was subverted by the arrival of the intelligence that Shah Mahmud and Shah Zadah Kam Ran were in progress

I

from Qandhar to fight against him; and at the same time that Mohammed Azim Khan had left Kashmir with the view that he, being the eldest of the brothers, should not leave Dost Mohammed to become master of the capital of Afghanistan. He, nevertheless, being elated with his victory, and at the same time fearful of his enemies on the south, and of his jealous brothers on the east, he proclaimed Shah Zadah Sultan Ali as king of Kabul, and made himself his minister. This intelligence more stirred up the jealousy of Mohammed Azim Khan and of the other brothers. They invited Shah Shuja to join with them for their common advantage, but some difference occurred and caused a battle between the Shah and his inviters, in which the latter were victorious, and the former was put to flight. They dared not, however, to move upon Kabul without being under the nominal authority and shadow of the Sadozai Prince; and they therefore sought, found, and proclaimed Shah Zadah Ayub as king. The Sardar Dost Mohammed Khan, under his own appointed king, Shah Zadah Sultan Ali, now left Kabul to meet Shah Mahmud and Shah Zadah Kam Ran. He soon discovered that it was impossible to gain a victory against such a

powerful army of the Shah, which was composed of
all the principal Durrani chiefs; and he therefore
thought it advisable to have recourse to his usual
intrigues and stratagems.   He accordingly forged
seals and letters, as if they were from some of the
high chiefs, which formed the army of the Shah
Mahmud, and which stated their discontent in serving the Mahmud, and a desire to enter into the
employment of the Shah Zadah Sultan Ali,—the
king made by the Sardar.   He also directed one of
his confidential chiefs to enter into correspondence
with the enemy, and to pretend to intrigue against
him (the Sardar Dost Mohammed Khan), and,
moreover, to enclose the forged letters for Mahmud
Shah, in order to convince him of his own (the
writer's) fidelity and attachment to the Shah, and of
his hatred against his employer Dost Mohammed.
This perfidy of the Sardar proved successful, so that
Mahmud Shah and Kam Ran became suddenly
alarmed, and showed the letters to the chiefs, whose
seals and names had been forged, and which they
now bore, and all of them solemnly denied being
the writers of these letters.   In the meantime Salu
Khan, called Shah Pasand Khan, stated to Shah

Mahmud that all the Durrani chiefs intended to go over to the enemy; and it so happened about that time the Shah Ghasi Dilavar, with a few horsemen, deserted the Shah's camp and joined the Sardar Dost Mohammed Khan. This frightened Shah Zadah Kam Ran and his father to the utmost, and they fled through Hazarajat to Hirat, leaving all the artillery and camp-equipage to the Sardar. Purdil Khan, the other brother, got possession of Qandhar, which was under Gul Mohammed Khan, governor for Mahmud Shah. This was the commencement of Afghanistan into the hands of the Barakzais—Sardar Dost Mohammed Khan and his brothers; and he considered that his good fortune had thus gained for him the possession of Kabul a second time.

Mohammed Azim Khan marched from Kabul with his own assumed king, the Shah Ayub, and the Sardar Dost Mohammed Khan took possession of the stronghold of Ghazni, where he appointed his younger brother, Amir Mohammed Khan, as Governor, with the view that if overpowered by Mohammed Azim and Shah Ayub, he may easily defend himself in this impregnable fort. However the Sardar's position was far from securing to him the enjoyment of the possession of the capital, for he found himself at the same time threatened by his brothers at Qandhar, and by those with Mohammed Azim Khan. Numerous negotiations and altercations were exchanged: and at last it was arranged that Mohammed Azim, being the eldest of the brothers, should enjoy Kabul; that Yar Mohammed Khan should possess Peshavar, and Purdil Khan should receive Qandhar, and the Sardar Dost Mohammed Khan, Ghazni. Thus the country was divided between the brothers of this family, and the nominally proclaimed King of the Sardar was set aside. All appeared happy with this arrangement, and were occupied in planning to repel any external real or apprehended danger. But the Sardar Dost Mohammed Khan was discontented, and searching for an opportunity to secure his own particular advantage.

Mohammed Azim Khan, with Shah Ayub, left Kabul to proceed against Shah Shuja, who was organizing troops in Shikarpur. When the former passed Ghazni, the Sardar Dost Mohammed Khan returned to the capital, and reproclaimed Shah Sultan Ali as king; and this made Mohammed Azim Khan

to retrace his steps.   When he reached Kabul with
his own appointed king, Shah Ayub, the monarch
who had been set up by the Sardar abdicated and
retired.   It is a matter of great difficulty to determine here whether the Sardar did all in his power
to subvert the designs of his rival brother, or joined
him to dethrone Shah Sultan Ali, who undoubtedly
was a prince of high talent and of some wealth.
However, he waited upon Sultan Shah, and said to
him, that if he was anxious to secure for himself the
sovereignty, he must murder Shah Ayub.   To this
he replied with wrath, that he was not so inhuman as
to steep his hands in innocent blood ; and he even
added, that he will try to destroy any man who shall
ever perpetrate such a murder.   The Sardar, after
making him easy for a few days, persuaded him, for
the safety of his person, to retire into the Bala Hisar,
which he did.   Mohammed Azim Khan explained
to Shah Ayub the necessity which existed for putting
an end to the life of Shah Sultan Ali,—on the promise that he (Mohammed Azim) will get rid of the
Sardar Dost Mohammed Khan in the same manner,
and with this view Ayub meanly agreed.   Both of
the Shahs were living together on friendly terms, till

after an evening party the poor Shah Sultan Ali retired to repose, when Prince Asmail, son of Ayub Shah, strangled him to death ; and now the cruel Shah requested his instigator, Mohammed Azim Khan, to fulfil his promise, of killing the Sardar Dost Mohammed Khan. To this request, however, he answered, " How can I murder my brother ?" Such was the end of Shah Sultan Ali, by the intrigues of the Sardar who had once elevated him to the throne.

After some time the Sardar Dost Mohammed Khan commenced to contrive schemes for reducing the power of his elder brother, Mohammed Azim Khan, and for gaining possession of all his wealth, which he had hoarded up from extortions and all kinds of oppression when Governor of Kashmir. He pretended to appear as if he was really fond of his brother, and could not part with him even when he retired, adding, that he thinks proper to attend him always, and to guard him against his enemies, whereas, in secret, he intended to annihilate him at a favourable opportunity. He had nearly succeeded in his base design when, luckily, Navab Samad Khan became acquainted with the plot, and informed Mo-

hammed Azim Khan immediately. He then increased
the number of his personal guard; and to divert the
attention of his brother the Sardar he marched with
all his treasure and family towards Qandhar, with
the intention to receive tribute from the Mirs of
Sindh. The Sardar assembled his Qizalbash adherents, such as Mahmud Khan Bayat, &c., and
stated that they had abandoned the legal cause of
Mahmud Shah, and joined Mohammed Azim Khan
in the hope that the wealth he had brought from
Kashmir will be circulated amongst them in Kabul;
and that now, on the contrary, he goes with it to
Qandhar, and enriches its inhabitants. He would
therefore advise them to use every energetic exertion
and to follow him, and seize him with the Mammon
he possesses. They all agreed to this, and started
off. Meanwhile Mohammed Azim Khan precipitated
his march, and took shelter in the fort of Ghazni;
and as he had plenty of money he collected a large
force to preserve himself. However, he induced
Navab Samad Khan to dissuade the Sardar Dost
Mohammed from such an act of hostility against his
own brother. The Sardar accepted the terms of
peace on condition that a sum of money should be

advanced to him to distribute amongst his followers, which was gladly done.

Easiness of mind was restored to Mohammed Azim Khan by this peace, or rather truce, with the Sardar Dost Mohammed Khan, and he proceeded from Ghazni to Qandhar, where, leaving his cumbersome equipage, and being lightly equipped, he started to demand tribute from the Mirs of Sindh; and the Sardar, under the name of a coadjutor, followed him. When the army arrived at Shikarpur, negotiations began between the Mirs and the invader; and, when about to be satisfactorily concluded, here the arch-intriguer, the Sardar Dost Mohammed Khan, sprung his ˙ secret mine, and dispatched his uncle Alahdad Khan clandestinely to Mir Ismail Shah, the Minister of the Mirs of Sindh, with the proposal, that if he were to advance him only one lakh of rupees, in lieu of four lakhs which had been demanded by his brother Mohammed Azim Khan, that he, in conjunction with the other brothers, Sherdil and Pir Mohammed Khan, would march back to Qandhar; which deed, by diminishing the strength of the army, and depriving Azim of all brotherly support, would compel him to follow them with whatever the Mirs chose to give him, or even with nothing. The minister knew well that the stratagems of the Sardar Dost Mohammed have always been unquestionably successful; and that he was the first man who, for his own little personal advantage, would aptly sacrifice the material interests of his powerful brother. He therefore made the above-mentioned proposal known to the Mirs, and lost no time in sending the amount of money asked by the Sardar, who, being delighted with this success, which otherwise would never have attended him, deserted Mohammed Azim Khan; and Sherdil and Pir Mohammed Khan of course went with him. Now Azim Khan soon discovered that he was treacherously abandoned by his brothers, and by a larger number of forces than what he had with him: and he therefore considered it proper to fall back upon Qandhar, where Purdil Khan received the intelligence of his failure, by the conduct of the Sardar, before the latter reached the city. He received him coolly on account of this: and the Sardar thinking that Mohammed Azim and Purdil

Khan might join to destroy him, and consequently considered that it was the wisest plan for himself to go to the brothers at Peshavar.

On his route from Qandhar he plundered villages, caravans, &c., and extorted money from every one he met till he reached Kabul. Here he created a tumult, but Azim Khan followed to check his progress. The Sardar had already formed a party of his own in the city, and immediately went to Istaliff, for collecting the Kohistanis against Azim Khan. The Navab Samad Khan caused peace between them, on which the Sardar, plundering all he could on the road, came to Peshavar. Here the brothers of course were aware of the danger which would befal them if they were not liberal and polite to their embarrassing guest, and they instantly gave up the district of Kohat, with its revenues, for his support. Mohammed Azim Khan, with the king of his own creation, Shah Ayub, came to Peshavar, and demanded the revenue of that country for his Majesty from his brothers. When this was settled, he thought, imprudently, to leave the Sardar in the rear, in the possession of Kohat; and he promised he would give him a larger country, affording much more revenue, if he will come with him to Kabul. He then appointed Navabs Samad Khan in Kohat, and Mohammed Zaman Khan at Hashtnagar, he himself retiring to Kabul with the Sardar.

In Kabul the Sardar Dost Mohammed became again restless, and began to quarrel with his brother, Mohammed Azim Khan, and demanded larger sums of money than he could conveniently give. When he pressed hard, Mohammed Azim Khan unwisely said to the Sardar that he may go any where he likes, and that he does not want his services. This was the object of his desire, which proved highly beneficial to himself and injurious to Azim Khan. The Sardar hereupon quitted Kabul, and on the road contrived schemes how he might gain possession of the stronghold of Ghazni. He assembled all his brave followers, and desired them to enter the fort, four persons together; concealing their arms, and to continue so doing until he gives further orders. He added, that they are to avoid the suspicion of the commander at the gate, and if questioned, say they want to buy provisions. When the Sardar found that a sufficient number had gone into the fort for offensive operations, he himself, in disguise, with two

servants, joined the party. The commandant of
the guard at the gate was shot by him; and a
skirmish took place, which, after some injury on
both sides, gave the Sardar possession of the whole
gate. He now easily hastened to increase the number of his retinue from his camp; and he soon
proclaimed himself the master of Ghazni, and
restored confidence and peace among the inhabitants.
He engaged himself in repairing and strengthening
the fortifications, and stored the place abundantly
with ammunition and provisions. He then waited
in confidence, ready for the assault of Mohammed
Azim Khan.

The intelligence of the Sardar Dost Mohammed
Khan's possessing Ghazni heightened the wrath of
Mohammed Azim Khan; and at the head of a
strong force, and with battering guns, he came and
besieged that fort. For eight days a continued
firing was kept up on both sides, and the guns from
the citadel caused great slaughter in the camp of the
enemy, who, at length, hopeless of subduing the
garrison, thought best to negotiate with the Sardar.
Navab Samad Khan was then deputed from the
camp to confer with Dost for that purpose, but the

Sardar neither opened the gate nor asked him to come in; but hanging out a rope from the rampart he descended by it himself to meet the envoy outside of the fort. The ambassador used every sort of art to deprive the Sardar of the fort, but he swore that he will rather sacrifice his head than give up Ghazni to Mohammed Azim Khan. A second deputation was sent the following day, and another conference was held, in which it was agreed that the Sardar should continue to keep possession of the fort, but that he must come and wait upon Mohammed Azim Khan, as a token of his homage, and so prevent the appearance of disgrace and weakness to be attached to him (Azim). On this the Sardar appointed his younger brother, Amir Mohammed Khan, the governor; and manned every tower and bastion for defence. Having thus secured the place, the Sardar came out and had an interview with his besieger, and they both embraced, and yet accused each other for the breach of brotherly respect. A treaty of peace was thus concluded, and Mohammed Azim Khan again resolved to levy tribute on the Sindhians.

The Sardar Dost Mohammed Khan was now

strengthening himself much, and enjoying repose by
the possession of Ghazni, the first stronghold of
Afghanistan.   Even now nothing could keep him in
peace, nor induce him to secure the internal welfare
of the country, and he planned to bring external
embarrassment on his brother, and on the whole
family.   With this view he deputed a mission to the
Maharajah Ranjit Singh, and kept an unceasing
correspondence with the Lahaur court, and hoped by
this alliance to elevate himself, and to subdue his
brothers, and especially the powerful Mohammed
Azim Khan.   This excited the alarm of Mohammed
Azim Khan, who lost no time to fall back upon
Peshavar for the purpose of checking the progress of
the Sikhs.   The Afghan and the Sikh armies were
now near enough to have occasional skirmishes;
however, all the Barakzai brothers sent Yar Mohammed Khan as an envoy to the Maharajah Ranjit
Singh.   He betrayed the trust reposed in him; and
with or without the advice of the Sikh invader, he
wrote letters to Mohammed Azim Khan, that it
was the intention of the Sikhs to take a different
route, and to seize his family and treasure then left

at Michni. The Sardar Dost Mohammed Khan was to be sure connected with the enemy for the destruction of Azim Khan; and these sad circumstances marred his intrepidity. Upon one hand he considered that he ought to prevent the seizure of the wives and treasure by the Sikhs at Michni, and on the other, that retiring from the face of the enemy without hazarding a battle, was a most cowardly deed. In the meantime his heart was bitterly wounded by finding that not only the Sardar Dost Mohammed Khan had attached himself to the Lahaur chiefs, but that nearly all the other brothers had followed his example. In this disturbed state of mind he sometimes resolved to fight and keep his ground; and at other times he thought best to break up the camp, for the purpose of preserving his wives and his money. Soon after this his followers became disheartened at the uncertainty of his determinations, and every one began to strike his own tent, and to leave the camp; while no one knew a sufficient cause for so doing. Mohammed Azim Khan, sadly vexed, plucked out his beard, and lamented for the treachery of the Sardar Dost Mohammed Khan, and of the other brothers; and for being thus compelled to retire with the outward show of weakness and disgrace.　On his return to Kabul Azim Khan was attacked by dysentery, and soon after died broken-hearted.

CHAPTER IV.

Succession of Habib-ullah Khan—He is defeated by the Sardar —Peace is concluded between them—Habib-ullah's secret intentions—Flight of the Sardar—Sherdil Khan and the Sardar join against Habib-ullah—Policy of Dost—He takes the Bala Hisar—Intrigues and rupture between Sherdil and Dost— Siege of the Bala Hisar—Peace between the brothers— Death of Sherdil Khan—The Sardar sole master of Kabul —Sayad Ahmad's war with the Sikhs—Rebellion at Tagav, and defeat of the Sardar.

SARDAR MOHAMMED AZIM KHAN, by the turn of fortune, was the first in wealth amid the sons of Sarfraz Khan, the brothers of the Sardar Dost Mohammed Khan. Knowing the incapacity of his son Habib-ullah Khan, he implored Navab Jabbar Khan, as he breathed his last, to take care of his son, whom he requested and charged to wipe away the stigma he had sustained before the Sikhs. After his death Habib-ullah Khan succeeded him; and these two became his favourite and immediate advisers—Hafizji, son of the late

Mir Vaiz, and Aminullah Khan Laho-gardi.* He
also wrote and invited Purdil Khan from Qandhar,
and treated him with consideration and liberality.

It must not be forgotten that Shah Ayub, the
sovereign created by the late Mohammed Azim
Khan, was still in the Bala Hisar. He disbelieved
his son Shah Zadah Ismail, and paid no attention
to his prudent advice,—namely, to seize Habib-ullah
Khan with the treasure of his father. Purdil Khan
therefore entered the citadel by force, with a large
retinue; seized the Shah, and killed the Shah Zadah.
He set Ayub at liberty, however, after having caused
him to pay the sum of one lakh of rupees; and he
then made his way towards the Panjab.

Habib-ullah Khan, surrounded by the abandoned of all classes, immersed himself in base
dissipation. The courtiers of his father's time became disgusted; some retired, and some were dismissed. Sardar Dost Mohammed Khan discovered
that he had now an open field for his hypocrisy and
ambition. Regardless of the difference of age, and
of the dignity of an uncle towards a nephew, he pre-

* Who took a prominent part in the rebellion against the
English in 1841.

tended to respect Habib-ullah Khan, as older and
chief of the family, and therefore as superior to himself. He often ran, and even placed shoes under
his nephew's feet, wiping them with his own hand-
kerchief. While the Sardar was cunningly gaining
ground and time for the display of his real object,
Habib-ullah Khan was fool enough to pride himself
by fancying that he already exceeded the power of
his late father in reducing the Sardar to the condition
of one of the vassals. There was no limit to the
false and sweet words of his devotion and affection
towards Habib-ullah Khan, and no bound to the
pride and vanity of the latter on this occasion.
However some old and experienced persons about
him, as Aminoollah Khan, &c., always cautioned
him against the mask of homage which the Sardar
Dost Mohammed Khan had politically put on. At
length he discovered that the Sardar was paying
him a false homage, and was only watching for a
favourable opportunity to upset his power. He
thereupon disclosed his fears of the Sardar to his
unwise companions; and with their consent resolved
to seize the Sardar when he comes to his court, and
to deprive him of his eyes. Dost Mohammed Khan

proceeded to the Bala Hisar, as usual, in the morning, and it was fortunate for him that Haji Khan Kakar became acquainted with the plot, and on the Sardar's entering the room, where he sat with Habibullah, he caught the sight of the Sardar, and put his fingers on his own eyes; which sign the Sardar, of quick understanding, instantly knew meant that Habib-ullah had contrived and conspired to blind him, and consequently he lost not a moment to return and ride off on his horse.

The Sardar Dost Mohammed Khan induced Yar Mohammed Khan to take his part, and prepared to wage war with Habib-ullah Khan. The latter was supported by the son of Mir Vaiz and by many other influential citizens. The followers of both parties came out by the gate named Shah Shahid, and after a long fight the Sardar was victorious. The enemy was besieged, and would have been easily assailed had Dost Mohammed Khan not feared the plunder of his treasure and property, which the Sardar was desirous to procure for his own use. He therefore used his exertions in preventing his followers to enter the residence of Habib-ullah Khan, and stopped in the fort of Baqar Khan Moradkhani,

hemming in the enemy all the night. Next day
Amir Mohammed Khan came to aid his brother the
Sardar, and Habib-ullah Khan also received reinforcements from Lahogard, when another battle ensued near the fort of Kashif. However, the no-
bilities interfered and put a stop to the bloodshed.
It was agreed that the Sardar was to receive twenty
thousand rupees and the revenue of Vardak in addition to that of Ghazni, and Habib-ullah Khan must
remain the undisputed master of Kabul. On this
the Sardar went to Ghazni and continued to improve
the military strength of the place in every way for
some time. But Habib-ullah, conscious of his sagacity, could not enjoy rest, for the constant fear of
being destroyed by the Sardar was destructive of his
happiness: consequently he dispatched agents with
valuable presents to the Qandhar chiefs, and sought
their alliance. Purdil Khan immediately came to
relieve him from anxiety, and to lend him aid if
necessary. After some days spent in festivals and
parties of pleasure, the real Afghan character showed
itself in a misunderstanding which took place between the host and the guest, and this presented an
opportunity for the Sardar Dost Mohammed Khan

to appear again as the enemy of Habib-ullah Khan.
In the plain near the fort of Qazi both sides met for
battle, but bloodshed was prevented by the interference of some silver-bearded chiefs. On this Habib-ullah placed the Sardar on the elephant with
himself, and brought him into the city with every
pomp and show of cordiality, as if he was reconciled
heartily with him for ever, while yet he conspired
for his murder. He presented him with a large sum
of money to distribute among his forces, and thus
pretended to show the sincerity of his disposition and
attachment. The Sardar meanwhile became acquainted with the conspiracy, and while it snowed
heavily he fled from the city, placing his family also
on the elephant. The cold was so keen, and the
rapidity of the flight was so necessary, that one of
his little daughters fell down in that hurried march
and expired immediately. Habib-ullah was informed
of his escape, and immediately followed and overtook
him. He had, however, secured a fort near Maidan
for his head-quarters, and was able to sally out and
thence to skirmish with his pursuers. Amir Mohammed Khan, the younger brother of the Sardar,
started from Ghazni to relieve him; but Habib-ullah,

having known of this, met and routed him on the road. The Sardar now thought proper to leave the fort in the dark of the night, and go to his brother at Ghazni unseen by the enemy.

Meanwhile Sherdil Khan was invited by Habib-ullah, and the quick-sighted Sardar Dost Mohammed Khan, found that their union with each other would be injurious to his own advancement. He therefore left Ghazni for Kohistan, where he remained for a few months, making the chiefs his partisans, and thus prepared to render himself strong enough to encounter his united foes. Sherdil Khan was not less active in the city. He was intriguing to pro-claim himself the principal chief, and to destroy Habib-ullah Khan, for whose assistance he had origi-nally come. The latter's influence was merely a shadow of the nominal chiefship, while Sherdil Khan managed the affairs of government. He allowed thirty thousand rupees per month for his private expenses, and appointed Khodai Nazar Khan, his own maternal uncle, deputy governor in Kabul. His habits were tyrannical, and he very soon made the whole population disgusted with the existing rule of Sherdil. Many people began to hold correspondence

with the Sardar Dost Mohammed Khan, and assured
him of their co-operation in his behalf. The Sardar
came to Kabul, and adopted his usually successful
policy of adjusting matters by stratagem rather than
with the sword. He asked for an interview with
Sherdil, and after a long-continued discussion on the
propriety and importance of the past and present
conduct of each other, a new agreement was made,
in which it was arranged that Sherdil Khan was to
remain the paramount Lord of Kabul; while the
Sardar was to keep the government of Ghazni,
Maidan, and Kohistan, marrying at the same time
the widow lady of Mohammed Azim Khan, with all
her property. She was the daughter of Sadiq Khan
Javan Sher, and the step-mother of Habib-ullah Khan.
Although Sherdil was considered a braver man, as
well as a shrewd diplomatic character, yet after all he
could never penetrate into the deep-bottomed hypocrisy of the Sardar. He was quite senseless, indeed,
not to apprehend the great influence which Dost
Mohammed gained by his connexion with the widow
lady. He obtained through this marriage quarters
and friends among the very warlike and heroic Qizalbashes, where he could raise brave and numerous

cavalry, and where in adversity he could shelter himself against any of his powerful brothers.

After the conclusion of this agreement the Sardar Dost Mohammed Khan thought that nothing could advance his interest farther than to cause a struggle in the town.   He therefore presented a series of fictitious alarms relating to perfidious dangers from Habib-ullah to his new ally Sherdil Khan, and induced him at last to make the other his prisoner. The Sardar, to show his sincerity in the cause, counselled Sherdil that he should confine him also (the Sardar) with Habib-ullah, which will show the other party that they are not united, and which will thus give him the opportunity of promoting his pretensions secretly!   This was accordingly done, and the mother of Habib-ullah Khan was exasperated as well as distressed at the custody of her son; and closing the gates of the Bala Hisar, she declared war against Sherdil.   Thus happened what the Sardar Dost Mohammed Khan wanted; and as Sherdil found himself in an awkward position, he asked counsel of the Sardar, then his prisoner, on mutual understanding.   He was immediately released, made deputy governor under Sherdil, and commenced to negotiate with the warrior-lady. He sent to her deputations repeatedly, and after assuring her, with his usual solemn oath, of his fidelity towards her, and promising her safe escort with her treasure, as well as the wealth of her son Habib-ullah, he succeeded in having the gates of the citadel opened, and lost no time in placing his guards on the different towers. On this Sherdil Khan immediately repaired to the Bala Hisar, and placing the widow lady of Mohammed Azim, the step-mother of Habib-ullah, on an elephant, sent her to Sardar, who married her according to the concealed agreement. The Sardar resolved not to violate the oaths he had made with the lady when she caused to be opened the gates of the Bala Hisar for him, and not to satisfy his perfidious avarice by plundering her himself; but he induced and gave opportunity to Sherdil Khan to do this, on the condition of equal shares in the spoil. The pillage took place accordingly, and went so far, that every woman of the family was searched and deprived even of her dress, if it was not torn. Sherdil possessed himself of the whole remaining mammon of the late Mohammed Azim Khan, and drove every member of the household of Habib-ullah with infamy out of the citadel. Sherdil now became avaricious of this very considerable booty, and determined not to give even a little to the Sardar Dost Mohammed Khan, as had been originally stipulated. To effect this object of his imprudence, he sent off Habib-ullah Khan as prisoner into the distant fort of his Mama, and then contrived schemes to blind the Sardar Dost Mohammed Khan, if not to destroy him altogether. In the mean time the brothers, chiefs of Peshavar, also arrived in Kabul to take advantage of the disorder, and to share the riches if possible. Sherdil intended to seize the Sardar and perpetrate his deed of cruelty when he attends his court, but he was again informed of the plot, as before, by the motion of Haji Khan Kakar; and instantly leaving the presence of Sherdil, on the pretence of ablution, he rode off on his horse and came to his residence. This was the second time when the Sardar had a providential escape from his deadly enemies but pretended friends.

It was now evident that Sherdil Khan could not remain in the enjoyment of his ill-gotten power, as the Sardar Dost Mohammed Khan could not be entrapped. The latter lost no time in collecting a strong body of men at the expense of his new rich wife; and, exasperated at the faithless behaviour of Sherdil Khan, he insisted upon having his own will for the delivery of Habib-ullah Khan. He then laid siege to the Bala Hisar, and all the brother chiefs of Peshavar joined him with the view of enriching themselves from the plunder of the besieged. Sherdil Khan also sent an express to his brothers at Qandhar, intimating to them that he was possessed of considerable wealth, which, if he were not protected by those who were his real brothers, would fall into the hands of the Sardar Dost Mohammed Khan and the chiefs of Peshavar, and would make them extremely powerful in the family. This communication stirred up the chiefs, and they left Qandhar immediately for the purpose of defending their brother Sherdil Khan in Kabul. They arrived at length to aid the besieged, but the Sardar had surrounded the citadel so closely that provisions began to diminish; and in the mean time he sent a message to Sherdil Khan that the brave never shut themselves up in a house or fort, but come out and feel a proud desire either to fall or to gain in the open field. It is well known that Sherdil Khan was

really a person of great intrepidity, and braver than
all the sons of Sarfraz Khan. This message stirred
him up and he sallied out. Many days at first
passed in skirmishes, and at last a general action was
intended. Sherdil arrayed the line of his forces
towards the tomb of Shah Shahid; and the Sardar,
with the flower of his Qizalbash adherents, appeared
on the opposite hillock, called Tappah Maranjan.
The Qandhar chiefs, after reconnoitring the position
of the Sardar, discovered that there would be only
useless bloodshed in fighting with him while supported with such well-equipped cavalry and in possession of such a commanding position. Sherdil
Khan, just like an Afghan, came into the camp of
the Sardar, and stopped at the tent of the Navab
Mohammed Zaman Khan. Counsel after counsel
continued for many days, and the leaders of both
parties were cherishing themselves on fruits and rich
dinners together, while their respective followers
were fighting for their employers in the field.

It would be tiresome to the reader to detail here
the numerous treaties which were concluded and then
violated, the struggles which were renewed and which
again ceased,—oath after oath being exchanged, till

finally it was settled that the Navab Samad Khan should be empowered by both parties to adjust their differences. He proposed that neither Sherdil nor Dost Mohammed Khan should possess Kabul, which should be entirely left to be governed by the influential citizens, headed by the Sultan Mohammed Khan, one of the brother chiefs of Peshavar. It was further arranged that Sherdil Khan with his brothers must retire to Qandhar, and the Sardar to his government seat at Ghazni or Kohistan. This peace, however, was soon disturbed, for the followers of the Qandhar chiefs fell into a quarrel with those of the Sardar, and this ended not without much bloodshed. In the mean time, the widows of the late Mohammed Azim Khan deafened the ears of the hearers by shrieks, and begged the Sardar and the Navab to revenge on Sherdil Khan the insult and disgrace he had shown to the ladies of their deceased brother, demanded that he should be compelled to liberate their sons, Habib-ullah and Akram Khan. The Sardar again, exclusive of his other brothers, went and made a secret agreement with Sherdil Khan, that the Sardar will join him against any one who may attempt to impede his progress, or may wish to seize his property which had belonged to Habib-ullah Khan, on the condition that Sherdil Khan will bind himself to assist the Sardar against the Peshavar chiefs, if necessary, and will give up his prisoners into his hands. On this Sherdil Khan loaded on beasts of burden all the moveable wealth from the Bala Hisar, and after delivering Habib-ullah Khan to the Sardar, set out for Qandhar.

The Sardar Dost Mohammed Khan meanwhile knew that the brother chiefs of Qandhar and of Peshavar, in concurrence with each other, had established Sultan Mohammed Khan Governor of Kabul, with the view of having influence in the capital, and that he himself was set totally aside. Consequently he insisted upon leaving Habib-ullah Khan with Sultan Mohammed Khan on his part in the city; and he succeeded in doing so. Some time, however, passed before the Sardar could recruit his means and troops in Kohistan, and in the interval the death of Sherdil Khan happened. The talents and bravery of this chief of Qandhar were respected and dreaded by the Sardar, who now found that no one else remained in the family capable to frustrate his designs in any way. Sultan Mohammed Khan was exceedingly partial to the citizens of the "Sunni" sect; and to counterbalance this, the Sardar took the "Shias," or Qizalbashes, under his wings; and he employed clandestinely emissaries to kindle religious misunderstanding and offences between the two parties. In the meantime Habib-ullah Khan left Kabul, annoyed with the treatment of Sultan Mohammed Khan, and this created a fine excuse for the hostilities of the Sardar.

Finally, the Sardar Dost Mohammed Khan communicated to Sultan Mohammed the alternative to leave Kabul, or to be ready to fight with him. The latter, however, treated this message with ridicule, till the Sardar actually had opened a fire on the city. The citizens made a few skirmishes, and at length Sultan Mohammed Khan consented to evacuate Kabul; and so the Sardar entered the Bala Hisar by one gate, while the Sultan went out by another. The Sardar was now so fortunate as to be the sole sovereign of Kabul, where he ruled till the British Government dethroned him; and he is now again ruling where his English enemies could not govern. He was proud of having the chief seat and government of the capital of Afghanistan; but he was not

L

happy in his new position. He was sure that as soon as the brother chiefs of Qandhar and of Peshavar had no fear of attacks from Kam Ran and the Maharajah Ranjit Singh, they will not allow him to remain in the undisputed possession of Kabul. He therefore entered into correspondence with the fanatic Sayad Ahmad, who had raised a religious war on the Sikhs, in the Yusaf Zai country; and who kept the chiefs of Peshavar also engaged so as to prevent their attempts to disturb the Sardar. By this diversion of the attention of the Peshavar chiefs he had nothing to fear from the East; but his brothers on the South marched from Qandhar to oppose him. He thereupon led forth a large force, and met his antagonists near Qarabagh. A few skirmishes took place between the Kabul and Qandhar armies, which were obliged to fall back on their respective capitals by the sudden appearance of the cholera.

The Sardar Dost Mohammed Khan made a discovery that Habib-ullah was intriguing with the ill disposed chiefs to supplant him from the throne of Kabul, and he thought the best and safest mode of putting off this impending danger, was to bribe and

induce the followers of Habib-ullah to desert their
master, and to join him. He succeeded in this, and
afterwards confiscated all his estate. Annoyed at this,
he went over to the chiefs of Peshavar, where he received a district yielding one hundred and twenty
thousand rupees for his support, yet after a year he
quarrelled with them and returned again to Kabul.
The Sardar, however, paid him no attention, and this
induced him to go to Qandhar with all his family.
Distress from want, and the neglect of the ruling
uncles, broke and deranged his spirits, and he became
quite insane. Even then he did not stop much
longer there, notwithstanding the chiefs offered him
twenty-five thousand rupees a-year for his maintenance, but he crossed the Ghoeleri range of mountains with his families, and on reaching the Esa
Khail district near Derah Ismail Khan, he massacred all his wives and children, and threw them into
the Indus. Such was the dreadful deed and sad fall
of one who was once respected, flattered, and dreaded
by the Sardar Dost Mohammed Khan, and by the
other uncles.

The Sardar Dost Mohammed Khan had not firmly
established his authority in Kohistan, for robberies

and murders were still in practice, and some persons in existence there, who threatened death to his collectors and magistrates. He therefore assembled a select force, but, avoiding every occasion for the use of arms, he, with his natural sweetness of tongue, ensnared the ringleaders, as Nurak Shakardarari, Sayad Baba Qushqari, Zaman Istalafi and Mazu Tagavi, &c., assassinated them all, and forced the petty ones into banishment.

The inhabitants of Tagav, in the meantime, rebelled against the Sardar Dost Mohammed Khan and subverted the tranquillity of the suburbs of Kabul. The Sardar collected a good force and placed over it the Navab Jabbar Khan to punish the rebels. The Navab remained for some time in Tagav negotiating with them, and thought that he will be able to settle the disturbance without having recourse to arms, but it proved to be quite contrary. The Tagavis made a night attack upon the Sardar's army, which, with its leader Navab Jabbar Khan, was defeated and dispersed. All the camp equipage fell into the hands of the rebels, and the remains of the forces returned successful to Kabul. This failure did not incense the Sardar Dost Mohammed Khan, but created in him an apprehension that rebellion would soon appear on every side, if the honour of his arms was not recovered, and if the Tagavis were not punished.

CHAPTER V.

Haji Khan joins the Sardar—The Sardar punishes the rebels—
Takes Bala Bagh and Jalalabad—Jealousy of the brothers—
His escape from assassination—Marches against Shah Shuja—
His letter to the British political agent at Loodianah—Sir
Claude Wade's answer—The Sardar writes to Shah Shuja—
Reaches Qandhar, and defeats Shah Shuja-ul-mulk — Cor-
respondence discovered among the spoils—Ingratitude of the
Qandhar chiefs towards Dost Mohammed Khan—The Sardar's
interview with his dying brother—Flight and evil designs of
the Peshavar chiefs—Haji Khan Kakar.

WHILE the Sardar Dost Mohammed Khan was
making preparations for marching an army in
person against Tagav, his principal and secret
object was to subdue Bala Bagh, Jalalabad, and the
people of Zurmat and of Bangash. The Sardar had
at this time with him Haji Khan Kakar, a man of
great treachery and hypocrisy, similar to himself.
This person was formerly in the service of Habib-
ullah Khan, and then in that of Sherdil Khan the
Qandhar chief. He knew well that among all the
brothers Dost Mohammed Khan was the only man
to prosper, and therefore, on two former occasions

when he informed the Sardar of the plots which his
(Haji) master had laid for blinding and killing him.
Knowing also that at length the Sardar will gain the
paramount power over the other brothers, he stole
his escape from the camp of the Qandhar chief, his
employer, and took shelter in the shrine of " Shah
Ashqan Arefan," and pretended to be tired of this
world, and to devote the remainder of this life for
gaining the happiness of the next. The Qandhar
chiefs did everything to induce him to follow them,
but he seemed determined to retire from the world
and live quiet in the mosque, yet this was merely a
pretence. The Sardar went to him after the Qandhar
chiefs went away, and persuaded him to quit the
Mausoleum, and to co-operate with him for the
aggrandisement of his power and of his country.
Haji Khan accompanied the Sardar to his residence,
and commenced a new career under a new master,
as he had anticipated, and he will be found, on many
occasions, to play a double part and to abound in
treachery. Haji Khan advised the Sardar Dost Mohammed Khan first to proceed towards Zurmat and
Bangash; and, though the Sardar at first thought it
not good to undertake this expedition, yet at length

it proved successful.   He destroyed many rebellious
forts, collected revenues, punished the refractory, and
established peace and governors in that district. The
cholera in the mean time spread and affected the
Sardar; and fearful of the result, he returned to
Kabul.   Some time afterwards · he declared war
against Tagav, as he had originally intended. This
declaration made Sultan Mohammed Khan and the
other brothers alarmed on account of his increasing
power, and they communicated to the Navab Mohammed Zaman Khan their earnest desire and urgent advice to make himself ready to oppose the
Sardar, who after the conquest of Tagav would certainly subdue his country of Jalalabad.   While the
Navab was preparing for defence, repairing the fortress, and storing up provisions at Jalalabad for siege,
the Sardar was engaged in razing the strongholds of
the Tagav rebels.   They fled to the mountains, and
the Sardar possessed himself of their very considerable flocks, and of all their various quadrupeds.
From that day no one from that country ever at-
tempted to give him any offence, and the captured
guns of the Navab Jabbar Khan were also restored
to the Sardar.

The Sardar Dost Mohammed Khan now turned his attention to the projected conquest of Bala Bagh and of Jalalabad. The former was ruled by Mohammed Osman Khan, and the latter by the Navab Mohammed Zaman Khan. After a siege of two days, the chiefs of Bala Bagh surrendered, and then the fort of Jalalabad was invested by the forces of Dost Mohammed Khan. Here the siege continued for a few days, and then the Sardar commanded his Kohistan force to mine the fort. It was accordingly mined and blown up, when his army made an assault and captured Jalalabad. The Navab Mohammed Zaman Khan entered the room of his wife, who was the daughter of the late Vazir Fatah Khan, and thought himself safe under her protection. On this the Sardar gave orders to his son, Mohammed Akbar Khan, to go in, seize, and conduct the good Navab to his presence. Regardless of the respect due to him, he forced the Navab to leave his lady's protection; and with no turban on his head he was conducted by Akbar Khan into the presence of his father, who brought him away and gave him as his state-prisoner a sufficient allowance to live upon.

It must be borne in mind that the daily increase of power and influence, and the aggrandisement of territory by the Sardar Dost Mohammed Khan, was the source of the odious jealousy of his brothers, both old and young, the chiefs of Peshavar and of Qandhar. Knowing their own weakness they left and acknowledged him to be the master of Kabul, but yet they always murmured on account of the great expenses incurred by them on various occasions in proceeding to Kabul, and in restoring order there before the Sardar possessed it; and consequently they wrote to him to repay to them certain sums of money, and sometimes they asked for protection against Kam Ran and Ranjit. The Sardar always laughed at these reckless and murmuring demands for money and aid; but said, in reply, that he had nothing to give them, and that if it was convenient to him he will lend them military assistance against any real and general enemy. The Sardar Dost Mohammed found out that the Navab Jabbar Khan, instead of adjusting differences between him and the other chiefs, increased the difficulties for him by his unceasing intrigues with the malcontents. He thought best therefore to deprive him of the Ghilzai country, and to fix for him an adequate and respectable stipend in the city. He stated to the Navab he has received numerous complaints from his (Navab's) subjects, and that for the stability of his rapidly and progressively increasing government, he thinks to take up the administration of that district himself, and to provide for him in lieu of it by some other means. This made the Navab feel more hostility towards the Sardar, who had always been successful against the base conspiracies and intrigues of his brothers, of the Navab, &c. It has been said that while at Jalalabad the Sardar found a person armed and concealed at night in his private tent, who was bribed to murder him. The Sardar felt or rather heard the breathing of a man under his bed; and without making any noise, he got up in the manner as if he was to retire for a minute, and then to return to his bed immediately. He then very quietly took the arms from the guard at the door of his tent, and pointing the musket in the direction of his bed, he commanded the culprit to come out. He was seized, yet at the interference of the Navab, and of the Peshavar chiefs, he was pardoned, or else he would have been blown up by the firing of a gun.

It was immediately before or soon after the Sardar gained possession of Jalalabad, that the Shah Shuja, the ex-king of Kabul, appeared and raised an army at Sindh, with the intention to try to recover from his repeated failures of fortune in recovering his dominions and invading Qandhar; but the chiefs of this place wrote and applied for the assistance of the Sardar Dost Mohammed Khan. He knew that if he was not to proceed at their call, his brothers will not be able to oppose and to frustrate the designs of the Shah, who if once in the possession of that city, would place him in a most dangerous situation in Kabul; and he therefore prepared an army, to start forth with it towards Qandhar. The Navab Jabbar Khan, with the rest of the discontented chiefs, was in correspondence with Shah Shuja, who had agreed to restore the Ghilzai district to him, and in like manner to restore Jalalabad and Bala Bagh to their respective masters, the Navab Mohammed Zaman and Usman Khan; and they had resolved to join the Shah, when the Sardar Dost Mohammed Khan arrives suddenly before the Shah's camp at Qandhar. The Navab was of opinion that Shah Shuja had resolved to recover his lost kingdom under the auspices

of the English government, and he had inculcated a
similar belief into others. To effect the purpose of
his intrigues, or to secure his profit, he planned of
course numerous schemes, and at last on arriving at
Ghazni he supplicated the Sardar Dost Mohammed
Khan to allow him to go on with his plans and to
make some favourable terms with the Shah for him,
as he was sure that he (the Shah) would at last be
victorious. The Sardar, knowing that the Navab
wished to go over to the Shah, and believing that
then all the chiefs from his own camp and from the
Qandhar camps would follow his example, leaving
him alone in the field, replied thus: " Lala,* there
will be plenty of time for your negotiations if I be
defeated."

Dost Mohammed Khan thought it advisable to
ascertain whether this expedition of Shah Shuja (as
rumour described it) was framed by the desire of the
British government; and he therefore addressed a
letter to Sir Claude Wade, then political agent at
Loodianah, and requested that functionary to inform
him whether the Shah was supported by the English

* An affectionate term for addressing personally to a brother,
and sometimes to a very intimate friend.

government to invade Afghanistan, or was marching
thither on his own account only. He added, that if
the former was the case, he would take all these matters into his own deliberate consideration; and if the
latter, that he was on the way to meet the Shah with
arms. Sir Claude Wade replied that the British
government had no participation in this expedition
of the king against the Barakzai chiefs, but that he
wishes him well. Dost Mohammed Khan dispatched
also a letter to Shah Shuja, saying that his brothers,
the chiefs of Qandhar, are not capable to meet the
wishes of his Majesty, and that he (the Sardar) is
making rapid marches, and trusts to settle all differences satisfactorily. This mode of writing seemed
to promise that he will fight with and defeat the
Shah, which his brothers at Qandhar were unable to
do. The Sardar had also written to Gulistan Khan,
the Hazarah chief of Qara Bagh, to reinforce him
against Shah Shuja; although he had one year before shown designs of revolt, but had not actually
taken up the cause of the Shah. Whether he did
not or could not spread dissensions in favour of the
monarch, is a matter of investigation; yet it is evident that he made a very fair excuse for not accom-

panying the Sardar Dost Mohammed Khan to Qandhar. He stated that he was moving with followers for
the assistance of the Sardar, and on the road met
some Afghan maliks,* with their heads cut on their
shoulders, who advised him not to proceed; but he
paid no attention to them, thinking that probably
they wished to mislead him by false advice. He
continued marching on, he said, till he met Mir Yaz-
dan-bakhsh,† with his head also in his hand, who cried
out and said to me, " Oh unfortunate man! where
are you going? Do you wish to fall into the mouth
of a serpent? Is not this head disunited from my
shoulders a warning to you?" The chief added, that
when he heard thè above words from the lips of a
Hazarah, he could not hesitate a moment to disbe-
lieve him; and that he therefore was obliged to go
back to his home with his followers, and thought it
safest not to accompany the Sardar. The most re-
markable thing in the Hazarah's answer is, that he
showed his Afghan ruler (by mentioning the Afghan
and the Hazarah men with their heads cut in their
hands) that the Sardar being an Afghan was not to

* Head men of the villages.
† Whose account will hereafter be found.

be believed, and that therefore he could not trust himself to him.

On arriving at Qandhar the Sardar thought it prudent to fight at once with Shah Shuja-ul-mulk, rather than allow his troops to recover from the fatigue of their rapid marches. He was wise enough to know the duplicity of certain chiefs and relations in his camp, and thought even the least delay might mature their intrigues and induce them to abandon him. Shah Shuja-ul-mulk had occupied a very strong post opposite to the city, but his vanity, and the idea of securing a safe route, excited him to quit his entrenched camp and to choose another place for battle in spite of his wiser counsellor, Samandar Khan. Dost Mohammed Khan on his side made the disposition of his army, and the plan for attacking the Shah; and he placed his son, Mohammed Akhbar Khan (renowned as the murderer of the late Sir William Macnaghten, the British Envoy), at the head of his well-mounted cavalry; and the infantry was commanded by Nayab Abdul Samad Khan,* as

* A Persian adventurer, who came into Bombay as a horse merchant, and thence went to Sultan Mohammed Khan at Peshavar. He entered his service, and raised a regiment of

well as by his other sons. Dost Mohammed Khan,
being always the first for cunning in Afghanistan,
now desired to know, and tried to find by some hypocritical manœuvre, whether the troops that were
with him had any design to support him or to abandon him. He drew his sword consequently, and galloped forward as a general towards the enemy. He
had not proceeded more than fifty yards when he
stopped to find whether the troops followed him with
or without hesitation. He then looked at his forces,
and what he read from their countenances it is impossible to say; but he ordered Mohammed Akbar
Khan to make an immediate attack with his cavalry.
The battle was very hard fought, and the infantry of
the Shah, under Mr. Campbell, though in a very weak
state, made a brave resistance. It defeated at once
the Barakzai force, and the chiefs entered the city
of Qandhar. Sardar Dost Mohammed Khan was,

infantry. Afterwards he fled to Kabul, and received a similar
command under Dost Mohammed Khan. He continued with
him for some years, and then finding his position dangerous he
stole his escape to Bokhara, and gained the favour of an infantry
regiment from the half-mad monarch, the Amir of Bokhara,
where his proceedings in regard to the British authorities shall
be mentioned in their proper place.

M

however, still keeping his post, and Mohammed Akbar Khan causing great havoc by his cavalry and by his intrepidity amid the line of the Shah. The Sardar having discovered that the army of the Sadozais with the Shah was gaining, and his brothers the Qandhar chiefs had retreated into the fort; determined either to lose or to gain, he, with his son, Mohammed Akbar Khan, made a general attack upon his Majesty, and after a desperate resistance and loss they at last succeeded to defeat and disperse the army of the enemy. The weak but brave regiment under Mr. Campbell was still in the engagement, and at last surrendered when it was known that Shah Shuja with his Khavanins (nobles) had run away, and that their commander, Mr. Campbell, had fallen wounded on the field. He was taken prisoner by Dost Mohammed Khan, and was handsomely treated by him. All the tents, guns, and camp equipage of the ever fugitive Shah Shuja, fell into the hands of the Lion of Afghanistan, and a large bundle of the papers and correspondence of various chiefs in his country with the Shah. Among these he found many letters under the real or forged seal of Sir Claude Wade to the address of certain chiefs, stating that any assistance given to Shah Shuja shall be appreciated by the British government.

Nayab Abdul Samad Khan, the commander of the infantry of Dost Mohammed Khan, had sent a letter to the Shah by his own orderly; and when detected, he (the orderly) was blown up by a gun to prevent the disclosure of his master's intrigues with the Shah.

The chiefs of Qandhar prepared to pursue and seize the person of the fugitive king, and begged the Sardar Dost Mohammed Khan for leave to do the same. He replied that he would not take the trouble to pursue the Shah; but that he would be delighted to get possession of Shah Zadah Mohammed Akhbar, the son of the fugitive Shah by his own sister, whom in time of necessity he could make a useful instrument, and under his royal shadow advance his own interest. It was evident that the defeat of the Shah and the preservation of the Qandhar chiefship was owing to the active intrepidity and brisk assistance of the Sardar Dost Mohammed Khan; and yet the chiefs, forgetful of this cause for gratitude, began to treat the wishes of their champion with contemptible neglect and disinterestedness. They boasted of their superiority and bravery, after the battle had been fought and gained by him for them, and even did not trust him so far as to enter the city of Qandhar. Perhaps herein they were influenced by the remembrance of the mode and success of his stratagem in taking possession of the fort of Ghazni ; and thus were mistrustful of his designs, and too fearful of the probable consequences to allow him to come into the citadel.

The prospect of appearing disorders in Kohistan, and the cold treatment he received from the chiefs of Qandhar, as also the arrival of the unwelcome intelligence of the serious illness of his brother, Amir Mohammed Khan, compelled the Sardar Dost Mohammed Khan to return to his capital, Kabul. On the road he thought it prudent and politic to connect himself with the Tukhi Ghilzai chief, and he proposed the connexion and instantly married his sister, in order to make an addition to the circle of his wives, and at the same time to establish confidence in the Ghilzai chief. When he reached Kabul he found his dear brother, Amir Mohammed Khan, just breathing his last. He was able only to say to his brother the Sardar what he had purposed to do, for the selling his old grain from Ghazni, and for storing up the new crop; and desired him to see that the money is received, and that all sorts of pecuniary matters are duly settled, for these he was ever most passionately fond of.

Before we make mention of the preparations made for his next expedition, it would be necessary to describe the circumstances which led to it. While the Sardar Dost Mohammed was engaged at Qandhar, his brothers the Peshavar chiefs, Sultan and Pir Mohammed Khan, were deprived of the government at Peshavar by the Sikh army; they were compelled to return and take refuge at Jalalabad. They were led to believe that the Sardar Dost Mohammed Khan would be routed by Shuja, which would give them an opportunity to gain possession of Kabul, and they had actually sent and placed their own governors in some of the districts; but the news came that the Shah was defeated, and that the Sardar was returning successful. This was, to be sure, sad tidings for them, which destroyed all their prospects and all the castles the deposed chiefs, the brothers of Peshavar, had built in the air. In the mean time, showing

the usual fraudulent character of an Afghan, they
fired a salute to celebrate the victory at Qandhar,
and accused their own officers of taking the possession or the management of certain villages belonging to the Sardar, pretending that it was contrary
to their wish and order. They proceeded towards
Kabul, and went to meet the victorious Dost Mohammed Khan on his way back from Qandhar.
The interview was nothing apparently but indica-
tive of cordiality and brotherly unanimity. Here
it is worthy of notice that the double-game player
Haji Khan Kakar bowed lowly to him. This will
show the feelings and disregard of honour characteristic to an Afghan, while having no shame or
repentance for his past ill conduct, but repeatedly
committing himself to similar disgraces and making
excuses if necessary. This person had deserted
Sherdil Khan to join the Sardar, and then deserted
the latter to connect himself with the Peshavar
chiefs, who were now deposed; yet his personal
safety was secure as being under their protection.
In the meeting, however, the Sardar said to this
deserter that it was evident that his brothers of
Peshavar could expect little good from him after

his past conduct towards himself; to which Haji Khan replied, that if he had deserted him he had gone to his brother, and not to any Sikhs or other strangers.

CHAPTER VI.

Preparations for a new expedition against the Sikhs—Design of
the Sardar to assume the Royal title—He is surnamed Amir-
ul-momnin—His method of procuring money—Barbarity
exercised towards a rich trader—New coinage—The Sikhs
depute Dr. Harlan to Sultan Mohammed Khan—The Amir
is incensed, and threatens Dr. Harlan—He encamps at
Shekhan—Truce with the Sikhs—The Amir's treacherous
designs—His violent altercation with Pir Mohammed Khan
—His plans and counsellors—Ranjit Singh arrives, and sends
an embassy to the Amir—Oath of friendship between the
Amir and Sultan Mohammed Khan—The Amir seizes the
Sikh envoys—Breaks up his camp—Sultan Mohammed takes
the captive envoys with him—Rage of the Amir.

THE Sardar Dost Mohammed Khan stated on his
return from Qandhar, that he had got rid of one
enemy in the person of Shah Shuja, now defeated,
but another was powerfully wounding his heart and
honour by the constant turn of affairs, and by the
remembrance of the inroads made by an infidel into
the Mahomedan land. In this he alluded to the
conquest and possessions of the Sikh army at Peshavar; he planned to declare a religious war, in the
view that having no money himself to levy troops, he

AMIR DOST MAHOMED KHAN.

could hardly persuade the people to take up his
cause; whereas, under the name of a war for the sake
of religion, he might be successful.   The priests were
accordingly consulted, and all the chiefs, as well as
his counsellors, and Mirza Sami Khan, concurred in
the opinion that the Sardar Dost Mohammed Khan
should assume the royal title, and proclaim himself
as king; because the religious wars, fought under the
name and flag of any other than a king, cannot en-
title the warriors to the rights and honours of mar-
tyrdom, when they fall in the field.   The Sardar was
not altogether disinclined to assume royalty; but the
want of means to keep up that title, and the unanimous disapproval of his relations, prevented him
from adopting the name of a king.   The Sultan Mohammed Khan was so jealous of the Sardar's taking
the royal title, that he left Kabul on the pretence of
going to Bajaur.   In the meantime the Sardar,
without any preparation or feast, went out of the
Bala Hisar with some of his courtiers; and in
" Idgah " Mir Vaiz, the head priest of Kabul, put a
few blades of grass on the head of the Sardar, and
called him " Amir-ul-momnin," or, Commander of
the faithful.

The change of title from Sardar to the higher grade of Amir-ul-momnin, made no change nor produced any effect upon the habits, conduct, and appearance of Dost Mohammed Khan, except that he became still plainer in attire, and in talk, and easier of access. The only difference we find now is that of addressing him from this time as Amir. Before the Amir came to the final determination of extortion, the head priest, Khan Mulla Khan, satisfied him by saying that it was not contrary to the Mahomedan law to snatch money from infidels, such as Hindu bankers, if it was disbursed amongst warriors of the true faith. As the Amir was really in pecuniary wants, and had the sanction of the priest, he therefore seized all the Shikarpuri merchants, and demanded three lakhs of rupees from them. The Amir sent openly, as well as clandestinely, his confidential men into all parts of the country, who spared no time in forcing the payment of the demands of their employer; and where he had given orders to raise a certain sum from certain bankers of a district, the persons employed on this occasion did not forget to fill their own pockets besides. Those who fell into the hands of these official banditti were tortured and deprived of their health before they would part with their wealth; and those who escaped suffered by the confiscation of their moveable property. Sham-shuddin Khan at Ghazni, Mohammed Usman Khan at Balabagh, and Mohammed Akbar in Jalalabad, as well as the other petty governors of the various small districts, received instructions from the Amir to follow his example in seizing and torturing, and thus depriving the wealthy of their money. This method of extortion did not remain limited in application for the infidels alone, but gradually it involved the Mahomedans. In the city many principal persons suffered, and among them a rich trader of the name of Sabz Ali, who was commanded to pay thirty thousand rupees, and having refused the payment of so large a sum, he was confined in prison, and torture of every horrid description was inflicted on him by the Amir. Some days he was branded on his thighs, and on other days, cotton, dipped in oil, was tied over his fingers, and burnt as a torch; and after many days of agony the poor man expired. On this occasion the Amir only uttered a word, that he wanted his money and not his death; which, how-

ever, could not make him a loser, for he forced the
relatives of this victim to pay, and thus obtained
this sum. The whole country at this time was an
appalling picture of extortion and torture, and he
continued to spread havoc all around till a sum of
five lakhs of rupees was thus unjustly gathered up for
the religious war of the faithful.

The title and the money were now provided for
the Amir, but another conversation took rise amongst
the learned Mirzas of the court before the " Commander of the faithful" could march; and it was
discussed what words or verse should be struck with
the name of the Amir on the coin. Numerous
persons of skill in verse exhibited specimens of their
own composition, and the one which Mirza Sami
Khan, the prime minister, formed, at length succeeded in being struck on the coinage. The gold
coin was scarce, but many pieces of silver and copper
were circulated, bearing the stamp of Dost Mohammed Ghazi. The value of the silver was twelve
sharis, each of which was formed of the value of five
copper pence.

Intelligence of these preparations for a religious
expedition by the Amir Dost Mohammed Khan

against the Sikhs reached Peshavar; and the Maharajah Ranjit Singh deputed Dr. Harlan* to the
Sultan Mohammed Khan, who was not on good
terms with the Amir, hoping that by gaining him
over to himself he would succeed in making a division in the Mahomedan camp. This did not escape
the notice of the Amir Dost Mohammed Khan, who
dispatched the Navab Jabbar Khan with the view
to frustrate the designs of the Sikh mission, and to
induce the Sultan Mohammed Khan to join his
camp with the Bajaur militia. On the arrival of the
Amir the Navab joined him with the Sultan Mohammed Khan, and with Dr. Harlan from Bajaur.
It was now evident that the Sultan Mohammed was
bought by Dr. Harlan for the Sikhs, and therefore
the Amir accused him sharply for interfering and
causing differences between his brother Sultan Mohammed and himself. Dr. Harlan found that he
was not in a safe position after being suspected by
the camp followers, and accused by the Amir, whom
he could not induce to listen to him like the Sultan
Mohammed Khan. He therefore went at night to

* An American gentleman.

the Amir with the "Qoran," as a token of suppli-
cation; and next day he considered himself fortunate to get permission to pass safely to the Sikh
camp at Peshavar.   The Amir quitted Dakka, and
encamped at Shekhan, in the , plain of Peshavar,
opposite to the mouth of the Khaibar pass.

The Maharajah Ranjit Singh had not then arrived,
and is said to have sent orders to his general to lull
the designs of the Amir Dost Mohammed Khan
by exchange of negotiations until he himself joins
the camp; and these were accordingly commenced.
The Navab Jabbar Khan and Agha Husain were
the negotiators of the Amir, who had enjoined the
latter to watch the former.   The Agha was found
to be bribed by the Sikhs to cause a truce; and
at length the Sultan Mohammed Khan went to the
Sikh camp, and became a medium for maintaining
the truce until the arrival of the Maharajah.   Meanwhile the Amir had refused to give the Government
of Peshavar to Sultan Mohammed, whether it were
taken by arms or obtained by negotiations; and he
was likewise denied when he proposed to have Jalalabad.   He therefore now thought that it was right,

and that he was free to seek for his own interests while in the Sikh camp.

The Amir Dost Mohammed Khan was sensible of his own danger, from the presence of his discontented brother in the enemy's camp; and, contrary to the rules of the truce, he clandestinely stirred up some of the Ghazis to attack the Sikhs with the most foul and dishonest view, namely, to endanger his life. There were, in consequence of this, several desultory assaults made by the Afghans, who brought some heads from the enemy's side, along with some little plunder from their tents. The Sikh army only waited the attacks, and thus obeyed the commands of the Maharajah to stand on the defensive. Pir Mohammed Khan, brother of Sultan Mohammed Khan, who had remained in the camp of the Amir, pretending to be unwell, now waited on him, with a drawn dagger in his hand, and threatened to stab it into his own breast, adding his own opinion of the baseness of his act in causing this hostility in spite of the existing truce; alleging that it would excite the Sikh general to cut the head off his brother in retaliation. The Amir replied, and even swore falsely, as usual, that he had never given any such directions, and that he had no control over the Ghazis—the champions of the true faith. However, he affected to say that they should preserve the truce, while in the mean time he excited their avarice by pointing out to them the golden bangles which will fall into their hands by killing a Sikh soldier. The advanced guard was changed every day by the Amir; and when Pir Mohammed Khan's turn came, the Amir commenced negotiation with the Sikh of such a tenour that a severe conflict occurred;—but Pir Mohammed Khan being a good soldier, as well as commander, behaved bravely, and said that that atrocious scoundrel (the Amir) had brought a heavy calamity upon him, but that he had got well out of it.

It was not an easy task for the Amir to decide what course to pursue. His prime minister, Mirza Sami Khan, supported by Mohammed Afzal Khan and a few other chiefs, was advising the Amir to wage war; and Abdul Samad, the commander of his infantry, stated boastingly that he would defeat the whole Sikh army with his own regiments, and would bring Avitabile prisoner. On the other hand the Navab Jabbar Khan, considering the

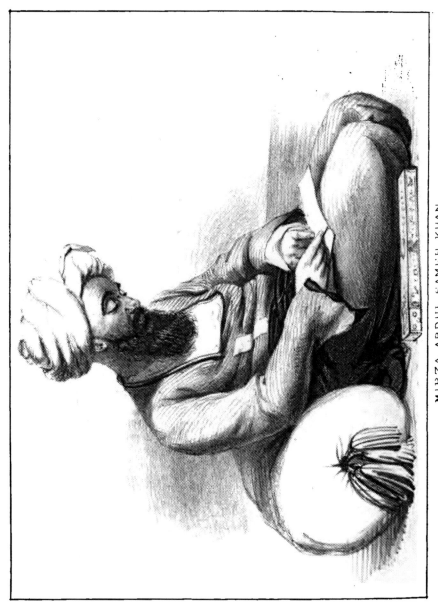

MIRZA ABDUL SAMEH KHAN

superiority of the enemy, proposed to retire without the hazard of battle, and the Amir wisely agreed
with him.

Meanwhile the Maharajah Ranjit Singh arrived
in the camp from Lahaur, and his appearance gave
fresh and bold spirits to the Sikhs. He lost no
time in arranging the troops and the plan of attack,
if necessary; but at the same time he sent his confidential physician or minister, Faqir Aziz-uddin,
along with Dr. Harlan and the Sultan Mohammed
Khan, to the Amir Dost Mohammed Khan, with
the message either to retire or to fight. While the
agents were conferring with the Amir, intelligence
was brought that the Sikh army had already surrounded the Afghans with a heavy park of artillery,
and that there was no chance of success by waging
war, but of much good by retreat. However, the
Amir was fearful that his followers might become
disorderly at sounding the retreat, and then he
might lose his guns and ammunition, which would
reduce him to the level of his rival relations, as Mohammed Zaman Khan, &c. He consulted at this
crisis with his minister Mirza Sami Khan, and during
the conversation he fixed on a scheme for carrying

N

off the Faqir Aziz-uddin and Dr. Harlan, the Sikh
agents, to Kabul.   He thought that this arrangement
would compel the Maharajah to give up Peshavar,
or at any rate a very large sum, for the ransom of
the Faqir, without whom the veteran ruler of the
Panjab could not live.   The Amir, however, thought
at the same time that this act of seizing the envoys
would bring an everlasting disgrace on him, and
therefore he resolved to gain his object by casting
the odium on the head of his brother the Sultan
Mohammed Khan.   He sent for him, therefore, and
referring to all past misunderstandings and discord
between them, he made a new engagement; and
swearing on the Qoran, he solemnly bound himself
to maintain a perpetual friendship and brotherhood.
The Sultan Mohammed Khan learnt and knew immediately that the intention of the Amir was to gain
the persons of the envoy at the expense of his disgrace, yet he feigned, and also swore, to adhere to
the wishes and plans of the Amir.   The latter gave
up the charge of the Faqir and Dr. Harlan to him,
stating his wish to keep them as hostages till the
Maharajah restores half the territory of the Peshavar
to him, and sends a sum of money besides for his

own expense, proclaiming at the same time that he had not come to fight with the Maharajah, on whom he looks in the light of a father, but to establish peace with him for the future. The Sikh envoy begged in vain to permit him to return to the Maharajah in the first place for the purpose of informing his Highness of the agreement he had concluded with the Amir; but the latter replied that this can easily be done by means of a letter.

The camp of the Afghans was now broken up, and the Amir Dost Mohammed Khan used great caution and exertion to see that his guns and ammunition had passed safe to the mouth of the Khaibar, but he could not prevent the Ghazis from plundering the bazar and his own camp equipage. When he was quite safe and far within the valley he heard the firing of cannons from the Sikh camp, in their rejoicing at his flight. The Amir, believing that he had treacherously secured his game in the persons of Faqir Aziz-uddin and Dr. Harlan, the Sikh envoys, and that they were following him in the custody of the Sultan Mohammed Khan, turned his face towards the Sikh camp, ridiculed their firing, and expressed his own pride that he had carried off

the soul (the Faqir) of Ranjit Singh. In this, however, he himself was the person deceived. In the
mean time he continued his march; and the Sultan
Mohammed Khan, conscious of the evil intentions of
the Amir, and having a favourable opportunity to
gain the kindness and attachment of the Maharajah
Ranjit Singh, conducted the envoys, the prisoners of
the Amir, to his own camp, instead of securing them
in that of Dost Mohammed Khan. At night the
Amir encamped at Jabar-ghi, and next morning
made inquiries where his brother the Sultan Mohammed Khan had put up with the Sikh envoys. No
one could find him or them in the camp, but still the
Amir continued his search. Meanwhile the arrival
of a messenger from the Sultan Mohammed Khan
was announced, and a letter was delivered to him.
The contents were a tissue of violent abuse; and
after naming him the most faithless and the most
treacherous, with everything which was bad, threatened to attack his country if he would not instantly
send his guns and his brother Pir Mohammed Khan.
This appalling news wounded the feelings of the
Amir most bitterly. There were no bounds to the
sweat of shame and folly which flowed over his face,

and there was no limit to the laughter of the people at his being deceived and ridiculed. His minister Mirza Sami Khan was so much distressed by this sad exposure of his own trick, and still more by the failure of his plan in losing the Faqir, that he hung down his head with great remorse and shame, and then throwing away his state papers, he exclaimed that he would avoid all interference in the government affairs hereafter. In a tone of anger he stated to his master that his conduct was very unwise, and that he did not pay attention to his counsel when he advised him to fight with the Maharajah Ranjit Singh, adding, that his followers, the Ghazis, will never believe him that he had any intention of carrying on a religious war, and that none in future will come to support him. After a long-continued talk about right and wrong, and in referring to past intercourse with the Sikh camp, the Amir marched towards Kabul, and could neither keep his followers in order nor persuade them to allow him to review and thank them before they should depart for their respective districts. Such was the termination of the religious war of the commander of the faithful in Afghanistan. It commenced with extortion and oppression, and ended in an expensive rendezvous, gaining nothing but contempt and the ridiculous title of "Amir" to add to the name of Dost Mohammed Khan.

CHAPTER VII.

Difficult situation of the Amir—Duplicity of the Qandhar chiefs
—The Amir designs to seize some nobles—His plan betrayed
by Akhundzadah—He arrests Abdullah Khan Achakzai—
Releases him—Sisters of the Amir—Saddu Khan murdered
by a Kohistani bribed by his wife.

THE Amir Dost Mohammed Khan, after returning
to Kabul, was not easy in his mind, nor was his
authority respected. Theft, plunder, slaughter, dis-
obedience to him, were the predominant features of
the time. He always indulged in the idea that he
was betrayed by his own relations and brothers, in
the late expedition against the Sikhs; and that in
consequence of their increasing treachery he could
not execute his wishes in the arrangement of the
affairs of his own government. He was also surrounded by many chiefs and followers of the Sultan
Mohammed Khan, who from the time that Peshavar
fell into the hands of the Sikh rulers, had sought for
maintenance from the Amir. He did not know how
to restore confidence into his former adherents, and

to provide for the newly arrived Khavanins.* He communicated all these difficulties to the brother chiefs of Qandhar, and they sent their confidential " Mashir," Counsellor Mulla Rashid Akhundzadah, apparently to promote the interests of the Amir, but secretly instructed and advised to counteract them. This Counsellor arrived at Kabul, and by his famous possession and practice of hypocrisy, gained the entire confidence of the Amir, for he gave ready approbation and compliance to all his measures. The first object of Dost Mohammed Khan was to reduce the number and allowances of his former dependants, so that he might be able to support the Peshavar arrivals; and every one groaned at the appearance and application of this project, and above all there were no bounds to the hard and ill language of Haji Khan Kakar. The Amir then planned to seize his relations, with a great many other men of rank, and, after getting rid of them, finally to establish his own authority. His minister, Mirza Sami Khan, prepared a list of the persons who were to be imprisoned, and whose property was to be confiscated. He went himself into the country

* Petty chiefs.

on the excuse to look after his estate, but in reality
to keep himself free from the odium of taking an
apparent share in the plot; if it proved successful
he would appear to be perfectly unaware of its existence, and if it failed, he would become a mediator
to restore peace and order. While the minister
thus secured his own object, Mulla Rashid, who was
daily becoming more and more a confidant of the
Amir's plot, was not forgetful of his own peculiar
benefit. He kept the opposite party alert, and acquainted with the proceedings of Dost Mohammed
Khan, whose secrets and confidence he possessed.
He filled his own coffers with the presents which he
received from the Navab Jabbar Khan, and from
the relations of the Amir and other chiefs about him,
for betraying the secrets he knew, and making them
watchful of impending dangers from his conspiracy.
When the Amir thought that the plan was mature,
and time had arrived to secure the fruits of his perfidy, he sat with a dismal and anxious countenance
waiting for his confidential accomplice, Akhundzadah. Hereupon the latter appeared, and, throwing his
turban before him on the ground, feigned to pluck
at his own beard; and in a fearful and agitated tone

of voice explained to the Amir that his relations, the Navab, &c. have in some way been informed of his plot laid against them, and have collected their respective followers to frustrate his designs. The penetrating Amir instantly knew that the Akhundzadah was the very first person who made the opposite party acquainted with his proceedings; and he wrathfully showered a heavy load of abuse on his head, calling him a traitor coming from Qandhar to destroy his measures instead of furthering them. The Akhundzadah, by remaining quiet, pacified the furious Dost Mohammed, and then gradually began to advise him by saying that his violence in such critical circumstances was perfectly childish, and would probably produce serious injury by making it manifest that he had really conspired for the ruin of his brothers and relations, who, being alarmed and losing confidence in him, will then join to upset him. Whether the counsel of the double-faced Akhundzadah, or the necessity of the time, moved the Amir to swallow his own repentance, we cannot say, but it is certain that he instantly waited upon his brothers, and pretended to be uneasy in his inquiries for the reason of assembling their retinue,

and assuming a warlike aspect.   He commenced his
old and accustomed series of false excuses in a garb
of solemnity, with an oath that he had never thought
of any deliberate treachery against them.   The plot
which he had planned, he said, was to get hold of
Abdullah Khan Achakzai, with his property, and not
to injure them.   He thus cleared himself of the suspicion of his relations, and then set about to make
schemes to seize and gain possession of the person
and wealth of the Achakzai chief.   He instructed
his wives to send an invitation to the whole number
of the females of Abdullah Khan; who, of course,
will come as usual adorned with jewels, of which he
will deprive them without any difficulty.   He also
directed Mohammed Akbar Khan to send for the
chief personally, on pretence of consulting him about
some state affairs, and when in the room to seize
him immediately, accusing him that he has been
corresponding and intriguing with the Prince of
Hirat, the enemy of the Barakzai family, whom he
serves.   This measure proved successful, the Achakzai chief was apprehended, and his horses and property confiscated.   Now, however, the Amir discovered that his expectations are not realized, and that

all he had gained by this act of treachery, the seizure of Abdullah Khan, was nothing but a few horses, old carpets, and worn-out furniture. He thereupon thought that the odium and disgrace was heavier on his head than these things are worth, and therefore he set the chief at liberty, restoring to him his plun- dered property.

It has been stated before that the Amir Dost Mohammed Khan had only one brother, named Amir Mohammed Khan; and here we speak of his four sisters, because their character and deport- ment is worthy of notice. The eldest one was married to Shah Shuja-ul-mulk when in possession of the kingdom. She had four royal children, three daughters and one son.* The second was forced to be wife of Abdul Amin Khan Tobschi- bashi, at the time when she, with her mother, brothers, and sisters, were in distress on the murder of their father Sarfraz Khan. The Tobschibashi had by her seven children, and one of them was Abdul Rashid Khan.† Abdul Rasul Khan married the

* He was named Shahzadah Akbar, and died when the Shah was placed by the British on the throne of Kabul.

† He was bought by me to desert Haidur Khan at Ghazni,

third sister, who has four sons. She is a widow, and
known by the name of the mother of Madad Khan.
This lady resembles very much her brother the
Amir of Kabul, and bears an enterprising character.
She used every exertion to induce our authorities to
allow her, with her other sister, to remain in Kabul,
after the whole family of the Amir were sent prisoners to India. She was aware that her brother,
though an exile in Toorkistan, might return, and
that then a general commotion would arise in the
country. With this view she continued to pay her
visit to all the principal chiefs in the country, and
when the Amir appeared fighting with us in Bamian
and Kohistan, she was day and night engaged in
marching from one village to another, and in suppli-
cating the head men of the place, with the holy
" Qoran " in her hand, to rise against us, the infidels,—and to join her brother, the Commander of
the Faithful. When the Amir surrendered, she made
a wonderful escape to Jalalabad, and thence to

and came to the late Sir Alexander Burnes: his services were appreciated by Lord Keane and by Major Thomson, the engineer
officer, in the capture of that fort, and rewarded by a pension of
five hundred rupees.

Peshavar, in spite of our exertions to detect her while intriguing. Her conduct in other respects is not altogether without suspicion. The fourth sister of Dost Mohammed Khan was married to Saddu Khan, and had one daughter and one son, Mohammed Hasan Khan. Neither the behaviour of the husband nor wife was free from rebuke. His habits were very objectionable and mean. He was always stupified with opium and with all sorts of intoxicating things. His conduct towards his own daughter was unfather-like, brutal, and odiously abominable; and such, that at last it compelled him to take her far from the capital, and to put an end to her existence. He was passionate and dissipated, and his wife was equally regardless of the virtuous modesty of her own sex. She bribed a Kohistani to murder her own husband!! and while he was returning from a visit to the Amir at night he was shot in the Shor Bazar, and the culprit was seized. The Amir made the necessary investigations, and inquired after the reason which led him to assassinate a person of Saddu Khan's position, being a relative to himself. The guilty man replied that he had been desired to do this by his own wife, the sister of the Amir, who promised him a large reward, adding that he never dreamt that such a bold and desperate step of a female against her own comforter of life—her husband, would have originated in herself; but that, undoubtedly, there were some political circumstances which must have obliged the Amir to ask his sister to cause the annihilation of her own husband. The Amir made no further questions, and appeared sadly ashamed of his sister's conduct, while surrounded by the courtiers. However, he ordered the guilty one to be executed, and he was hanged near the gate of the Bala Hisar.

CHAPTER VIII.

The Amir fears the Hazarahs—History of Yazdan Bakhsh—
Dost Mohammed's plan for seizing the Hazarah chief—
Courage and devotion of his wife—Both are seized by the
Amir—They negotiate for their release—The Mir escapes,
and afterwards his wife—He consolidates his power—Haji
Khan and Mir Yazdan Bakhsh—The Khan plans the ruin
of the Hazarah Mir—His scheme to entrap him—Fails—He
makes Haji Khan Governor of the Hazarahjat—Becomes
suspicious of him—Haji Khan seizes Mir Yazdan Baksh—
Plunder of the Hazarahs—The Mir is strangled—The Sardar's
relations with Persia—His education—He humbles his rival
relatives, and increases his own power—Disgrace of Haji
Khan—The Amir's administration of justice.

It has been briefly described in the commencement
of the elevation and fame of the Amir Dost Mohammed Khan that his career was marked with
deeds of tragedy and perfidious bloodshed in Kohistan, and that he had no cause to be alarmed from
that quarter, except that he was not free from the fear
of a Hazarah chief of extraordinary character named
Mir Yazdan Bakhsh. To shorten the history of his
descent, and of the superiority and destruction of his

elder brothers and rivals, it may be sufficient to say
that he was the younger son of Mir Vali Beg of
Karzar, who was slain by a petty chief. On the
death of his father, the eldest son Mir Mohammed
Shah became the master of Behsud; Mir Yazdan
Bakhsh assembled a large force, and prepared to
revenge the wrongs of his family on the assassin of
his father,—and he apprehended him and slew him
on the very spot where the blood of his own father
had been shed. His attention was now turned to
subvert his elder brother, whom he defeated, and he
then made himself the principal chief or Mir of
Behsud. The more he grew in power in his Hazarah
tribe, and extended his territorial possessions, the
more did apprehensions arise in the mind of the
Amir Dost Mohammed Khan. He justly thought
that the Golam Khanah, a powerful body in Kabul,
are connected by the ties' of their faith with the
Shia sect and with the valiant Mir of the Hazarah;
and that as they were principally the instruments
of his prosperity, they might turn against him and
join the Mir to seek his adversity and destruction,
and he found no other way to entrap the object of
his apprehension but to cultivate for himself a deeper

o

confidence in the Shias of Kabul. He accordingly
showed them all attention and civility, and at length
persuaded them to establish a closer alliance between him and the Mir Yazdan Bakhsh by his visit
to Kabul. He wrote all the sacred oath and solemn
obligations of swearing on the Holy Qoran, and
affixing his own seal to it, he assured the Mir of
his personal safety and respectable treatment, and
the Shias of Kabul became responsible for the
veracity of the engagement. When the Besut Mir
received that communication of the Amir, guaranteed by the people of his own creed, he prepared
to set out for the city. One of his wives, however, the daughter of a Dehzangi chief, dissuaded
him from such a hazardous visit. She was a woman
of the most extraordinary qualifications and natural
powers of mind. She used to put on a masculine
robe, and ornamented herself with a sword and
shield, a bow and arrows, a spear, a dagger, and
a matchlock. She appeared in the field of battle
with her husband, and shared the laurels by his
side: thus, at home, she gave her lord comfort and
counsel,—and in the field of battle she killed his
enemies. Being wiser than himself in doubting the

fidelity of the Afghans, she always advised him not
to trust himself to them. On this occasion she
found that she could not succeed in forbidding her
husband to accept the invitation; and, therefore,
with her usual attachment and boldness, she accompanied him to Kabul, attired as a brave soldier.
The Amir Dost Mohammed Khan received them
civilly, but soon seized the opportunity to make his
guests his prisoners. The perfidious Dost Mohammed Khan would have killed the Mir without loss
of time, but the more talented prisoner knew well
that gold was the only thing which would melt the
strong feelings of the Afghan, and especially of their
treacherous host. He offered him, therefore, one lakh
of rupees if immediately liberated, and permitted
to go and collect from his own country, and in the
meantime to make the Shias of Kabul security for
the payment. The Amir, being always notoriously
in exigence, contracted the orders for his execution, so that he might secure for himself possession
of the money. While the arrangements were going
on for obtaining the security of the Gholam Khanah,
with regard to the payment of the offered sum, the
captive Mir contrived his escape from the prison.

When this became known to the Amir Dost Mohammed Khan, there was no restraint to his wrath and disappointment. He had still, however, the brave wife of the fugitive in his custody, whom he summoned into his presence and rebuked very severely. The Hazarah fair, turning towards the Amir Dost Mohammed Khan, in the court, exclaimed in a heroic tone of voice—" Oh, son of Sarfraz Khan, dost thou not feel ashamed to match thyself against a female ?" It is said, that on hearing this, the Amir and all his Afghan courtiers hung down their heads and were abashed. They applauded the spirit of the lady, and said to the Amir that they will not permit him to offer her any violence: and the Amir having recovered his senses, agreed to place her in the custody of the Shias, thinking that she will be treated by them better than by her former Afghan guard, and she was conducted to the Persian or Shia quarter—Chandaul. After some days she made her escape from the gaol, and dressing herself like a man, well armed and mounted, set off towards the high and bleak hills of the Hazarahs. The Amir was soon informed of her flight, and dispatched immediately a party of

horsemen to seize her: she was overtaken, but succeeded in keeping off her pursuers by firing her gun
and pistols towards them. The skirmish continued
while she was sometimes halting, and at other times
ascending the valley, till at last she reached the
boundary of her own country, and the party sent by
the Amir was now obliged to go back to Kabul,
ashamed of not being able to secure a female;
while the enterprising lady joined her husband with
deep sensations of satisfaction. The Hazarah chief,
however, never showed any ill will towards the Amir
of Kabul, never interfered with his extortions, and
the abuse which he made of his power in other districts of the Hazarahs. He was, moreover, very
prudent in paying his tribute,—but at the same time
engaged in erecting a very strong fort, and storing
it with provisions and ammunition, with the view to
have safe refuge in it when necessary.

Upon the other hand, the Amir Dost Mohammed
Khan had not lost sight of the increasing power of
his fugitive visitor, Mir Yazdan Bakhsh, the Hazarah
chief. He was watching his progress with bitterness
of mind, and searching for a favourable opportunity
to check and destroy it. He now appointed Haji

Khan Kakar governor of Bamian. By this he convinced him of his lasting gratitude in bestowing a
reward on him for the services he had rendered in
informing him of the intention of Sherdil Khan to
deprive him of sight; and at the same time he thus
placed an Afghan, one of a different creed, to watch
the conduct of his neighbour, the Mir Yazdan
Bakhsh. This person, by his cunning manners, had
cultivated a friendly sentiment and intimate connexion with the Shias of Kabul; and had secured
their confidence by pledging himself to support their
cause against the Amir if circumstances required it.
In consequence of this they always wrote to Mir
Yazdan Bakhsh, advising him to rely on the word
and counsels of Haji Khan, who, on the other hand,
gained the sincere friendship and intimacy of the
Hazarah Mir, by binding himself to destroy all the
ill intentions of the Amir towards him; and he even
said that he would stand by his side if he was to
rebel from necessity. After some time, the agent of
Haji Khan, at Bamian, entered into some agreements with the Tartar chief of Saighan, the enemy
of Mir Yazdan Bakhsh. This frightened the Mir,
who thought that this proceeding was a league made

for his destruction, and that not without advice from
Kabul. He therefore turned out all the Afghan
soldiers from all forts where he had himself formerly
placed them. He subdued and took possession of
all the castles of the petty Hazarah chiefs dependant
on the Afghans, and he became the ruling master
of the Bamian valley. This alarmed the Amir of
Kabul; and Haji Khan, whose interests were connected with the Bamian territory, showed him the
necessity of reducing the Mir Yazdan Bakhsh, and
he also took upon himself to settle the matter. He
showed himself liberal on every occasion to the
Hazarahs, the tribe of the Mir; and through the
Qizalbashes of Kabul he convinced the Hazarah
Mir that his agent at Bamian had acted contrary
to his orders; and in order to show the sincerity of
his false friendship, he dismissed Rahimdad Khan,
and appointed a new governor. He also sent the
"Qoran" with oaths that the past is forgotten, and
that the future will daily increase their mutual
friendship and confidence. He proceeded with
the Amir Mohammed Khan, the brother of the
Amir of Kabul, towards Hazarahjat; but Mir
Yazdan Bakhsh did not join their camp, but in-

stead of that he went on a pilgrimage to Band Barbar.

After the Mir Yazdan Bakhsh had discharged his religious duties, he bent his attention to arrange his political affairs. He accordingly came with a large force to subdue Mohammed Ali Beg, the Tajak chief of Saighan, but the latter shut himself up in a fort, and showed no inclination to fight. Another year rolled on, but neither the Amir of Kabul nor Haji Khan were careless about the means of weakening the Hazarah Mir, whom they could not entrap during the last season. In 1832, Haji Khan again volunteered to collect the revenues of the Hazarahjat, and to establish the authority of the Amir in Bamian on a firmer footing. Dost Mohammed Khan allowed him two years to effect this purpose, reinforced him with two thousand troops, and gave him an elephant in present; and Haji Khan farmed the whole country of the Hazarahs for forty thousand rupees, from the Kabul government. He then proceeded thither, and through the medium of Khan Shirin Khan, the Hazarah Mir made known that he agreed to co-operate with the governor, whose aim was to ensnare the Mir by professions of cordiality, and of good understand-

ing with him, and with the people of his creed. In
the mean time, a religious conflict took place between
the Shias and the Achakzai Afghans of Kabul, and
Haji Khan cunningly took the side of the Shias.
In so doing he had two objects in view; firstly, to
convince the Shias of his attachment to them, and
by this also to entrap the Mir Yazdan Bakhsh; and,
secondly, if the Javan Shers or Shias should gain
the ascendancy in this warfare, the subversion of the
power of Dost Mohammed Khan will take place of
course; and this was his principal desire. However,
these affairs ended at last in a peaceable manner:
but this duplicity of the Khan, as well as his correspondence with the Uzbeks, the Panjab, and the
Biloch chiefs, did not escape the penetration of the
able Amir, who naturally grew suspicious of the
Khan. Sometimes, therefore, he thought to deprive
him of the power he held, at other times he determined to put him to the sword; but while he continued in this state of irresolution, Haji Khan became acquainted with the alarming fact that he now
held no safe position. The Mir Yazdan Bakhsh in
the mean time paid him all the revenues, and waited
upon him, and this meeting seemed likely to give

perfect satisfaction on both sides; for it induced all
the other chiefs in the Hazarahjat to send in their
revenues that were due to the Khan, who thus collected sooner and more than his predecessor, the
brother of the Amir.

Haji Khan now set out for an expedition towards
Saighan; and, finding himself well supported and able
to execute his long nourished desire, he summoned
Mir Yazdan Bakhsh and his relations in the morning
to come to his tent; and as soon as the brother of
the Khan, with a strong body of armed men, came
in, Haji Khan took an angry tone of voice and
accused Mir Yazdan Bakhsh of intriguing against
him: and forgetting all the often-repeated oaths of
friendship, he seized the Mir with all his relatives.
The merciless Afghans began to plunder the Hazarahs, who, notwithstanding the inclemency of the
cold, were even deprived of their clothes. The
faithless Haji Khan allowed only the Mir Yazdan to
be left in his usual attire, and even his relations
were obliged to give up their robes. It was a heart-
rending sight to see the poor Hazarahs, barefooted
and without clothes, pursued in all directions by the
Afghans, who were now desirous to inflict on them

wounds and every act of tyranny, because they were
Shias. Mir Yazdan Bakhsh was pinioned with his
adherents, and their feet bound with fetters; and
the locks were fastened with melted lead, to prevent them from being opened by any one, and the
chief of Saighan advised Haji Khan to execute his
captive. The perfidious Khan accordingly ordered
the "Pesh-khid-mat" to put an end to the life of
the chief who only a few days before held sway over
the whole country, and commanded a large force.
The Qizalbashes of Kabul, now with Haji Khan,
made a clamorous remonstrance against his dis-
honesty and treachery towards the Hazarah Mir;
but this availed nothing, and the unfortunate Yazdan Bakhsh was strangled to death. It is said that
he met his fate with extraordinary composure of
mind, and that no sign of fear or sadness was found
in his appearance. Haji Khan said to the Qizalbashes that he was obliged and compelled by Dost
Mohammed Khan to put the Mir Yazdan Bakhsh to
this end. Such, however, was the termination of
the life of the Hazarah chief, and thus was the Amir
of Kabul relieved from the fear of the only remaining antagonist left in his kingdom.

It must here be stated that the elevation of the
Amir Dost Mohammed Khan to power was procured merely by the adherence and assistance of the
Persians. The grand point of the policy of Nadir
Shah was to colonize the distant regions he subdued
from his own extensive country of Persia. On his
death Ahmad Shah Durrani, who first held and
strengthened the sceptre of the realm of Afghanistan,
wisely took these foreigners under his protection,
and trusted them with his personal safety and with
the charge of the royal family; and they were surnamed Gholam Khanah, or the household slaves.
He treated them with every consideration, and by
a course of unceasing cordiality he attached them to
himself, and thus showed his Afghans that he had
the warrior Qizalbashes to put them down if they
ever stirred against him. Dost Mohammed followed
the same policy; and the Qizalbashes, strangers in
land, in customs, in habits, and in faith, thought it
prudent to attach themselves to him when he was
nothing, and was looked on with jealousy by his
most powerful and rival brothers. They supported
his cause in every extremity, and he was at last so
successful as to become the superior of all in Af-

ghanistan. Through their arms he reduced all the old and influential men of his own tribe and blood, and then patronized young adventurers of obscure origin in order to diminish the strength of those to whom he owed gratitude at least for his prosperity. These Qizalbashes were twelve thousand families in number in former days, all men of arms, and not of trade; but now they are reduced to plough the land and to sell vegetables, and are craftily managed and placed by the Amir Dost Mohammed Khan against each other. Their clans are different, and they bear various names, as Javan Shers, Afshars,* Rikas, Kurds, Bakhtyaris; and, in fact, they thus show their origin and descent from every tribe of Persia.

The chiefs in Afghanistan do not value education as the first quality, for they must only know how to ride, fight, cheat, and lie; and whoever excels in these acquirements gains the renown of the time. Amongst the sons of Sarfraz Khan, the brothers of the Amir Dost Mohammed, few knew the letters of the alphabet. Their early life was spent in poverty, danger, treachery, and bloodshed; but when they came to power, the constant sight of the orders

* The tribe of the great Nadir Shah.

submitted by the Mirzas (Secretaries) for their signature at last enabled them to read plain writing. Mehardil Khan, one of the Qandhar chiefs, qualified himself more than the others. He composed poetry, and made himself distinguished by his literary taste in Persia; yet there are some of his brother chiefs who can neither write nor read. The Amir Dost Mohammed Khan learnt the "Qoran" only at the meridian of his glory, and Nayab Amir Mohammed Akhundzadah was his tutor. However, his local knowledge, and the information he possesses in ancient and modern history, in proverbs, and in adventures, as well as in the administration of various distant kingdoms, will not fail to show him as being well stored with extraordinary talents and science. He speaks Persian, Pashto, Turkish, Panjabi, and the Kashmir languages.

Haji Khan Kakar, the perfidious murderer of Mir Yazdan Bakhsh, came from Bamian on a visit to Kabul; and on his arrival in the city he went straight to pay his respects to the Amir Dost Mohammed Khan. He, with polite attention, took the Khan, his visitor, into the palace, and introduced him to his favourite wife, the mother of Mohammed

Akbar Khan, with a cheerful voice; and to show
him a false respect, he said to her that her father
had arrived, whom she was so long desirous to see.
The crafty Haji Khan knew instantly that this flattering title from the Amir was not destitute of some
treachery. He waited the result, therefore, with
anxiety, and the next day he was informed by the
Amir that his wife, who looks upon him (the Khan)
as her father, has begged of him a favour; and that
he will not disapprove of her appointing Haidar
Khan to the Government of Bamian, and the Amir
will equally provide the Khan with a larger yearly
sum in cash. This awoke Haji Khan from mental
slumber, and he thought that his fortune was now
commencing to decline; wherefore, after some days,
he waited upon the Amir Dost Mohammed Khan,
and showed symptoms of being deeply offended and
discontented with these measures. The Amir hereupon angrily accused him of the atrocious murder of
the Mir Yazdan Bakhsh, on which the Khan inquired whether it was not perpetrated by his own
orders:—" No," replied Dost Mohammed Khan;
" it was never my wish that you should take a false
oath, and kill the man afterwards. I repeatedly

wrote to you to be kind to him, and induce him to come to Kabul, and to give him many dresses of honour. I would have been friendly to him, and permitted him to go back to his own country." Haji Khan then continued his remonstrance by saying, that it is most surprising that the Amir should accuse him of false swearing, and asked him how he had himself entrapped, and then had cut off the heads of the Kohistan chiefs. The Amir replied, by his own expertness, because he always sent a piece of wood wrapped up instead of the Holy Qoran. While this altercation was going on, the Amir did not tell him to disband his dependants, as he thought it would create an illiberal idea of his own feeling towards the soldiers; while Haji Khan, having no means to maintain them, would disband them himself. The Khan, however, retained them still, for he entertained for some time the hopes of having back Bamian; but he at length was compelled to discharge his followers.

There are no courts of justice in Kabul, and the matters of consequence are therefore all decided by the Amir Dost Mohammed Khan himself: hence a great criminal, or murderer, has a general hope of being released unpunished, if money, and sometimes influence, may interfere with his decision. The petty offences, and religious business, are entrusted to the care of the Mulla, or head of the Shara, or the Mahomedan law. He has appointed a kotval, or constable, who keeps watch at night, and has the privilege to seize the persons who may be found committing adultery, drinking wine, gambling or stealing. He puts such persons into prison, or "Bandikhanah," without limiting the time, and they can be released only through the medium of some man of rank, or by the discharge and payment of a certain sum. The criminal is neither fed nor clothed in the winter by the government, wherefore his subsistence depends upon begging alone. Even in these two departments of the "Mulla" and "kotval," if there is even the slightest chance of squeezing money from any sort of offender, he will not escape the tortures, long imprisonment, and even threats of the Amir personally. A most singular case happened a little before the arrival of the English mission in Kabul. The wife of Khairuddin, the son of Mulla Badruddin, the great merchant of Kabul, whom the Amir respected and called by the appellation of

P

father, bore only a suspected character, and the Amir got information of her being out of doors at a late hour of the night. He was aware that her seizure would be productive of a very large sum, and he dispatched a person of trust to apprehend her when she returns from her visit, and to conduct her into his presence; and this was accordingly done. The Amir kept her very close and concealed, and the relations felt disgrace as well as anxiety from her prolonged absence; and knowing her habits, were still more vexed to think that she was in custody. However, the Amir, for his own sake, allowed her to communicate her apprehension to her husband, but said, as she was a lady of a rich family, she was to pay him ten thousand rupees before she would obtain her liberation. Mulla Badruddin, although he was every day in court with the Amir, yet feeling ashamed to speak on such a disgraceful subject as his daughter's imprisonment, never uttered a word to Dost Mohammed Khan. He, on the other hand, being aware that the delicacy of the case will seal the old rich merchant's mouth, persisted not to diminish ought of the demanded sum. The absence of the lady from home was now the talk of all the neighbours;

and to put an end to this, the relatives were compelled to send her the amount secretly into the prison. She gave it all to the Amir, who, after depriving her of the jewels and shawls with which she was covered, dismissed her from custody. A similar case in some respects followed this deed of extortion.

There was a young man of moderate income, related to Sufi Naqshbandi, who is the only person that repairs watches and other European articles of the kind in Kabul. He fell in love with a handsome girl of a rich Khatri, whose heart was also won. She left the house of her parents, who were grieved at her choice, and unwilling to see their child married to a person of a different religion, and of strange customs; while he, on the other hand, bribed the Amir, and requested his interference. The girl was accordingly caught, and ordered to be sent to the palace. She remained there for a considerable time in charge of Dost Mohammed Khan; and the parents, considering that she was not worthy to mingle with them any more after living in the "Haram serai" of the ruler, where she must have drunk and eaten with Musalmans, showed no anxiety to have her restored to them. On this the Amir communicated his will to her paramour, that if he will give him a certain sum of money, he may have the possession of the fair object of his desire. The money was accordingly paid; and the young damsel, after thus causing the coffers of the Amir to be filled by the plaintiff and by the defendant, was sent out of the palace. Such is a sample of the mode in which the Amir Dost Mohammed Khan sometimes distributes justice.

When Haji Khan Kakar was governor of Bamian, he had made a close alliance with the Tartar chiefs of Turkistan. He went among them and had conference with several of them, and in particular he paid a friendly visit to Mohammed Morad Beg, Mir of Qunduz, and on his coming to Kabul, the Uzbek envoys accompanied him. The Amir did not wish to recognise their mission to him, as he thought it was framed by the advice of Haji Khan, for his own purposes; yet at the same time he received them in his court, and was civil to them until he had secured to himself the presents brought for him. After they left his presence, he neither gave them a residence nor appointed any person to entertain them; and they thus were left to the feeding and maintenance of Mulla Badruddin, and of Haji Khan himself, whose repeated applications to show them civility made no effect on the Amir.

CHAPTER IX.

The Wives of the Amir—Their jealousies—Cruel treatment of
one of them by the Amir—An anecdote—A Kashmirian wife
—Her escape from the Amir—Bitter enmity entertained
towards the Amir by Sultan Mohammed Khan—Wives, Sons,
and Daughters of the Amir—His policy of depressing his
brothers and raising his sons to power—Expedition against
the Sikhs—Mirza Abdul Sami Khan arrives at the camp—
Victory of the Afghans—Honours bestowed on Akbar Khan—
How to estimate the sons of the Amir—State of the Amir's
dominions—Revenues—Encouragement of Commerce—Character of the Amir—His military force.

It should not be omitted to mention that while the
Amir Dost Mohammed Khan was occupied by day
in endeavouring to increase his power and territory,
he was not less active at night in planning the aug-
mentation of the number of his wives, that he might
complete the cabinet of his pleasures. In some instances, however, his matrimonial connexions were
merely political expedients, and not for any domestic
comforts. The number of his married wives is not
under fourteen, besides the numerous retinue of slave
girls. At present the mother of Mohammed Akbar

is his favourite, and takes the freedom to give him her opinion on important occasions. She is descended from a high family, but is very jealous of the other wives of the Amir. Every one of them has a separate allowance, a slave girl, and a slave boy, and they occupy different rooms in the Palace or Haram Sarai, which is encircled by a high wall. Only one door is there for communication, where a few men, generally of old age, " Qabchis," are stationed. When the slave boy is absent, the slave girl brings orders from her mistress to the " Qabchi" for a purchase, or for any other purpose from the inside. If I remember the name well, one of the wives of the Amir who is named Bibi Gauhar, excited the great jealousy and animosity of the mother of Akbar Khan, who always sought for an excuse to create the suspicions and the wrath of the Amir against the rival lady. One evening there was a demand of firewood in the establishment of Bibi Gauhar, and her slave boy brought a quantity of it piled on the back of the seller. His eyes were, on entering the palace door, blindfolded, and his face wrapped in a cloth while he was conducted by the boy. After unloading the burthen from his back, he was in the same

manner brought back and let out of the Haram
Sarai. Hereupon the penetrating and jealous mother
of Akbar Khan thought this the best opportunity
to excite some abusive, but unjust suspicion of her
character in the heart of the lord. The Amir was
quietly asked in through Mohammed Akbar Khan,
and the mother of the latter, taking him aside, stated
that it was a disgraceful thing that her " Ambagh,"
rival wife of the Amir, was visited by her paramour,
who came in under the disguise of a wood-seller;
and she then fabricated sufficient stories to make the
Amir prepared to meet her object, for he appeared
incensed, and considered that it was not a fabrication;
and the poor lady, who a little before was the charm-
ing idol of the Amir, was sent for and ordered to be
punished for her misconduct. Her assertions of
truth were not listened to, and he told Mohammed
Akbar Khan to wrap her all in a blanket, and
throwing her on the ground to strike her with sticks.
The son was now perfectly aware of the jealousy of
his own mother against her, and did not fail to inflict
many most severe and cruel blows upon her. She
was not released until she fainted, and appeared
quite motionless in the bloody blanket. After some

time when she recovered, the Amir found that he
had been deceived by his wife, the mother of Akbar, and he apologized to the sufferer for his sad
mistake, and punished the fair inventor of the story
(Akbar's mother), only by not going to her apartments for a few days. Bibi Gauhar was the widow
of Mahmud Shah, afterwards of Mohammed Azim
Khan, and is now one of the Amir's wives.

At breakfast one day the Amir Dost Mohammed
Khan asked one of his guests to eat an egg, to which
he replied that he had already eaten a considerable
number of slices of roast mutton, and feared an egg
might cause an attack of indigestion. This made the
Amir burst into laughter, and he said that the Amir
Bangashi's wife bore a more masculine taste and
appetite for eggs than his noble guest, who appears
to yield in this affair to a female. In an amusing
tone of voice Dost Mohammed Khan entertained the
circle of his courtiers with the following anecdote:—
When I went to the Bangash country to collect the
revenues of that district, political circumstances
induced me to marry the daughter of the chief, afterwards known as the mother of Mohammed Afzal
Khan. According to the custom of the Afghans,

the parents of the lady place several baskets of fruits
and of sweetmeats, and one or two of boiled eggs,
coloured variously, in the chambers of the newly-
married pair.   After the dinner was over the Amir
with his bride retired, and while amusing themselves
with conversation, he took a fancy for some grapes,
and the bride handed him an egg, which he found in
fact to have a better taste than any he had ever had
before.   He added that he saw his bride using her
fingers with admirable alacrity in taking off the
skin preparatory to swallowing an egg, and that
this activity continued till she finished the whole
basketful, to his astonishment, and he remarked
that there were not less than fifty eggs in the
basket!

   Before we speak of the other ladies of the Amir
Dost Mohammed Khan it would not perhaps be
uninteresting to the readers to mention a singular
instance of fidelity and perseverance in duty of a
Kashmirian wife, named Bibi Karmi, in the face of
danger and of every temptation.   I have already
mentioned her being formerly married to Mohammed Rahim Khan Amin-ul-mulk.   When this
chief was confined by Kam Ran at Qandhar,

his son Prince Jahangir heard much said in commendation of the prisoner's wife, and he endeavoured to get possession of her. His threats and his offers of good fortune were equally received with contempt by the lady, who at length was informed that the prince had sent a party to seize and conduct her to the palace. Without saying a word to her dependants she left the house immediately, and threw herself into an adjacent well, in order to preserve her chastity and to avoid the dishonour of violation by her royal captor. Fortunately the well was dry, and was filled with rubbish, &c.; and although she suffered several bruises, yet she remained alive, and unseen by all, except by one merchant, who was standing at the time on the roof of his house. He had heard the report, and became convinced that the female who had thrown herself into the well must be Bibi Karmi, wife of the Amin-ul-mulk. He was also aware that there was in it no water, and therefore he secretly conveyed to her some meal and water at night. Jahangir could not find anywhere the object of his rash passion, and he plundered the houses of the neighbours when they failed to give him accurate information of her move-

ments. The prisoner chief was forgetful of his own
sufferings at the idea of the capture of his fair wife,
which was bitterly marring the peace of his heart, for
he did not know that she was safe, though suffering
a strange kind of safety in the well. After some
days the husband was liberated on paying two lakhs
of rupees to Kam Ran, and permitted to proceed to
Kabul. He was on his way overtaken and joined by
his wife Bibi Karmi, after her wonderful escape.
The merchant who had fed her in the well for his
own good will, and expecting a high reward from
Amin-ul-mulk, brought a horse, and mounting the
Bibi Karmi on its back, started off from the city, and
after a continued march of sixty hours, delivered the
lady to the Khan, who felt no bounds to his unexpected joy, and rewarded the man liberally. On
the death of Amin-ul-mulk the Amir Dost Mohammed Khan communicated the wish of his marriage to her, which was received with great hatred
by the Kashmirian widow. The Amir, stimulated
by the reputation of her beauty and wealth, determined to possess her, and ordered his counsellor,
Agha Husain, to proceed to her residence, and
placing her forcibly in the "jampan" (a kind of

open litter), to escort her to his "haram sarai."
The order was accordingly executed, and the qazi, or
the priest, was desired to solemnize the ceremony of
marriage, while the sad shrieks of the widow were
rending to the ears of the hearers.   When the party
broke up and the Amir retired, he was overpowered
by the charms of her beauty.   Now as to Bibi Karmi,
she was never at rest from the moment she was married without her own consent, and her tears flowed
in torrents.   All the endeavours of the Amir to make
her his friend were fruitless, and she plainly told him
that she would rather poison herself than allow him to
approach.   She stated that in her opinion it would be
a most disgraceful and cold affectation to profess to
enjoy his society, and to forget all the good and love
of her deceased husband; adding, that it is an un-
becoming and vain hope of the Amir to expect love
from her; but that if he was desirous to possess the
property she has, she would be glad to give him all.
On this she placed all her jewels before the Amir
with her slave girl, who was also admirably well
favoured, and left the room.   In short, when he had
well considered that nothing could gain the favour
and attachment of the lady towards him, he kept her

jewels, and she was permitted to leave the palace
after an unpleasant stay of a few months. She is
now in Kabul, respected and liked by all, and her
fidelity has become a proverbial saying among the
Afghans.

In the number of his wives the Amir Dost Mohammed Khan has one from the royal family, which
case is unprecedented in record or even in rumour,
for no one ever was allowed to make a matrimonial
connexion with the royal or Sadozai females. On
the contrary, it was considered a great honour if any
descendant of the Sadozai would marry a female
from the Barakzai tribe, namely, that of the Amir,
or indeed of any other tribe besides their own.
When the decline of that dynasty commenced, she
attracted the sight and attention of the Sultan Mohammed Khan, the brother chief of the Amir, at
Peshavar, and a correspondence began between
them. She prepared to leave Kabul to be married
with her intended husband, under whose escort
she was proceeding. The Amir had also lost
his heart for her beauty, and got hold of her
by force and married her immediately. This at
once created, and has ever since maintained, a fatal

animosity between the brothers; and the Sultan
Mohammed Khan has often been heard to say that
nothing would afford him greater pleasure, even at
breathing his last, than to drink the blood of the
Amir. Such is the nature of the brotherly feeling
now existing between them; and the Amir has
often and justly mentioned that these three words,
commencing with the Persian letter "ze," and pro-
nounced like z in English, are the principal and
deadly causes of quarrel among men, namely,
"zan" (female), "zar" (money), and "zamin"
(land).

Descent or Relationship of the Wives of the Amir Dost Mohammed Khan.	Sons.	Names.	Daughters.
1. Sister of Mulla Rashid			
2. Daughter of Mulla Sadiq Ali, the Bangash Chief . . · . .	2	Mohammed Afzal and Azam Khan	
3. Daughter of Baqa Khan, the Parvan Chief	1	Mohammed Akram Khan	
4. Daughter of Khojah Khanji, whom the Amir murdered in Kohistan, as is already men-tioned	. .	. .	1
5. Widow of Shah Mahmud, and afterwards of Azim Khan . .	3	Mohammed Aslam, Hassan and Hu-sain Khan.	
6. Granddaughter of Jahangir Khan, Tori Chief	1	Vali Mohammed Khan.	

Descent or Relationship of the Wives of the Amir Dost Mohammed Khan.	Sons.	Names.	Daughters.
7. Daughter of Prince Abbas, who caused enmity between the Amir and Sultan Mohammed Khan	3	. .	1
8. Daughter of a wealthy merchant, Nazir Khair-ullah.*	. .	. .	1
9. Sister of Mehtar Mosa, Chief of Zurmat			
10. Daughter of Sadiq Khan Javan Sher, widow of Azim Khan .	1	Sultan Jan, Step-son.	1
11. Sister of the Chief of Kalat and Ghilzai			
12. Bibi Karmi of the Amin-Ul-mulk, who acted as above related			
13. Daughter of Haji Raihmat-ullah-Khan, famous for being the mother of Akbar Khan, and favourite of the Amir . .	5	Mohammed Akbar† Ditto Haidar. Ditto Sherali. Ditto Amin. Ditto Sharif Khans.	1
14. Daughter of the Chief of Mo-rad Khani, married on his restoration to Kabul or re-turning from India in 1843.			

The Amir Dost Mohammed Khan's best policy

* He left Kabul for fear of being seized and deprived by the Amir of his riches, and resided at Bokhara. Amir married his daughter to soothe his fear, and thus induce him to return to Kabul, and plunder him. He knows the Amir's craft, and will not come back.

† This son of the Amir is well known to the world for his treacheries, cruelties, and murders.

for the security of his authority is very judicious, though it has made him disliked by his rival relations. In the commencement of his power we find him occupied in bestowing the administration and charge of various districts upon his relations, or in some instances allowing them the enjoyment of their own possessions. Thus Navab Mohammed Zaman held Jalalabad; Mohammed Usam Khan, Bala Bagh; Jabbar Khan, Laghman and the Ghilzai; Shamshuddin Khan, Ghaznin; Haji Khan, Bamian; and so were also the other petty districts shared among them: but when he gained the stability of his position, he deprived every one of them of all authority, placing his own sons in their places. These feared him more than the others, and followed his example in the administration of their respective territories. Now at length the Amir was firmly established, and looked upon as the supreme Lord of Afghanistan. He was of course surrounded by his intriguing and dissatisfied brothers at home, but yet he entertained no fear of their upsetting him. The alarms, however, were daily increasing from the fear of an enemy abroad,—the powerful ruler of the Panjab.

The Sultan Mohammed Khan, brother of the Amir Dost Mohammed Khan, influenced by the Sikhs, commenced intrigues and designs for taking Kabul. The Amir ordered Mohammed Akbar Khan to proceed to Khaibar, and then he reinforced him by means of his eldest son, Mohammed Afzal Khan. He did not take this step merely as one frightened by rumours, but he had actually received repeated communications from the chiefs of the Khaibars, demanding the dispatch of some troops, and offering him their co-operation against the Sikhs, stating that otherwise they will be obliged to acknowledge the authority of Ranjit Singh. The army of the Amir encamped at the mouth of the Khaibar Pass, towards Peshavar, and every day skirmishes took place between the Afghans and the Sikh force garrisoned at Jam Road. The Amir considered it proper that his sons and the army should have some person of good judgment to regulate their conduct and the plan of the battle or of the negotiations. He was well aware that he had no more trusty servant nor any wiser man than his minister Mirza Abdul Sami Khan, and him he commanded to join his sons. The Mirza arrived in the camp, and observed that a large number of Mahomedan fanatics had assembled under the standards of Mohammed Akbar and of Afzal Khan, whether stimulated by religious feelings, or moved thereto by their avarice of plunder; but at the same time he was sure of sustaining one or two very strong battles with the Sikhs then present. He determined on attacking the enemy, and reported all the circumstances and prospects to the Amir at Kabul, and he sent fresh reinforcements under the Navabs Jabbar Khan, Usman Khan, and Sham-shuddin Khan. The fort of Jam Road was besieged, and the garrison prevented from fetching any water or grass from outside the citadel. They wrote to Sardar Hari Singh at Peshavar, telling him of their distressed and fearful condition, and solicited his immediate succour. The Sikh chief, with an army of about ten thousand men, twenty pieces of artillery, and a great quantity of ammunition and provisions, came to the relief of the garrison at Jam Road. He attacked the Kabul forces, and compelled Mohammed Akbar Khan to quit his ground; while Mohammed Afzal Khan, his brother, with his conspicuous bravery and judgment, managed to penetrate into the left wing of the Sikh troops, on which

Hari Singh retraced his steps. He then, however, assailed the Navab, defeated him, and captured two of the guns. Many Afghans were fleeing back towards Kabul; but Shamshuddin Khan, noted for bravery, happened to reach the place at this crisis, and by a most daring assault regained the lost field. Hari Singh was mortally wounded, and soon after died; and this gave the Afghans the victory. The Sikhs, after losing their leader, entrenched their position round the fort of Jam Road, and the army of the Amir of Kabul was recalled.

It is a general topic of conversation that, had not Mohammed Afzal Khan shown his judicious valour, and Shamshuddin Khan his rash boldness, the victory would never have been gained by the Afghans. However, all the merits and praise due to them were attributed by the Amir Dost Mohammed Khan to Mohammed Akbar Khan, the son of his favourite wife. She gave feasts and illuminated the city in commemoration of the victory gained by her son, and prevailed upon her husband to think and say that every honour and all applause was due to him. Since that period the eldest son of the Amir, Mohammed Afzal Khan, with other heroes of the family, is very much disheartened. No feeling of pure regard has since existed between the father and these sons; and Akbar Khan continues gaining the favour and strength of the Amir.

It is a matter of unquestionable truth, that Mohammed Akbar Khan, by his most extraordinary and successful intrigues, cruelties, and murders has gained the highest pitch of influence in Afghanistan and renown in England, but Mohammed Afzal Khan is the first of all the sons of Dost Mohammed Khan who possesses a sound judgment and the laudable quality of heroism. On the death of the Amir there will be no doubt a general commotion in Kabul. If Sultan Mohammed Khan, the ex-chief of Peshavar, or any of the present chiefs of Qandhar, be in existence at that period, no doubt he will then exert himself to become the master of the capital, and many chiefs, and even the sons of the Amir, will co-operate with any of these against Mohammed Akbar Khan. On the other hand, none of the sons of the Amir stands so high in the estimation of the population and of the chiefs, and the Barakzai family, as Mohammed Afzal Khan, and all these will join him against Akbar Khan. Mohammed

Azam Khan, also the brother of the former, will not hesitate to intrigue for killing the latter, while Akram Khan, and the other sons of the Amir, will unite with him. Akbar Khan will have no supporters but his own younger brothers, as Haidar Khan, &c. The whole dominion of Kabul, now under the possession of the Amir, will be divided into small principalities, governed by his sons, and independent of each other; and continued warfare, intrigues, assassinations, and plundering of the merchants, will be the predominant features of the government.

It is well known that the Amir Dost Mohammed is not the master of the whole of Afghanistan. He has, of course, seated himself on the throne, or in broad words, in the capital of that dominion—Kabul. The city is divided by the river "Jue Shir," which springs from Sirchashmah, on the road to Bamian; has a population of about sixty-five thousand souls; lat. 34° 30', long. 69° 6'. The whole province of Kabul, or the authority of the Amir Dost Mohammed Khan, extends from Hindu Kush-Parwan, lat. 35° 10', long. 69° 12' on the north, to Mukar, south of Ghuzni, lat. 32° 52', long. 67° 41', and little higher from Bamian in the west, lat. 34° 50', long. 67° 48', to the Khaibar pass in the east, lat. 33° 58', long. 71' 30',* making a length of two hundred miles from east to west, and the breadth of about one hundred and seventy miles from north to south. All the distances above detailed are often traversed by the Amir's cavalry from three to five days. The principal towns and marts of the country are Jalalabad, Ghazni, and Charkar, with some other petty places of renown, as Istalif, Shakardrah, &c. &c.

On the revenues of the province of Kabul a great many assertions are in existence, varying from each other very considerably. My information on this point is derived from the records of the chief collectors of the Amir Dost Mohammed Khan, as Mirza Sayad Husain, Divan Mitha upon one side, and Divans Birbal and Daya Ram on the other. These parties, however, differ in the total sum, but the connexion of Sayad Husain with the minister of the Amir, is the manifest reason of his pocketing large sums undetected from the revenues, while the latter Divans proved the truth on their own side, by putting

* Thornton's ' Gazetteer of the Countries adjacent to India.'

down the additional sums only on the paper which were realized for the government, and paid in accordingly. By the Sayad's account, the annual sum of money derived from the land, custom-house, extortion, and other unjust sources (Bidat), amounts to 2,431,271 rupees, while Divan Birdal collected 2,509,238 lakhs. It would be better and perhaps the shortest way to put down here the list of the collections of the latter, and I shall mention the amount of the revenue under its proper heading or name by which it is raised, namely, "Asal," or just, and " Bidat," or unjust. The accounts of Divan Birbal make an additional sum of 77,967 rupees in favour of the government.

Names of the ——, or of the Places the Revenue is collected from.	"Asal," or just Amount of the Revenue.	"Bidat," or unjust Amount of the Revenue.	Total Sum in Kabul Rupees.
Duties from Custom House	207,580	92,340	299,920
Vajah Shahganj, Arghande, &c. &c. .	109,054 and 2 abbasi	11,920 and 1 sannar	120,975
Bilok-i-Kohdaman, Char Yakar, and Lahogard	389,914 and 3 shahis	23,635 and 1 shahis	413,549 and 1 abbasi
Istalif	24,834 and 1 abbasi	1,525 and 6 shahis	26,360
Khalsah, Government Land	159,179	..	159,179
Rezah Kohistan and Bulaghain . . .	18,831	2,805	21,636

Names of the ——, or of the Places the Revenue is collected from.	" Asal," or just Amount of the Revenue.	" Bidat," or unjust Amount of the Revenue.	Total Sum in Kabul Rupees.
Ghorband	23,480	2,732	26,212
Tajakyah Maidan	21,825	921 and 5 shahis	22,746
Charkh	23,306	1,000	24,306
Ghilzai	222,595 and 1 senar	7,631 and 1 shahi	230,226 and 3 shahis
Behsud and Bamian	69,964	..	69,964
Ghaznin	397,971 and 7 shahis	37,451 and 3 shahis	435,423
Taefah Kharauti, Shinvari, &c. . .	18,321	740	19,061
Zurmat, Gardez, and Kharvar . .	64,240 and 2 abbasi	950	65,190 and 8 shahis
Hazarah Turkam, and Parsa . .	6,599	..	6,599
Khurm and Khost	95,000	..	95,000
Jalalabad and Lamghan-i-Tajakyah .	435,588	29,940	465,528
" Darkat-i-Mut-faraqah Havai," . .	5,870	3,850 and 6 shahis	9,720 and 6 shahis
Total	2,292,380	216,902	..
Grand Total . . .	..	..	2,509,238

The Amir Dost Mohammed Khan has acquired great celebrity for the encouragement of commerce in comparison with the conduct of his brothers, the chiefs of Qandhar and Peshavar; and in this he has acted wisely, both for his own benefit and for that of

the merchants. The roads under his government
are safer than they were in former days; and there
are no further demands on the merchandise made by
the petty officers of the customs, as there were under
the Sadozai dynasty. But I have heard from Mulla
Rahim Shah, Gholam Qadir, and Gopaldas Shikarpuri, merchants of first rank, that the consumption of
goods, and the circulation of money, was upon a
much larger scale under the disturbed state of the
late kings' governments only in Kabul than it is now
under the Barakzai chiefs, including Qandhar and
Peshavar, as well as Hirat.* The chief of Kabul has
established some new duties on the exports, the imports, and the transit of goods in Kabul, under
various names, commonly called " Bidat," which has
already been stated under the head of revenues. The
Amir has encouraged commerce indeed, but yet he
has often forcibly extorted large sums of money from
the merchants, wherewith to maintain his troops for
sake of the extension and stability of his government.
Whenever traders with shawls from Kashmir, or
horses from Bokhara, pass on their way through
Kabul, the Amir avails himself of the first descrip-

* Independent of the Barakzais.

tion of the articles, and of the animals, and giving no
value to all the cries of the owner, he pays any sum
he likes; which, of course, is much less than the
original price. The merchants bring a great quantity
of gold in Russian ducats, and the Bokhara tilas for
Amrat Sar and India; but a good deal more from the
former place. They bring these openly in the
smallest quantity only, for fear of being seized by the
Amir; and being thus forced they practise smug-
gling. At one time, while the British mission was
in Kabul, a Lohani merchant was seized, if I remember well, with twenty thousand ducats; and on
application made on his behalf several times by the
late Sir Alexander Burnes, the Amir reluctantly
restored some portion of it to the merchant.

Amount of duties levied at the different offices of customs in the
province of Kabul, given to me by Mirza Sami, the minister
of the A'mir :—

Names of Places.					Amount in Kabul Rupees.
Kabul	.	.	.	.	. 212,000
Ghazni	.	.	.	.	80,000
Bamian	.	.	.	.	55,000
Kafshan	.	.	.	.	4,500
Charkar	.	.	.	.	10,000
Istalif	.	.	.	.	6,000
Sarae Khojah	.	.	.	.	4,000
Arghande	.	.	.	.	16,000

Names of Places.	Amount in Kabul Rupees.
Jalalabad	7,000
Basaval or Hazarah nau . .	2,500
Gandumak	2,500
Lahogard	6,000
Sardari	6,000
Goshi Qandhar	2,000
From the city gates called "Chiraghi" (lamp)	2,000
Total . .	415,500

It must be understood that the above mentioned sum is included in the revenue of the government, and the total amount of 2,509,238 rupees is nearly equal in Company's rupees to 2,262,943, or about 226,294*l.* sterling. All the government and mercantile accounts are received and paid in Kham rupees, equal to ten shahis each. This is not a current coin, but is used in the accounts.

In the person, in the manners, and in the public proceedings of the Amir Dost Mohammed Khan, there is manifest the existence of every thing imaginable most suitable to support his own view. He is calm, prudent, and wise in cabinet, and an able commander in the field. In treachery, cruelty, murder, and falsehood, he is equally notorious. He is not at all a popular ruler, but he is the first man in Afghanistan who knows how to keep his authority undisturbed, and to deal effectually with the vagabond Afghans. He is certainly very much liked in regard to one thing, namely this: any man seeking for justice may stop him on the road by holding his hand and garment, once his beard, may abuse him for not relieving his grievances; and the Amir will continue to listen to him without disturbance or anger. Upon several occasions people in companies come near to the palace, and by the shouts of "Dad," justice, deafen the ears of the hearers; but seldom do they receive what they want. On the whole, whatever odium may be attached to the Amir of Kabul, it is an unquestionable fact that he is the only person fit to rule Kabul. Dost Mohammed Khan is of the Sunni religion, being the son of an Afghan; but as his mother is a Shia, he is therefore suspected to be of her creed, though he does not confess it openly. He has indulged in all sorts of dissipation, and experienced all kinds of hardships. When he gained power, he prohibited the sale and the use of wine, and prevented dancing girls from remaining in his kingdom, while the dance performed by boys was considered lawful! One day he was informed that some women were drinking and dancing privately in the house of Husain, the servant of Nayab Abdul Samad, on which the Amir sent people to seize them. The punishment inflicted upon them for drinking wine against the Mohammedan law and his own notification was the infliction of deformity instead of their beauty, in order to prevent them from appearing again in drinking parties. Their heads were shaved, and the beard of the host was burnt by the flame of a candle! The Amir Dost Mohammed Khan always gets up before it is dawn, takes a bath, makes his prayers, and reads a portion of the "Qoran" every morning. After that Mahmud Akhund Zadah gives him some lessons in history as well as poetry. He receives afterwards the state people privately in the dressing-room of the bath, and then comes out to hold his court. He sits there generally till 1 P.M. Now he had his breakfast, or I may say his dinner, as it is just the same as he receives after sunset. When he has finished his breakfast or mid-day meal he sleeps till 4 P.M. He then discharges his prayers, and proceeds usually to ride, sees his stud, and returns to the palace, where he dines with his immediate courtiers and friends.

There is then some talk of his early proceedings and of his future plans; and the wonder, the jealousy, and the ascendancy of foreign powers are discussed. Sometimes chess, and at other times music, were the favourite amusements of the evening. He amused himself generally in this manner till one hour past midnight. All the chiefs are then dismissed, and on retiring the Amir resides in the apartments of his wives. They live in separate parts, and the Amir pays a visit to one lady one night, and to another wife the next night, and no one is visited two nights successively except the mother of Mohammed Akbar Khan.

The military strength of the Amir Dost Mohammed Khan does undoubtedly exceed and excel that of any other of the chiefs of Afghanistan; and if I am rightly informed, the Sadozai kings never had such a large park of well-mounted guns as the Amir has. Whatever his occupations were during the day or night, his sole aim was bent towards the improvement and increase of his military power. He had fifty pieces of cannon, some of them well cast, besides those which were captured from the Sikhs when Sardar Hari Singh fell in the battle of Jam Road;

he has also about two hundred of " Shahnaks," good ones of their kind; these being light and small are placed on the backs of camels, and used by the driver. His cavalry amounted to twelve thousand in number, and is composed of two different brigades, the one called " Khud Aspah," riders of their own horses, and the other, " Amlah Sarkari," mounting the government horses. These are placed under the petty " Khavanins," in various numbers, from two to two hundred horses, and then attached to, and commanded by, some one of his own sons. Mohammed Akbar Khan usually leads two thousand, Mohammed Afzal Khan six hundred, Gholam Haidar Khan one thousand, and so on, the other sons and the Navabs, and the rest of the relations of the Amir, have few followers. He has also more than two thousand of " Jazayarchis," or infantry, bearing a large musket, like a wall piece of ordnance, which they use with a rest. This arm has gained great improvement under Mohammed Akbar, and his best and most confidential Ghilzai are armed with them, and he superintends the manufacture of them in person. The infantry of the Amir, organized by Nayab Abdul Samad, Mr. Campbell, and Dr. Harlan,

cannot be compared to the cavalry of that chief, but
as they are generally the men of the mountains, they
are by the position of their country and mutual warfare well adapted to fight under the shelter of bushes,
walls, and hollow places, where the uniform movements of our foot regiments will not permit them to
exercise their discipline as the Afghans can. Their
muskets are also better for throwing balls to a long
distance than those of England. This portion of
the Amir's force is limited to about fifteen hundred
men.

The pay of the troops is not properly distributed,
for neither the cavalry soldiers nor commanders,
" Khavanins," receive an equal sum; the increase
of pay and rank both depend entirely upon the
influence and patronage of their friends. They
are paid yearly in cash, grain, grass, sheep,
blankets, and butter, which, after obtaining an
order from the paymaster, they get from the
local collectors and the headmen of the villages
in the country. The general pay of a horseman
is 12 tomans, or 120 Kabul Kham rupees, that
is about 10*l.* a-year, which feeds and clothes him
with his family, as well as his charger—such is the

R

wonderful cheapness of provisions in that country. The foot soldier has no more than 84 rupees, or 8*l.* a-year, in the same manner, but a greater number of them are engaged for only about 6*l.* per annum.

(243)

CHAPTER X.

Connection of the British with Afghanistan—Policy of Russia
—Her alliance with Persia—The Afghans lean towards. the
British Government—Claims on Peshavar—Policy of Lord
William Bentinck—Of Lord Auckland—Letter from the
Amir to the Governor-General—Reply of the latter—Mission
of Sir Alexander Burnes—The Amir demands the restoration
of Peshavar—Sir Alexander's Reply—Dissatisfaction of Dost
Mohammed Khan—His letter to the King of Persia—His
plan of balancing Russia, Persia, and England against each
other.

I HAVE now fully related the adventurous commencement of the career of the Amir Dost Mohammed Khan, and brought him gradually to the
zenith of his glory. It is evident that the Afghans
never put any circumstances on record, nor do they
take the trouble to keep past events fresh in their
memory. Whatever they do remember is preserved
by the memory only, in the rudest manner. My in-
formants always failed in giving the precise dates,
or even the years of the Amir's progress, as noticed

R 2

in the preceding pages, and therefore no blame can be justly attached to this narrative for misplacing the events of his career. I shall now begin to describe the circumstances which opened the way for making the British more familiar with Afghanistan, and which also made the Amir Dost Mohammed Khan desirous to correspond with the Indian authorities.

Upon the one hand the English Government always sought for information in an independent state, lying between the confines of the Indian Empire and the Caspian Sea, and its officer felt an anxiety to secure that object. That political foresight was even worked upon so far back as 1808, when the mission of the Honourable Mountstuart Elphinstone was directed and proceeded to that quarter. The valuable "Account of the Kingdom of Kabul," published by that functionary, opened the eyes of the British nation to explore its curiosities, and in a political view the attention of the Government was most earnestly directed to that part of the globe. Hence also some Englishmen of mature sense and much ambition were induced to penetrate into that despotic country, and thought that, by making important and improved additions to the already gained knowledge of that extensive tract, and close familiarity with its vast number of inhabitants, they might gain the patronage of their Government and high estimation in their own country. With these deliberate views of advantage, therefore, they set out to carry their objects into effect. First of all Mr. Moorcroft entered Afghanistan, but unfortunately he expired on the other side of the Hindu Kush. Mr. Sterling, Captain Arthur Conolly, and after all the late Sir Alexander Burnes,* walked in the same path as marked out by his predecessors. The more new knowledge we gained of that region the more interest we felt in relation to its importance, both in a political and commercial point of view. For this purpose the navigation of the river Indus was opened, and a favourable alliance made with the Sindhians, the Daud potrahs, and the Sikhs.

Upon the other hand, the Persians and the Afghans having much more inland communication with each other, and dwelling on the frontiers of Russia, nourished a magnified idea of her ambitious policy, of her great power, and of her jealous eyes towards British India, and thus they considered themselves

* When the author of these Memoirs accompanied him.

the fortunate favourites of both these rival nations.
The Persians, being wiser and nearer than the
Afghans, set the example of acting on this universal
feeling, allied herself to Russia, while she continued to profess the holding of intimacy with
England, and in this manner thought she obtained
her wishes. The Afghans, though not so polished
as their neighbours in Persia, were not altogether
unaware of the interest which the English took in
their extensive country, which commanded the passes
or doors leading to India. With this thought the
late King Shah Shuja sought asylum in British
India, and hoped to be supported by us, and in this
he was not disappointed. Also in the same opinion
the late celebrated Vazir Fatah Khan sent communications to the Indian Government. The same
impression was on the heart of the Amir Dost
Mohammed Khan, but his crafty manœuvring
brought all the secret designs of the parties concerned
in them to light, and he thought that he possessed
the key of Hindustan, which no doubt will be too
dearly bought by the English if there should happen
the slightest shadow of another bidder.

With these well matured sentiments he desired to

make himself known to the governments of India, Persia, and Russia ; and while his brother, the Sultan Mohammed Khan of Peshavar, was alive, and held the Kohat and Hasht-nagar districts of that province under his acknowledged superior, Maharajah Ranjit Singh, the Amir Dost Mohammed Khan, whom both always despised and feared, made claims upon Peshavar.   There were always warfare and negotiations between him and the Sikhs upon this subject, and the Amir despatched communications and agents to the governments of British India, Persia, and Russia, soliciting the interference of each of these powers to recover the Afghan territory from the ruler of the Panjab, and promised his alliance and services to them (of course against each other) if there should happen the necessity of employing such services in future.

The late Lord William Bentinck, however, did not take a prominent interest in the politics of Afghanistan.   In fact there did not seem any necessity during his government to demand attention so seriously in that quarter as it unavoidably happened to require in the time of his successor.   The regretted Governor-General nevertheless seemed inclined to

share so far in the politics of that country that he
appointed Sayad Karamat Ali,* Mr. Masson, and
myself† in Afghanistan to convey to him information
of the passing events in that state.   This produced
an easy way for the Amir to effect his long-nourished
objects, and he therefore lost no time in corresponding with the British government.   His communications to his Lordship and Sir Claude Wade, the
political agent, implored the mediation of their
authority to adjust differences between him and his
powerful enemy the Maharajah Ranjit Singh.   He
had strong reasons for fearing that he might be subverted by his foe, who, through the influence of his
brother Sultan Mohammed Khan, now with the
Sikhs, could injure him (Dost Mohammed) even in
Kabul.

In the mean time the Earl of Auckland arrived
as the new Governor-General of India, and the
Amir Dost Mohammed Khan addressed a congratu-
lating epistle to his Lordship.

* Fellow traveller with the most deeply regretted and distinguished Captain Arthur Conolly.

† I never joined that situation at Qandhar, being appointed in
the meantime to settle the disputes between the subjects of
Lahore and Bahavalpur during the absence of Major Mackinon.

The Amir Dost Mohammed Khan of Kabul to the
Governor-General of India.

(After compliments.)

              " As I have been long attached to the British Government by the ties of friendship and affection, the late intelligence of your Lordship's arrival, enlightening with your presence the seat of government, and diffusing over Hindustan the brightness of your countenance, has afforded me extreme gratification; and the field of my hopes, which had before been chilled by the cold blast of wintry times, has, by the happy tidings of your Lordship's arrival, become the envy of the garden of Paradise.

    " It may be known to your Lordship, that, relying on the principles of benevolence and philanthropy which distinguish the British Government, I look upon myself and country as bound to it by the strongest ties, and the letters I have received from that quarter have all been replete with friendly sentiments and attention,—and to the effect that, in the time of need, the obligations of friendship should be fulfilled. The late transactions in this quarter, the conduct of reckless and misguided Sikhs, and their breach of treaty, are well known to your Lordship. Communicate to me whatever may suggest itself to your wisdom for the settlement of the affairs of this country, that it may serve as a rule for my guidance.

    " I hope your Lordship will consider me and my country as your own, and favour me often with the receipt of your

friendly letters. Whatever directions your Lordship may
be pleased to issue for the administration of this country, I
will act accordingly."

This letter was followed by many others similarly
expressive of his anxiety and fear of the Sikhs; and
his alarms were truly increased when an army of
fifty thousand from Lahaur arrived at Peshavar, in-
tending to revenge the sudden attack of the Afghans
upon Jam Road, and the fall of the Sardar Hari
Singh in that battle. The Earl of Auckland sent
to the Amir Dost Mohammed Khan a very kind
answer, and at the same time resolved to relieve him
from the continued fear of the Sikhs, under the
name of holding a commercial alliance with him.

The Earl of Auckland to the Amir Dost Mohammed Khan.

22nd August, 1836.

(After compliments.)

    "I HAVE had the pleasure to receive
your friendly letter, which was transmitted to me through
Sir Claude Wade, and I am gratified at the opportunity
which it affords so shortly after my assumption of the
Indian government, to convey to you the assurances of my
unfeigned regard and esteem.

    "It is my wish that the Afghans should be a flourishing
and united nation; and that, being in peace with all their

EARL OF AUCKLAND G.C.B.

neighbours, they should enjoy, by means of a more extended commerce, all the benefits and comforts possessed by other nations, which through such means have attained a high and advanced state of prosperity and wealth.

"My predecessor, aware that nothing was so well calculated to promote this object as the opening of the navigation of the Indus, spared himself no pains in procuring this channel for the flow of industry and enterprise; and it shall be my study to second his philanthropic purpose, and to complete the scheme which he so successfully commenced. I feel assured that you cannot but take a lively interest in the success of this undertaking, so especially conducive as it must be to the prosperity of the people over whom you rule.

"It is probable that I may, ere long, depute some gentlemen to your Court, to discuss with you certain commercial topics, with a view to our mutual advantage.

"I have learned with deep regret that dissensions exist between yourself and the Maharajah Ranjit Singh. My friend, you are aware that it is not the practice of the British Government to interfere with the affairs of other independent states; and indeed it does not immediately occur to me how the interference of my Government could be exercised for your benefit. I shall be happy, however, to learn from you by what means you think that I can be of any assistance; and in the meantime, I have only to hope that you will be able to devise some mode of effecting a reconciliation with the Sikhs; it being not only for your own advantage but for the advantage of all the countries in

the vicinity, that two nations so situated should ever preserve the unimpaired relations of amity and concord.

"Begging that you will accept my renewed assurance of
friendship and regard,

"I am, &c. &c.

(Signed)   "AUCKLAND."

The receipt of this letter excited a great sensation
in Dost Mohammed Khan, and served as a new
reason for him to employ his tact in order to second
his own objects, by intriguing with Persia and
Russia.   On the other hand the Governor-General of
India made preparations for sending a special mission
to his court, and Sir Alexander Burnes was selected
to conduct it.   The equipage of the mission and the
presents for the Amir were nothing in comparison
to those of the Honourable Mountstuart Elphinstone
when deputed to Shah Shuja-ul-mulk: however,
Sir Alexander Burnes, in company with his assist-
ants, Major Leech, Lieut. Wood, and Dr. Lord, of
the Bombay Presidency, ascended the Indus, and
I was ordered by the Supreme Government to join
him on that river.

The mission was well received at Haidarabad,

Khairpur, and Bahavalpur, on its way up the river;
and in the latter place Sir Alexander Burnes received a letter from Mr. Masson, the news-writer
in Kabul, stating that the Amir has been delighted
to hear that he was nominated to confer with him;
and he added that whatever the objects of the
mission might be, whether commercial or political,
they will meet an unreserved welcome from the
Amir Dost Mohammed Khan. The more near the
British mission approached Afghanistan, the more
frequently the Amir of Kabul despatched letters to
Sir Alexander Burnes, conveying the expression of
his delight at the prospect of the interview, and his
readiness and desire to attach himself to the British
government by any terms the Governor may think
proper to propose. On entering the Khaibar Pass
the mission was met by a deputation from the Amir,
and a salute was fired; and it was honourably conducted and escorted by Shah Ghasi Gul, Mirza
Aghajan, and Sadat Khan, the Momand chief, towards Kabul. Dost Mohammed Khan sent another
deputation, headed by Nazir Ali Mohammed Khan,
who had directions to provide the mission with all
the Afghan cookery and the other luxuries of Kabul,

and to wait upon us all the way to Kabul. After
some marches it reached Butkhak, and next day
Mohammed Akbar Khan, with a large retinue, came
to receive and conduct the mission into the city.
The procession in entering was very grand, and
we were placed on elephants together with him,
and thus proceeded onwards between lines made
on both sides by the spectators and the respectable citizens, who were requested by the Amir
to welcome us. The anxiety and pleasure of Dost
Mohammed Khan at the arrival of the English envoy
was so great, that he desired his son to conduct us at
once to his own presence. He received us most
cordially; and near his own palace a beautiful garden, surrounded with the most comfortable apartments, was allotted to us as our place of residence.

On the 21st of September the Amir Dost Mohammed Khan assembled his nobles and received
the mission formally. Sir Alexander Burnes submitted his credentials from the Governor-General of
India to the Amir, and they were opened by himself,
and read aloud by his minister Mirza Abdul Sami
Khan; and the Amir seemed really flattered by
hearing the contents of them in the presence of those

THE LATE SIR ALEXANDER BURNES KT. C.B.

chiefs who, being older, and having seen the late kings of the Sadozai family, had never dreamt that Dost Mohammed Khan, one of the humblest of the sons of Payandah Khan, could become a person of such consequence as to be respected by the English power.

The credentials were these:—

The Earl of Auckland to the Amir Dost Mohammed Khan.

Fort William, 15th *May,* 1837.

(After compliments.)

"IN my letter to your address, dated 2nd August, 1836, I intimated my intention of deputing an officer to confer with you as to the best means of promoting the interests of commerce, and facilitating the intercourse of traders between India and Afghanistan.

" To your enlightened mind it cannot fail to be obvious, that commerce is the basis of all national prosperity, and that it is commerce alone that enables people of one country to exchange its superfluous commodities for those of another; to accumulate wealth, and to enjoy all the comforts and blessings of civilized life.

"The general diffusion of these blessings and comforts among neighbouring nations is the general object of the British Government. It seeks for itself no exclusive benefits, but it ardently desires to secure the establishment of peace and prosperity in all the countries of Asia.

" With this view the British Government prevailed upon

the powers occupying the banks of the river, to open the navigation of the Indus; and to this object, indeed, have all its efforts been invariably directed.

"I now send Sir Alexander Burnes, who will deliver this letter, to confer with you as to the best means of facilitating commercial intercourse between Afghanistan and India. I have no doubt that he will meet with a friendly reception at your Court, and that his personal communication with you will be attended with all the advantages which I anticipate.

"In conclusion, &c.,

(Signed) "AUCKLAND."

For a few days the Amir Dost Mohammed Khan continued to show us every civility, and appearing to act with perfect sincerity and candour; and in his conversation with Sir Alexander Burnes he always showed a moderation in his demands. Sir Alexander Burnes wrote at that time as follows :—"Up to this time my communications with the Amir have been confined to matters of compliment and ceremony, but I shall take an early opportunity of reporting on what transpires at this court, merely observing at present, from what I have seen and heard, that I have good reason to believe Dost Mohammed Khan will set forth no extravagant pretensions, but will act in such a manner as to enable the British Government to show its interest in his behalf, and at the same time to preserve for us the valued friendship of the Sikh chief."

However, the moderation of the Amir Dost Mohammed Khan was of short duration. He forgot that the presence of the British mission in his capital had prevented the Sikh army from revenging the sudden attack of Akbar Khan upon Jam Road, and placed no value on the mediation of the English, which was intended to secure his interests. The tenor of his previous correspondence and conversation was anxiously expressive of his fears of an attack from the Sikhs; but now, changing his views and his mind, he longed for the possession of Peshavar, and he accordingly demanded of Sir Alexander Burnes to write to his government to cause the restoration of that province to him. Sir Alexander Burnes replied to the Amir that Peshavar was never under his authority; and that his brothers, Sultan Mohammed and Pir Mohammed Khan, were the rulers of that part of Afghanistan, and had still "jagirs" in that district, granted to them from the sovereign of the Panjab. He added,

also, that the Maharajah Ranjit Singh was a faithful
ally of the English,—was powerful both in arms and
in money; and had lost his commander-in-chief,
Sardar Hari Singh, in an unprovoked assault of the
Afghans upon his handful of forces at Jam Road.
The British Government, he said, being desirous to
establish peace for the extension of commerce as far
as to the markets of Central Asia, and finding by
the Amir's letters and words that he was always
involved with alarms, resolved to adjust differences
between him and the Sikhs by amicable terms;
that is to say, the Amir will have no further necessity by extortions to make himself unpopular, to
raise troops and to shed blood in fighting with the
forces of the Panjab.   On the contrary, that he will
enjoy the comforts of his authority without fear, and
will reign in prosperity.   Sir Alexander Burnes
continued, that his Government will induce the
Maharajah, by friendly advice, to give up Peshavar
to its former master, the Sardar Sultan Mohammed
Khan, the brother of the Amir; but that the alliance, which so faithfully is maintained by the
Maharajah, cannot permit the British Government
to use its authority directly on this subject.

In my own presence the Amir Dost Mohammed
Khan replied, that this was not the good offices of
the English which he had expected; that his hopes
were quite different; that he had now a turban of
muslin on his head, but that on entering into a
friendly relation with the British he had sanguine
hopes that he would have a shawl one in lieu of muslin.
On the contrary, he finds that the English wish to
keep the old material on his head, with the obliging
promise that they will not allow any other power to
deprive him of it. To this act of amity he attaches
not much importance, as he was not afraid that any
one will ever wrest it from him. The Amir continued, that the restoration of Peshavar to the
Sultan Mohammed Khan will not be a token of the
British entertaining good wishes towards himself,—
nay, it will hasten the ruin of his government in
Kabul. He added, that his brother, Sultan Mohammed, though one of the family, and of one blood
with himself, was a more fatal enemy to him even
with a small force than the Sikhs with their large
army. The Sikhs will lend his brother money, and,
under his Mahomedan name, will send forth their
intrigues to the very heart of his capital.

Now, also, the Amir Dost Mohammed Khan was informed of the progress of the Persian mission towards Afghanistan, bearing presents and letters in answer to those which he and his brothers the Qandhar chiefs had despatched to the king, and which affair the Amir had kept till this time unspoken.

It must here be said with propriety that when he had communicated his grievances to the British Government, he conveyed the same to the other western powers of Russia and Persia, with the view of gaining his object by playing these three states against each other.

————

Letter from the Amir Dost Mohammed Khan to His Majesty Mohammed Shah, King of Persia.

(After Respects.)

"SINCE in former days the chiefs of my family were sincerely attached to the exalted and royal house of your Majesty, I, too, deem myself one of the devoted adherents of that royal race ; and considering this country as belonging to the kingdom of Persia, I on a former occasion despatched Haji Ibrahim to your Majesty's presence with the object of explaining certain affairs connected with this nation. I crave permission to state, that the cause of my addressing in the present instance is the following:—Your Majesty is the king of 'Islam,' yet throughout these territories disturbances and misery are caused by that detestable tribe, the Sikhs.

"Although four hundred thousand families of the tribe of Afghans, and the neighbouring tribes, wear the collar of obedience in subjection to this sincere well-wisher, my inability for the employment and arrangement of this multitude limits my forces to twenty thousand excellent horse and ten thousand foot, and fifty guns, which are ready at my capital, Kabul.*

"I have been long engaged in war against one hundred thousand horse and foot of the wicked infidels, who have three hundred guns; but, by the grace and assistance of God, I have not yet been subdued by this faithless enemy, and have been able to preserve the true faith; but how long shall I be able to oppose this detestable tribe, and how long shall I be able to resist their aggressions?† Without doubt an account of the difficulties of my situation has reached your Majesty; and your Majesty must have heard that, notwithstanding the inferiority of my power, I am perpetually engaged in war with the wicked Sikhs, without a moment's cessation. As the noblest of cities, Qandhar and the capital Kabul, and the countries bordering on Khora-

---

* Exaggeration. For the proper number, see his military power in the preceding pages.

† This is sufficient to show that the Amir feared the aggression of the Sikhs, but never considered that he had a right to seize upon Peshavar, and that it should be given to him, and not to his brother, Sultan Mohammed Khan, is not also known of this.

san, as well as the province of Khorasan, and the country
dependant on the above places, form part of the Persian
territory, and are within the kingdom of the King of Kings,
the misery and welfare of those dominions cannot be sepa-
rated from the interests of the Persian government.   Even
if my affairs should fall into disorder, and even if your Majesty should not direct your attention to the condition of
these countries, nevertheless I shall persist in contending
with the Sikhs as long as I am able ; but should it prove
that I be unable to resist that diabolical tribe, then I have
no choice, and must connect myself with the English, who
will thus obtain a complete authority over the whole of
Afghanistan; and it remains to be seen hereafter to what
places, and what extent the flame of the violence of this nation
may be carried.

"I considered it imperative on myself to represent these
circumstances to the King of Islam.   As for the rest, your
Majesty will act as seems expedient to your royal understanding.   All other affairs will be narrated by Mohammed
Husain Khan, who is a trusty person attached to your well-
wisher."

This letter will clearly show that the Amir, without having waited the answer of his former communication, sent through Haji Ibrahim, despatched
Mohammed Husain Khan with another letter in the
mean time into Persia; and from this proceeding the
reader will perceive that the Amir Dost Mohammed

Khan was not desirous to form any connexion with
the British government, unless the Shah of Persia
should relinquish his cause. He had also sent a
letter to the Emperor of Russia by Husain Ali,
stating that since Mahomed Shah, the centre of
the faith, had closely connected himself with his Imperial power, desiring the advantage of such alliance,
that he also being a Mahomedan, was desirous to
follow his example, and to attach himself to his Majesty. In that letter the Amir gave an exaggerated
account of his own military power and of his successful opposition to the Sikh army, whom he described
as commanded by English and French officers. He
added that if he was not assisted by the Emperor,
the Sikhs, who are in alliance with the English government, will at last overpower him, and that their
influence in Afghanistan will be a foundation for that
of the British, who, under a commercial name, will
become the superiors of this country, and will annihilate the trade which is now so briskly conducted
between Moscow, Bokhara, and Kabul.

He then added, "that Husain Ali will fully explain
to your Imperial Majesty the feelings of my respect
and attachment to your august government, and the

advantages which are likely to result to us all, Russia, Persia, and Afghanistan, from being heartily united, and considered to be but one body." This letter was recently shown to me by the son-in-law of Mirza Sami Khan, with the one which is already published in the Afghanistan correspondence.

The chiefs of Qandhar, the brothers of the Amir of Kabul, had also deputed Taj Mohammed Khan to his Excellency Count Simonich, the Russian ambassador in Persia, and his credentials were expressive of similar sentiments of concord and attachment to the Russian government as the letter of Dost Mohammed Khan, alluded to and given above. It is plain enough to observe that the Amir was raised to the supremacy which he enjoyed, by his bloody and treacherous but successful intrigues, and by the adherence to him of the Persian sect in Kabul. He was now, therefore, persuaded by his confidential counsellors, Mirza Sami Khan, Agha Husain, Mahmud Khan Bayat, and Haji Mirza Khan of Nanchi, not to come to a definite alternative in his negotiations with Sir Alexander Burnes, but to wait the arrival of the answers from the Russian and Persian governments.

CHAPTER XI.

A Persian Envoy arrives at Qandhar—The Chiefs of that place
make a treaty with him—Letter from the Shah of Persia to
the Amir—Instructions of the Persian Envoy—Mr. Ellis's
despatch to Lord Palmerston—Sir John Macneil at the Persian Court—The Shah marches against Hirat—Despatches of
Sir John Macneil—Russian intrigues—Various letters to the
Chiefs of Qandhar—Their treaty with the Shah, under the
guarantee of Russia—Negotiations of Sir A. Burnes at Kabul
—The Russian Envoy, Capt. Vikovich—Diplomatic etiquette
in Asiatic courts—Letters relating to Capt. Vikovich—His
proceedings at Kabul—Progress of Russian influence there—
The English mission retires—Various documents.

THE information which the Amir Dost Mohammed
Khan had previously received of the progress of the
Persian ambassador was now confirmed by his arrival
at Qandhar, which induced him to take open steps
with regard to particulars which he had hitherto kept
secret. He knew the weight and value of the
influence of his old adherents, the Javanshers of
Kabul, and was aware that the government of Persia,
advised by Russia, was marching against Afghanistan,
or at least Hirat, the gate of India. Qambar Ali

Khan, the ambassador of his Majesty Mohammed
Shah of Persia, along with Mohammed Husain Khan,
the agent of the Amir, had in the mean time arrived
in Qandhar. The chiefs in this place detained the
Persian envoy to enter into alliance with them; and
being jealous of the Amir of Kabul, and desirous to
gain the conspicuous favour of the Shah of Persia
and of the government of Persia for themselves alone,
they prevented him from prosecuting his journey to
Kabul until they themselves had concluded a treaty
of alliance with him.

" The Treaty which I, Qambar Ali Khan, here made
with the respected Sardars, Kohandil, Rahamdil, and
Mehardil Khan, on the part of His Majesty Mohammed
Shah, is as follows :—

" In case the Sardars should send one·of their sons to
His Majesty, I promise to the Sardars the following in
return :

" 1. That the country of Hirat, whether it be taken by
the power of the servants of the Persian Government, or by
that of the Sardars, must be left to the latter; and that
the Shah should not expect anything from them in return
but service, and likewise should make no interference of
any kind with their country or tribe in Afghanistan.

" 2. His Majesty is not to form any connexion with the
Afghans of any description, great or small, and also not to

employ them in case of any business with the Afghans;
but in such case His Majesty is to have recourse to the
Sardars.

" 3. His Majesty is never to make friendship with Shah
Zadah Kam Ram and Yar Mohammed Khan.

" 4. On the arrival of the son of Sardar Kohandil
Khan, His Majesty is to order the army at Meshid to
march towards Hirat; and if Kam ¦Ram and Yar Mohammed Khan resolve to take Qandhar, the Shah should
prevent them by coming to Qandhar; and if they do not
agree to this, then the Shah should come to Hirat.

" 5. The Shah is also to give the Sardars means to pay
the expenses of twelve thousand cavalry and infantry, and
twelve guns, and the extra expenditure of the troops in the
capture of Hirat; and, if the war lasts long, the Shah
must furnish the expenses of the army.

" 6. In case any harm befal the country of the Sardars,
the Shah is to give them, in his own country, land equal to
the value of their loss.

" 7. The Treaty which I have now made with the
Sardars, is to be approved of by His Majesty, and to bear
the signature of Haji Mirza Aghasi, Mirza Masud (the
Minister for Foreign Affairs), and also of the Ambassadors
of Russia and of England, to secure confidence to the
Sardars.

" QAMBAR ALI."

When Mohammed Husain Khan, the envoy of

the Amir of Kabul, who had returned from Persia
with Qambar Ali Khan, discovered that the Sardars
would not permit his companion to go to Dost
Mohammed Khan, and had made an engagement
with him, taking all the credit to themselves, and
casting altogether the interests of his employer, the
Amir, aside, he quitted Qandhar, and returned to
Kabul. Dost Mohammed Khan, when informed
of what had been done, secretly told him that he
(Mohammed Husain) was not to pay any attention to what he (the Amir) might speak slightingly of the result of his mission, of his own letter,
and of the power of Mohammed Shah; for such
things would be said by him in order to make the
British envoy believe that he did not care for the
alliance of Persia, but was desirous to connect himself with the English, and this deceit was to be continued until he received the reply to his letter from
" Petarpur " (St. Petersburgh). In secret he wrote,
at the desire of Mohammed Husain Khan, to the
chiefs of Qandhar, desiring them to send Qambar
Ali Khan to him in Kabul, and upbraiding them
that they had made a treaty with him for their own
advantage, without consulting him at all, or making

him a partisan in it. Now the cunning Amir, according to his arrangement with his envoy, made as if he looked upon the result of his mission as a matter of trifling importance, and did not show him much respect. He deceitfully pretended, in the presence of the British envoy, and of Mr. Masson the newswriter, to be dissatisfied with the terms of the letter (farman) which the King of Persia had sent him in answer to his letter (arizah), while privately he felt proud of the arrival of such an honourable token of His Majesty's favour on his behalf, and sent a copy of it to the King of Bokhara, with whom he was in correspondence on terms of equality.

Letter from His Majesty Mohammed Shah, King of Persia, to the Amir Dost Mohammed Khan of Kabul.

" His Excellency, the repository of honour and glory, the most Noble of Nobles, the opponent of infidels, the Amir Dost Mohammed Khan, Lord of Kabul, is honoured with our auspicious royal correspondence, and informed that the two letters addressed by His Excellency have been conveyed to our Royal presence by the hands of Haji Ibraham and Mohammed Husain Khan. The contents of each, displaying the rectitude of the intentions of that receptacle of

dignity, have been perused by us from the beginning to the
end, and the objects and wishes of his Excellency have
also been explained to us by the above messengers. All
these circumstances being proofs of sincerity and purity of
intention, they gave entire satisfaction to our Royal mind,
and disposed us to feel confidence in his devotion.

" With regard to your representation of your connexion
with this never-ending government, and with regard to
your observations that Kabul is to be considered as one of
the countries dependant on the kingdom of Persia, and that
you are incessantly engaged in war with the infidels, notwithstanding whose superior strength you had hitherto been
able to oppose them, and to preserve those dominions from
subjection, but that if you did not receive assistance from
us, you will be obliged to seek aid elsewhere, in order that
an end might be put to these disorders; in truth these observations are written with sincerity, and it is apparent to
our kingly mind that your Excellency is a distinguished
warrior of Islam, who fights with valour for the faith, most
surely expecting to prosper, both on account of his depend-
ence on this never-ending government, and for the protection of Islam, and for the defence of our kingdom and religion; and from kingly generosity we deem it imperative
on us to hold that refuge of dignity under the standard of
our protection, and not to grudge or withhold from him
assistance of any kind. Thus, before the arrival of the
messengers of your Excellency, we had firmly resolved to
march to Hirat, and to convey every description of aid to

your Excellency. We commenced our march from our
capital, Tehran, with this intention. After our arrival at
Bootan, it was represented to the ministers of this haughty
state, that the cholera was raging with violence throughout
the cities of Khorasan. We, therefore, for the sake of
change of air, and in expectation of the cessation of this
malady, moved to a healthy situation, and halted some days
in the plains of Kalpoosh. In the meantime, it was represented to us, that Makhdum Quli, the Yamut (Turkman),
having formed an alliance with Ala Quli Khan (chief of
Khiva), had arrived at Karakala, which is situated near
the Desert, with twenty thousand horse, the flower of the
Usbeg and Turkman cavalry; and having fortified himself in that position, was waiting for the opportunity of
the absence of our conquering army to produce disorder
and tumult on the confines of our dominions. When this
intelligence reached us we despatched our beloved brother,
Feridun Mirza, with eight thousand regular infantry and
four thousand cavalry, and twelve guns, to chastise these
marauders. As soon as they became acquainted with the
arrival of our troops, their courage failed them; and, not
daring to oppose our forces, they abandoned their provisions
and stores, and fled into the deserts. Our brother followed
in pursuit of this wicked tribe; and near Qirchul, the
cavalry, and some of the infantry, overtook and attacked
them. From morning until night the fire of war was in a
blaze, but the affair terminated in the defeat of the Turkmans. The greater part were killed, some were captured,

and the remainder fled into the barren deserts, and escaped from our warriors. After chastising this tribe we halted some time at the river Gurgam to arrange the affairs of that frontier; and then winter, and the season of snow and rain having arrived, it was impossible to continue the campaign. We despatched twenty thousand horse and foot, and forty guns, with ordnance and stores, to Khorasan, to be in readiness to march in the beginning of spring to Hirat; and we have resolved to march, with the assistance of God, with the remainder of the army, towards Khorasan, after the festival Nauroz. As there has been some delay in the advance of the victorious army, we have despatched Qambar Ali Khan to your Excellency; and have sent a diamond-hilted dagger to your Excellency, which is to be worn as the ornament of your faithful waist. We have commanded Qambar Ali Khan to detail the full extent of our royal favour towards your Excellency, and your Excellency will explain to Qambar Ali Khan your wishes and intentions, in order that they may be represented to us on his return."

Written in the month of Shaval, 1252.

Qambar Ali Khan, while detained and negotiating at Qandhar, was very brisk in his intrigues and correspondence with Mahmud Khan Bayat, and other Persians of influence, and in the confidence of the Amir. He had also employed secret emissaries to collect information of the resources of the country, and particularly about the provisions. He had also requested the rich merchants of the Persian tribe to secure supplies for the army of Mohammed Shah, who, by his statement, was to penetrate Afghanistan in company with the Russian ambassador, as soon as Hirat had tendered submission. He possessed the following instructions, bearing the seal and signature of Mohammed Shah, and of his prime minister Haji Mirza Aghasi, the copy of which he gave, with his own agreement, as a security to the various merchants. Among them was Mulla Nasu, a wealthy trader, in the confidence of the chief Kohandil Khan, who secretly gave the copy of it to my newswriter, Mohammed Tahar.

Translation of a Copy of Instructions from the Persian Government to Qambar Ali Khan, envoy to Kabul.

" When you pass beyond the boundary of Qayan, at each stage that you reach you will detail the following particulars in a book which you will present to His Majesty on your return, namely, the state of the towns and villages, and population, with an account of all circumstances that happen during your journey, an estimate of the population

T

and the strength of the tribes at each place, as of the Sistanis, Biloches, Afghans, and Qazalbashes, and an account of the revenue and expenditure of those countries,—their produce, their principal articles of cultivation, and from what course of cultivation the most profit is made, and an account of the taxes levied from the people, and the imports or commerce : finally, whether there is water on the road, and whether the latter is level or mountainous. In passing through Bilochistan you must raise great expectations of the munificence and benevolence of His Majesty in the minds of the Khans of Belochistan and of Sistan. If these persons are favourably disposed towards Kam Ran, you should endeavour to persuade them to attach themselves to the service of this government, and try to inspire them with perfect confidence. You should, in particular, extol the generosity of His Majesty to Ali Khan, and declare to him that tidings of his services had reached His Majesty. All these Khans should assemble and prepare their troops, &c., at the time of the arrival of the fortunate camp, for they are to join the Royal Stirrup. At Qandhar he will deliver the firman and robes of honour to Kohandil Khan, and to his brothers, and excite his hopes of the generosity of His Majesty. He will attach himself strongly to Kohandil Khan, and he will inquire from him why, after the arrival of that letter (some former one), he did not send his brother and his son. Kohandil Khan must endeavour to send one of his brothers in advance to this court, while he himself will remain in his present situation, and await the arrival of the Royal army. He will get his troops in readiness, and prepare as much cavalry as is practicable, for, please God, the campaign of Hirat will be entrusted to him. Qambar Ali Khan will declare to Kohandil Khan that if he has incurred any losses in the service of this government, reparation shall be made for them, and he shall experience His Majesty's generosity. Qambar Ali Khan will form an acquaintance with all the persons in authority, and with the Afghan and Qazalbash Khans, as well as with the Qazalbashes in general; and his object will be to excite their hopes of His Majesty's generosity. If they feel apprehensions, on account of the religious differences of Shias and Sunnis, he will endeavour to dispel their apprehensions, and will give them assurances that the justice and benevolence of His Majesty will not permit any distinction whatever to be made between them, and thus he will endeavour to render all persons desirous of serving this government. When he has finished his affairs in Qandhar he will proceed to Kabul, and deliver a dagger as a mark of His Majesty's favour to Dost Mohammed Khan, and he will convey the auspicious robes of honour to Navab Jabbar Khan. He will use the utmost endeavours to inspire them with earnest confidence in the sincerity of His Majesty's favour for them ; and he will give them the strongest assurances that, after the arrival of the Royal army in those countries, favours of every description shall be unsparingly lavished upon them. Publicly he will declare that the object of his mission is to convey an answer to the petition of Dost Mohammed Khan, and to deliver the auspicious robes of honour, but in private he will expatiate on the connexion of Dost Mohammed Khan with this country, and he will declare that, please God, Dost Mohammed Khan shall enjoy the royal favour to such an extent that those countries shall be placed completely in his possession, and he shall have entire control over them. Qambar Ali Khan will declare to Dost Mohammed Khan, that if he will avow his intimacy with this government, and will send one of his brothers or his sons to this court, it will prove of the highest advantage to him. In fine, his hopes of assistance from this country are to be excited, and he is to be persuaded that his only hope of safety is from this government. He is to be urged to prepare his troops, and he is to expect the arrival of His Majesty in spring. If the Amir is desirous of obtaining from Qambar Ali Khan a document declaring his connexion with this country, and prohibiting the Sikhs from molesting him, he is permitted to grant it."

While the Persian and the Afghan envoys were entering into alliance, and exchanging treaties for their respective governments, the Shah and his minister were not indifferent about other affairs, but busied themselves also in giving proof to the British ambassador that the court of Tehran was not only resolved to subdue Hirat, but that the reduction of the whole kingdom of Afghanistan into subjection was talked of and intended. The Right Honourable Mr. Ellis, who was sent from England to congratulate the Shah on his ascending the throne of Persia, writes to Lord Palmerston in the following manner:—

"I thought it desirable to bring again formally before Haji Mirza Aghasi, and the Minister for Foreign Affairs, the views of His Majesty's Government in respect of the foreign policy best suited to the actual condition of Persia; but they both protested against considering the Afghans as a government or consolidated state, with whom relations of peace or of equality were to be maintained. They declared that a large portion of Afghanistan belonged to the Shah of Persia, and that he was at liberty to decide for himself how he would deal with the Afghans, as being his subjects.

"I inquired how far they considered the dominion of Persia to extend, and their reply was, to Ghazni.

"I feel quite assured that the British Government cannot permit the extension of the Persian monarchy in the direction of Afghanistan, with a due regard to the internal tranquillity of India, for that extension will at once bring Russian influence to the very threshold of our empire.

"The success of the Shah in this undertaking is anxiously wished for by Russia, and her Minister here does not fail to press it on to early execution. The motive cannot be mistaken. Hirat, once annexed to Persia, may become, according to the commercial treaty, the residence of a Russian consular agent, who would from thence push its researches and communications, avowed and secret, throughout Afghanistan. Indeed, in the present state of the relations between Persia and Russia, it cannot be denied that the progress of the former in Afghanistan is tantamount to the advance of the latter, and ought to receive every opposition from the British Government that the obligations of public faith will permit.

" Aziz Khan (the Qandhar Envoy) held the same language to me as he had undoubtedly done to the Shah and his Ministers, namely, that the whole of Afghanistan was, with the exception of Hirat and its dependencies, ready to come under feudal submission to the State, who, in a fortnight, with the aid of the Afghans, like Nadir Shah, could push his conquests to Delhi.

" That the Russian Minister had had a long audience with the Shah on the preceding day, when the subject of discussion was the expedition against Hirat, in which the Russian Minister had recommended perseverance this year, on the ground that what now could be effected with ten thousand men, might not next year be practicable with a much larger force.

" It appears from the correspondence that Dost Mohammed Khan, on the 17th of September, despatched an agent, Haji Ibrahim, with letters to the Shah of Persia, placing himself, his country and its resources, at the disposal of the Shah, offering to co-operate in an attack upon Hirat, and seeking generally the protection of the Shah against the Sikhs."

SIR JOHN McNEIL. BART. G.C.B.

On the departure of the Right Honourable H. Ellis, Sir John Macneil was appointed by the Government of England the envoy extraordinary and minister plenipotentiary at the court of Persia. His long residence in that country and acquaintance with the feelings and politics of its people, promised fair that the intrigues of Persia, guided as they were by the Russian ambassador, will not be permitted to pass without detection; for as the latter continued still unchanged in his designs towards Afghanistan, Sir John Macneil, in his various despatches to Lord Palmerston, gives a full detail of the united policy of the Persian and Russian states. The British minister did all he could to dissuade the Shah from undertaking the hazardous expedition against Hirat, and reminded his Majesty that such proceedings will be contrary to the expectation of her Majesty's Government, and will, in fact, be injurious to the interests of British India. Nevertheless the campaign was formed, and the Shah marched against Hirat. The messenger of her Majesty's embassy in Persia, bearing letters from Major Pottinger, was seized, maltreated, and deprived of his letters and

property. The Russian minister was in the meantime urging the Shah to prosecute his journey
towards Hirat, and promised, on the part of his
government, that if Persia takes possession of Hirat,
she shall be released from the balance of the debt
due to the cabinet of St. Petersburgh. Colonel
Stoddart, accompanying the camp of the Shah, took
always an opportunity to beg his Majesty to come to
amicable terms with Hirat; but such remonstrances
were of no avail. Ghuryan was taken, and Hirat
besieged. Such disregard to the advice of the
British representative was productive of serious
injuries and insults to the agents of that government
in all parts of Persia; and the inhabitants of the
Residency at Bushir were threatened to be massacred by the populace. At length Sir John Macneil
determined to proceed to the camp, and try to
persuade Mohammed Shah fervently to accept the
terms of the defenders of Hirat, and induce him to
withdraw his army from the siege of that place.
His Excellency Count Simonich, the Russian ambassador, wrote to the foreign minister of his Majesty to prevent Sir John Macneil from joining the

camp; and Mirza Masud really directed a communication to him on the subject, and desired him
at least to postpone his departure till the instructions of the Shah were received; nevertheless he
sent no answer, but set out to his quarters. On
arriving at Ghuryan he received an official letter
from the deputy foreign minister, conveying the
orders of the Shah not to proceed beyond that place.
Yet he joined the camp, and induced the Shah to
allow him to mediate, and to adjust the differences.
Then treaties were framed; at one time agreed to,
and at another time refused through the advice of
Count Simonich. In the meantime the British
ambassador was not respected nor treated with the
usual cordiality, and was thus compelled to leave the
court and camp of the King of Persia.

*Extracts from the Despatches of Sir John Macneil, Envoy
Extraordinary and Minister Plenipotentiary at the Court
of Persia.*

" YET in this state of things, the Russian minister, as late
as the 23rd ult., still continued to urge the Shah to under-

take a winter campaign against Hirat, an enterprise which, even were the army in the best condition as to feeling and preparation, would be extremely hazardous.

"Agreeably to intelligence communicated to me by Colonel Stoddart, it appears, that when one of my couriers was returning from Hirat to the capital, some horsemen were despatched from the royal camp in pursuit of him, who prevented him from continuing his journey, and brought him to the camp, where he was treated with great violence and indignity. Subsequently, when Colonel Stoddart had waited on His Excellency the Hajee, and explained to him that the above person was in my service, and when the Persian government was apprised that he was attached to my establishment, even then an order was issued for placing him in guard, and he received extreme ill-treatment from Hajee Khan Karabreghee, who used every description of threat towards him.

"It is reported and believed at Tehran, that the Russian minister has announced the intention of his government, if the Shah should succeed in taking Hirat, to release Persia from the engagement to pay the balance of the debt due by her to Russia ; and the reason assigned for this act of grace is, that the Emperor desires to contribute that amount towards defraying the expenses of the campaign.

"I have the honour to enclose a copy of a communication I received a few days ago from the officiating resident at Bushire, by which your Lordship will perceive that a threat of exciting the populace to commit violence, with an allusion to the massacre of the Russian mission, has been held out by the government of Bushire.

" The most obvious impediment to the interference of Great Britain in the quarrel between Persia and Hirat is the stipulation contained in the ninth article of the treaty of Tehran ; but it can hardly be argued that this article binds us to permit the unjust and wanton destruction by Persia of the most valuable defences of India, while the Shah appears to be acting in concert with, and promoting the influence in those countries of, that very power whose exclusion from them has become the chief object of the alliance with His Persian Majesty.

" And as I find that the government of India entertains the opinion that the preservation of the integrity of Hirat is of vital importance, I have determined to proceed to the Shah's camp, and to endeavour, by every means in my power, to induce His Majesty to conclude a treaty with Shah Kam Ran, and to raise the siege of Hirat.

" Count Simonich has contented himself with despatching a messenger, and with inducing Mirza Masud to address me a letter, remonstrating against my going to the camp, on the pretext that, from the opinion entertained by people generally of the views on which I act, my presence in the camp will tend to strengthen the Afghans, which will be injurious to the Persian government.

" ' According to what you yesterday mentioned verbally in

the apartment of His Excellency the Beglarbegi, it would appear that you intend speedily to proceed to the camp of His Majesty, &c., &c., the Shah; and as, in consequence of certain circumstances which have occurred, and of certain others which friends and enemies have conjectured and imagined to be connected with these, your Excellency's presence during the siege of Hirat will certainly and undoubtedly produce greater confidence and resistance on the part of the besieged, and this is obviously injurious to the interests of this proud and ever-enduring empire, and the British government certainly cannot desire to cause an injury to this state; therefore I request your Excellency, if possible, to abandon this journey, or to postpone it for a time, till instructions on this subject can be received from His Majesty the Shah.'

"At Ghuryan I received a letter from the Deputy Minister of Foreign Affairs, conveying to me the Shah's desire that I would not advance beyond that place, as my presence could not fail to encourage the Hiratis in their resistance. I replied, that my duty to my own government, and even to the Shah, precluded the possibility of my complying with His Majesty's requests, which I greatly regretted, as it was at all times my anxious desire to comply with the wishes of the Shah. Next day I came in one march to the camp. All the attentions usually paid on such an occasion were omitted; and I have reason to believe that all my acquaintances in camp were either directly forbidden to visit me, or

received hints to the same effect which could not be mis-
understood; yet I took no notice of these slights.

"On the morning of the 20th, before I had yet left the
town, I heard of the arrival of Count Simonich in the
camp, and I ceased to hope that the adjustment of the differences between Persia and Hirat was on the point of being
effected. On my return to the camp, I found the Shah's
views had undergone an important change: his manner was
more abrupt and peremptory; and he at once rejected the
proposed agreement.

"In about an hour the firing recommenced; and from
that time the siege was prosecuted with renewed activity;
for Count Simonich gave his advice as to the best manner
of conducting it, and employed an officer of the Etat-Major,
belonging to his suite, to construct batteries, and to carry
on other offensive operations against the town. The Shah
became elated with success. The Russian minister furnished
a sum of money to be given to the Persian soldiers; and
his countenance, support, and advice confirmed the Shah in
his resolution to grant no conditions to the Afghans of
Hirat.

"I have had the honour to report to your Lordship that
more than one attempt at negotiation had failed.

"I need not repeat to your Lordship my opinion as to
the effect which such a state of things would necessarily have
on the internal tranquillity and security of British India;
and I cannot conceive that any treaty can bind us to permit

the prosecution of schemes which threaten the stability of
the British empire in the East. The evidence of concert
between Persia and Russia, for purposes injurious to British
interests, is unequivocal, and the magnitude of the evil with
which we are threatened is, in my estimation, immense, and
such as no power in alliance with Great Britain can have a
right to aid in producing."

Now I must come back to the proceedings of
Qambar Ali Khan, the Persian envoy, in connexion
with the chiefs at Qandhar. A treaty of an offensive
and defensive nature was formed between them, and
the chiefs despatched their agent with him to wait
upon his Majesty the King of Persia in his camp at
Hirat. The credentials were submitted to the Shah
with the treaty, and the letters of the chiefs delivered
to M. Goutte, the Russian assistant ambassador, and
General Bronski, with the camp of Mohammed
Shah. The latter officer, although Polish, and in
the service of Persia, was intimately connected with
the Russian embassy in this country, and was intriguing with the Afghans, in order to promote the
interests of the cabinet of St. Petersburgh. M. Goutte
promised the approbation and protection of Count

Simonich, and which was finally despatched to the chiefs. After perusing such documents, which contain the avowal of the Russian agent, and seeing that the Russian ambassador becomes a guarantee in arrangements concluded between Persia and Qandhar, there remains no place for any doubt concerning the aim and the intentions of the Russian Government. The treaty to which he becomes a party or guarantee must of course be thought to be good for himself. On consulting these matters deliberately, the Shah and the Russian functionaries addressed letters to the chiefs, approving of the treaty they had sent by their agents with Qambar Ali Khan.

Mohammed Shah to Sardar Kohandil Khan, Chief of Qandhar.

(After compliments.)

"ALAHDAD KHAN has arrived in my camp, and made known your requests, and the favour of the king towards you has increased. Whoever shall in confidence come to me shall meet with nothing but kindness, and shall gain his ends, and if you are still firm and true to your word, you may consider the favour of the king firm to you too. Always write the state of your wishes and hopes to me, and consider that you will gain all your ends."

———

M. Goutte, the Russian Agent with the Shah, to Kohandil Khan.

(After compliments.)

         "ALAHDAD KHAN and Mir Mohammed Khan have delivered your letter to me, and I was much delighted at its contents. You wrote to tell me you had determined on becoming subservient to Mohammed Shah, and had sought his protection. You may depend upon my fulfilling the engagements I have entered into with you, and consider it to be advantageous to yourself to perform any service to the government. I cannot express, in writing, my friendship for you, and care for your welfare. Regarding your making Russia the guarantee in this connexion, your wishes will meet the Russian ambassador, to whom I have forwarded your letter, and with it I have written my own opinions on the subject. I have cultivated your friendship at the suggestion of Haji Aghasi. It is better to despatch Omar Khan without apprehension, and I will write to the Persian government, to remove all apprehensions at your sending your son. He will be treated with great distinction by the Shah and his nobles. When you have despatched your son, the treaty, drawn up by Qambar Ali, will be entered into by the means of Hajee

Aghasi, and I, as your friend, tell you to be under no
apprehension at sending your son. After he arrives, everything you wish will be done through Haji Aghasi; send
your son quickly, and trust him to God. When I receive
an answer from the Russian minister (Simonich), I will
forward it."

Major-General Bronski to Kohandil Khan.

(After compliments.)

"ABDUL WAHAD BEG and Alahdad
Khan have arrived with Qambar Ali Khan, and have ex-
tolled to me your acts and nature. Consider the subjects
on which Captain Vikovich conversed with you, connected
with your welfare; besides these, I have other subjects to
speak on. You have done well in seeking the protection of
Persia; this Alahdad informed me you had done, and I am
much pleased with your messages. Alahdad Khan has requested me to write to you; he has himself witnessed my
influence here, and has been himself favourably received by
the Shah, and asked to know in what favour the Sardars of
Qandhar were with him (the Shah). Nothing but good
will result from this your connexion with the Shah; so
much good, indeed, that I cannot put it to paper. Be
convinced that your serving the Shah will turn out every
way to your advantage. The Shah treats every one according to his deserts, and your deserts are above all
others. By all means send Mohammed Omar Khan
speedily; he will be treated with nothing but kindness,

U

and on this subject the assistant to the Russian minister,
M. Goutte, has written, as also Haji Aghasi, who has
written to confirm what Qambar Ali had done (at Qandhar). By the fortune of the Shah, Maimana, the Hazarahs,
and Char Adinak (Annak) have been subdued as completely as could have been wished; and as the Asif of
Mashed had written, no doubt the son of Mizrab Khan
Wali, and the brother of Sher Mohammed Khan, and
Gurdzanum Khan and others will come over to the Shah
(as hostages). Persia is not what it was; I wish your
connexion with Persia were speedily accomplished. Mohammed Shah has hitherto avoided taking Hirat out of
kindness to its Mahomedans: but, by the blessing of God
and the fortune of the king, Hirat will be taken; everything will be for the best. It will be all the better the
speedier you despatch Mohammed Osmar Khan."

----

*Copy of the Draft of a Treaty sealed by Kohandil Khan, or
the proposed Terms of a Treaty between His Majesty Mohammed Shah and Kohandil Khan, the Sardar of Qandhar, under the sealed guarantee of His Excellency Count
Simonich, the Russian Ambassador.*

" I, as Minister Plenipotentiary of the Russian government at the Court of Persia, guarantee the fulfilment of
the following conditions of treaty between His Majesty
Mohammed Shah, and the Sardar of Qandhar.

" I. The principality of Hirat to be bestowed by the Shah

on the rulers of Qandhar, as a reward for their faithful services performed to him since his accession to the throne of Persia.

" II. The territories and tribes at present subject to the Sardars of Qandhar to be preserved to them free of violence, injury, or confiscation.

" III. The Persian government in no way to amalgamate with their own subjects any of the Afghan tribes, great or small, nor to employ them upon service unconnected with their own affairs, and all business relative to the Afghan states to be submitted by the Persian government to the rulers of Qandhar..

" IV. The Prince Kam Ran and his minister Yar Mohammed Khan to be excluded from all participation in the councils of Persia.

" V. Should any hostile movement be made against Qandhar by Shah Shuja-ul-Mulk, the English, or the Amir of Kabul, aid to be afforded by the Shah to the Sardars.

" VI. In the event of the sons or brothers of Kohandil Khan coming with an auxiliary force to the royal camp, no violence or injury to be in any way offered to the persons or property of them or their followers, and none of them to be detained as hostages, with the exception of a single son of Kohandil Khan, who will always remain in the service of the Shah.

" VII. A contingent of twelve thousand horse and twelve guns to be supplied by the Qandharis to garrison Hirat, receiving pay and rations from them, and to assist the Shah on occasion of service.

" VIII. On the arrival of the treaty duly ratified at Qandhar, Mohammed Omar Khan to be immediately despatched to the royal presence.

" IX. After the presentation of this prince, the necessary money for the outfit of the horse and artillery to be made over by the Persian government to the Sardars of Qandhar; Sardar Mehardil Khan to be then sent with a thousand horse to the royal camp. This prince being presented, and mutual confidence being established between the Shah and the Sardars, no other demand to be made upon the Qandharis by the Persian government than that of military service.

"Should Mohammed Shah fail to fulfil any of these several conditions, or depart in any way from the stipulations, I, as Minister Plenipotentiary of the Russian government, becoming myself responsible, will oblige him, in whatever way may be necessary, to act fully up to the terms and conditions of the treaty."

I have brought the lengthened arrangements of the Qandhar chiefs with the Persian and the Russian governments to a plain conclusion; and it would be desirable now to turn our attention to the affairs of Kabul, and the negotiations of Sir Alexander Burnes with the Amir Dost Mohammed Khan. Agreeably to mutual understanding, as has already been stated, he pretended to be angry with the style

of the letter of the Shah, and did not come to a
final settlement with the English envoy, waiting
the arrival of the Persian army in Hirat, and an
answer from the Emperor of Russia to his letter.
He was always in possession of the daily progress of
the Russian minister; and through the Hazarah
country received secret communications concerning
the movements of the Russian agent towards his
capital. He kept this under very strict secrecy; and
if any talk was made of the power of Persia, and the
influence of Russia, by any one in his court, while he
knew that there was a person to inform us of it, he
simply treated such ideas with contempt and laughter,
calling the Russians and Persians " Lotis," or buffoons.
In short, he always tried to keep off despair from
Sir Alexander Burnes by his pleasing manners and
eloquence, and thought that his craft was not known
to him. This was, however, not the case, for the
British envoy knew his meaning, and told and wrote
to him several times to come to an immediate understanding; but he put off from day to day, writing
letters to the chiefs of Qandhar and Qunduz, making
mention of his feigned intention to establish friendship with the British.

At length the expected news came of the arrival of Captain Vikovich, the Russian agent, in Ghazni, on his way to the court of the Amir Dost Mohammed Khan.   Hereupon the Amir, and his minister Mirza Sami Khan, planned privately, and it was soon conveyed by his " peshkhidmat " to Sir Alexander Burnes secretly, that Dost Mohammed Khan was to call upon the British envoy, and reporting the progress of the Russian agent towards Kabul, offer to act as guided by him (Burnes).   If the latter did not approve of his coming to the city, then the Amir was to secure for himself a document from Sir Alexander Burnes, binding his government to pay him money, and aid him with forces on the plea of giving an insult to the cabinet of St. Petersburgh ; and after having that paper he was at liberty to receive Captain Vikovich, and attach himself to Russia or to the English, whichever offered him the highest proposals.   However, the Amir called upon Sir Alexander Burnes, who, hearing his sayings, and knowing previously the meaning of his conversation and of his visit, said that the Amir would commit no wrong in -receiving Captain Vikovich, and, on the contrary, will make known his own

hospitality and good sense in distant regions. Here
the Amir was disappointed at the failure of his
scheme; yet still persevering in his design, he tried
to induce Sir Alexander Burnes to commit himself
in some other way. In our presence he spoke to his
minister in a manner that showed as if he felt no
interest in the mission of St. Petersburgh, and that
he therefore thought it was better to place him in
the house where the other Persian lier (Mohammed
Husain) was living, and again feigned to ask the
opinion of Sir Alexander Burnes on the subject.
He still adhered to his former sentiments, and replied that the Amir was ruler of Kabul, and knew
best to treat and receive agents and guests in his
own house. Finding that Sir Alexander Burnes
was not a man to become the subject of his fraudulent
proposals, he adopted at last what he had always
meant. He was aware that his brother Navab
Jabbar Khan, and also other relations, and certain
chiefs, were in favour of the English mission, and
might make intrigues with Captain Vikovich also.
He therefore found no better place and charge for
the Russian agent than that of his confidential
minister Mirza Sami Khan. He knew that the

people whom he suspects will be known there, and will thus fear to visit him in his house; and that this will keep his communication with the Russian envoy entirely secret. He was accordingly treated with great respect and civility, and was allowed to go and meet the Amir clandestinely in the private apartments of the minister. As he had not his own equipage, the son of the Mirza always accompanied him to sights and to the places of chief note, which attention was similarly shown to Sir Alexander Burnes for three days after his arrival in the Bala Hisar. This was the kind of honour paid to the envoy of the Emperor, which the British news-writer, Mr. Masson, mentions in his book, saying that he was under surveillance.

Captain Vikovich delivered his credentials, which consisted of a letter from the Emperor of Russia, and another from His Excellency Count Simonich, the Russian ambassador. These were written in the Persian and in the Russian languages. The Amir had no bounds to his joy and pride inwardly, but outwardly he feigned to show the English envoy and news-writer that he never knew till that very moment that he had even written a letter to St.

Petersburgh. He denied the transmission and the proceedings of Husain Ali, and of Mirza Sami Khan; and the latter took the credit upon himself (as Mr. Masson says) of gaining another ally for the Amir. All this ignorance of the Amir Dost Mohammed Khan, and the writing of the letter by the Mirza without his knowledge, was nothing but a fabricated invention of them both to mislead the English functionaries. By adopting this cunning line of policy he created a difference of opinion among a number of the persons who formed the mission of Sir Alexander Burnes, and at the same time he resolved to show them that he is an object so valuable and dearly sought by the united great powers of Russia and Persia, that the Emperor and his ambassador had addressed to him such flattering epistles while he never thought of seeking their friendship.

The Russian part of the Emperor's letter was copied by Major Leech, and the Persian was translated by me, which translation was unfortunately plundered from me at the time of the insurrection of Kabul, and could not be recovered afterwards, although I procured and purchased some of the

papers in Kabul. Mr. Masson says it bore no signature, and was written directly by the Emperor
himself; which affirmation, according to him, raises
some doubts of its authenticity. On the contrary,
according to Asiatic usage, these are the very reasons for confiding in the veracity of the letter. In
all countries of despotic government, as Afghanistan,
Turkistan, and Persia, and their neighbour the Russians, letters are forwarded under the seal and not
under the signature. There were several letters of
the Emperor of Russia shown to us by the late
minister, Qoshbegi, to the address of the King of
Bokhara, written direct from his Majesty, never
from his secretary. The letters addressed by the
minister do not stand so high in the estimation of
the Asiatic monarchs as those written from the
sovereign himself. It is considered a most strong
feeling of regard and friendship, and confidence on
the part of the writer. The cabinet of St. Petersburgh being aware of such a prevailing custom, and
desire of its neighbours the Ozbegs and Persians,
generally writes to them under the seal and name of
the Emperor: and so in the same way was the
letter written to the Amir of Kabul.

It is worthy of making such a remark in this place, and further to prove this, to the end that it may be clearly known how much the Asiatic monarchs are offended in being addressed by the minister or secretary, and not from the Sovereign himself. On the restoration of Shah Shuja to the throne of his predecessors, and the detention of Colonel Stoddart, the British Government was, on several occasions, obliged to begin communication with the King of Bokhara. More than fifty letters from Sir William Macnaughten, the British representative, and several others from the Earls of Auckland and of Ellenborough, were sent by special and highly paid messengers to the Amir of Bokhara; but he was always displeased at their arrival, and never returned an answer to any of them, and dismissed the bearers without any reply. He always told them, and also Colonel Stoddart, that he was an independent king, and should like to correspond with the British Sovereign directly, and not with the British representatives at Kabul, and the Governors-General of India,—(farman farma), whom he called the servants of the state. In the same manner it was felt by the Amir Dost Mohammed Khan. He considered the letter of the Emperor of so much more value and importance than that of Count Simonich, that the letter of the ambassador did not even stand in the first rank.

The contents of the letter from the Emperor of Russia to the Amir of Kabul, as far as I remember, from the translation I made of it at the time, to be sent to the government of India, were not of any political nature. It plainly acknowledged the receipt of the Amir's letter, and assured him that all the Afghan merchants shall be well received in the empire of Russia, justice and protection shall be extended towards them, and their intercourse will cause to flourish the respective states.

I have heard many people in their talking, say, that if the letter of the Emperor touched upon no other points but those of trade, there was no necessity for taking such alarm at its appearance in Kabul, and that it was exaggerated in importance, as it appeared to be felt by the Indian government. Though I do not boast of being well versed in the histories of India written by talented English authors, but from what I have learned from them I come to the conclusion that the disguised word or appellation for politics is commerce, and that commerce is the only thing which expands the views and policy of territorial aggrandisement. To my great surprise I read from the book of Mr. Masson the doubts he entertained of the true character of the mission of Captain Vikovich. These doubts must have arisen from some extraordinary sources of information, or else from the ambitious motive of making himself conspicuous in differing from the opinions of those who had more apparent, wise, and just means to consider that agent a true representative of the court of St. Petersburgh. Count Nesselrode is the best authority on such a subject, and he has plainly acknowledged this mission to Kabul, and the following letters will further show that he was not an adventurer, but an accredited envoy from Russia.

Mohammed Shah of Persia to the Amir Dost Mohammed Khan of Kabul.

(After compliments.)

"AGREEABLY to my affection and kindly feelings towards you, I wish to bestow great favours on you, and anxiously wait to hear from you.

"In these days the respectable Captain Vikovich, having been appointed by my esteemed brother the Emperor of

Russia, to attend your Court, paid his respects on his way, stating that he had been honoured by his Imperial Majesty to deliver some messages to you: on this I felt it incumbent on me to remember you by the despatch of this Raqam, to convince you that your best interests are deeply engraven in my mind.

" Concerning the favours of my brother Majesty attached to you, let me hear occasionally from you; and by rendering good services to him you will obtain the protection of this Royal house."

His Excellency Count Simonich, the Russian Ambassador at Tehran, to Amir Dost Mohammed Khan of Kabul.

" THE respectable P. Vikovich will wait upon you with this letter.

" Your agent Haji Husain Ali has been attacked by a severe illness, and therefore he stopped at Moscow: when the intelligence of his bad health was conveyed to the Emperor, a good physician was ordered to attend, and endeavour to cure him as soon as possible. On his recovering I will not·fail to facilitate him in his long journey back to Kabul.

" Knowing your anxiety to hear from this quarter I have hastened to despatch the bearer to you. He was ordered to accompany your agent to Kabul, and I hope on his arrival at your court that you will treat him with consideration, and trust him your secrets. I beg you will look upon

him like myself, and take his words as if they were from
me. In case of his detention at Kabul you will allow him
often to be in your presence, and let my master know,
through me, about your wishes, that anxiety may be removed.

" Though the great distance has often prevented the
regularity of my correspondence with you, I am always very
happy to respect and serve your friends, in order to show
my friendly opinions towards yourself.

" The cause of our often hearing from each other merely
depends upon friendship and acquaintance.

" I have some Russian rarities to forward to you: as the
bearer (P. Vikovich) is lightly equipped, it was beyond
his power to take them along with him; but I will take the
first opportunity to convey them safely to you, and now
have the pleasure to send you the under-mentioned list of
them.

First Kind of Samur.

	Piece.
Gilt and silvered cloth	1
Cloth with do. flowered	1
Ditto with gilt do.	1
Ditto with green gilt flowers	1
Zari Abi, with gilt do.	1
Ditto qirmiz of gold	1
Ditto do. of silver	1
Parcha hazir, red and white	1
Ditto painted	1

		Piece.
Parcha hazir, white with gold flower . . .	1
Alachah with do. . . .	1
Ditto yellow with silver do. . . .	1
Ditto red and green	1
Ditto light blue	1
Ditto with red flower	1
Ditto green	1
Ditto banassh	1
Ditto red and light blue	1

Before we proceed to notice the negotiations of Captain Vikovich in Kabul, it will be desirable to describe here briefly his conference with the chiefs of Qandhar. He told them that the King of Persia does not pay any attention to the advice of the British ambassador, but has attached himself to the Russians, who avowedly and secretly will lend him every aid to promote his object. Major Leech also reports thus :—

" Regarding the Russian officer, now in Kabul, with a letter from the Emperor, Mehardil Khan informed me that the following were his messages to them from the Emperor : that if they would make friends with the Amir Dost Mohammed Khan, the Russians would assist them with money to make war upon the Sikhs, and to regain Multan and Derajat ; and that they would also aid them in regaining Scinde; that Mohammed Shah owed them one and a half crores of rupees, and they would give an order on him for that sum, the money to be divided between the Amir and them equally, as also the countries thus gained; that the Russians could not furnish men, but would furnish arms; that they in turn expected the Sardars to become subservient (farman bardar), and to receive a Russian resident; that they were to make war when desired, and make peace equally at the Emperor's will. This officer told them that the English had preceded the Russians in civilization for some generations; but that now the latter had arisen from their sleep, and were seeking for foreign possessions and alliances; and that the English were not a military nation, but merely the merchants of Europe. Sardar Mehardil Khan also informed me that several merchants had seen that officer in Bokhara, but were ignorant of the object of his visiting that city."

" With regard to the active part that Russia is taking in the movements of Persia, the Sardar assured me he had good authority to state that Russia had taken measures to keep the kingdom of Mohammed Shah tranquil in his absence, by means of letters where they were feared, and of troops where they were not feared."

The residence of Captain Vikovich in the house of the minister was very favourable to his general deportment and secret negotiations or intrigues.

x

His intercourse and negotiations with the Amir, conducted only through his confidential Vazir, were not
made public, as were those of the British envoy.
With him the communication was held sometimes
through the Navab Jabbar Khan, or the Mirza
Imam Vardi, and sometimes the Nayab Amir. If
anything was ever known to us of the proceedings of
the Russian envoy, it was only through the secret
information of the Peshkhidmat of the Amir, and
of the minister. In some circumstances the intelligence gained by Mr. Masson, the news-writer, was
satisfactory, and without the slightest doubt. The
Russian envoy told the Amir Dost Mohammed
Khan that he has been instructed by his government
to assure him of using its influence to adjust matters
with the Sikhs, and to request the Court of Lahaur
to restore all the Afghan territories to the ruler of
Kabul. On the day of the festival of Nauroz (equi-
nox) the minister Mirza Sami Khan had a party of
some selected persons of state, to which Captain Vikovich was also invited. In the middle of their
enjoyments, it was considered by him that his not
asking the English envoy, while the Russian agent
was present, will openly reflect a suspicious and uncivil

light on his conduct, and on this consideration he sent
his son to ask Sir Alexander Burnes to favour him
with his company. He justly refused to accept the invitation, saying that if the Mirza did not think proper,
for his own convenience, to invite him previously,
like his other guests, he need not take the trouble to
join his assembly. After a long and frequent intercourse Sir Alexander Burnes asked me to go to the
minister. Here all the Persian and the Ghilzai chiefs
were present. The minister and Captain Vikovich
sat a little higher than the others, on the "Nihali;"
and the former, to show his civility, removed from
his seat, where he placed me by the side of the
Russian envoy. While the music was going on, the
minister was conversing on politics, sometimes with
M. Vikovich and sometimes with me, inquiring the
number of the English troops stationed at Lodiana;
the distance between the divisions of Karnal, Merat,
and Kanpur; and whether the Mahomedans were
the major part of the army, or the Rajputs; and
what were the feelings of the natives of India towards
the decayed household of the great Taimur. Understanding the manner in which the inquiries were
made, I came to the conclusion that every question

was put to me according to arrangements made previously to my joining the party; and therefore,
confining myself only to the answer of his questions,
without commenting on politics, I pretended to show
my astonishment at the great demand for Kashmir
shawls in the Russian dominions.   This afforded an
opportunity to Captain Vikovich, who said, although
the valley of Kashmir was nearer to the boundary of
British India, yet the good treatment which the
merchants receive from his government, along with
the high price for their commodity in Moscow and
at St. Petersburgh, had gained good will for the
inhabitants of this valley.   He then said to the
minister it is wonderful that the Amir of Kabul
lays his claims upon Peshavar, while he keeps the
name of Kashmir exclusively to himself, though it
is a principal source of the wealth of the Durrani
empire.   The minister replied that the policy of the
Afghans is different from that of the other nations.
They first catch hand, and then the arm, meaning, let us first gain Peshavar, and the claims on
Kashmir will soon follow.   Captain Vikovich said
that, if it pleases God, his presence in Lahaur with
the letters of the Emperor and of the Shah of Persia,

of which he was the bearer, will induce the ruler of
the Panjab to accede to the terms of the Amir in
giving Multan, Derehjat, Kashmir, and Peshavar to
their original masters, the Afghans. He added that
he was authorized to say to the Maharajah Ranjit
Singh, that if that chieftain does not act in a
friendly manner towards the Afghans, Russia will
send money easily to Bokhara, whence the Amir
can make arrangements to bring it down to Kabul
to raise troops, and to fight with the Sikhs for the
recovery of his country. The Russian agent also
issued a report that fifty thousand men of Russian
regiments were in readiness to land in Astrabad, in
order to keep peace in the rear of Mohammed Shah,
who would then march towards the Panjab; that
such movements would rouse all the discontented
chiefs of India to rebel; and that the English, who
are not soldiers, but merely mercantile adventurers
of Europe, would not dare to assist Ranjit Singh,
knowing that the Afghans are succoured by the
warlike nation of Russia.

The presence and the promises of the Russian
envoy changed now even the outward deportment of
the Amir towards the British mission. He de-

manded a written bond for the restoration of Peshavar, besides a large sum of money to enable him to
make himself the Supreme Lord of Afghanistan.
In the mean time Captain Vikovich stated that the
law of England does not permit the Governor-
General of India to act without consulting the
Council and the three authorities; whereas he and
Count Simonich, or any other Russian agent, had
the same power as the Emperor himself, and need
not seek nor wait for the advice of the others. All
these proceedings were communicated to the Governor-General of India, who judiciously placed not
much credence at first in the professions of the
mission; but when the state of things took an unfavourable attitude for the preservation of the tranquillity of India, he was then obliged to treat the
whole subject not slightingly, but as an important
affair. Some people, who do not know the real character of the Afghans, and especially that of the
Amir Dost Mohammed Khan, say, "Why did not
the Earl of Auckland give the small sum of money
demanded by the chiefs of Qandhar or the Amir?"
but there are hundreds of old nobles living in Kabul
who will agree with me, that the refusal of the money

from the Governor-General was judicious and wise.
It would not have served to bind the Amir to co-
operate with the British, nor to promote their interests; but it would have afforded him ample means
for using his arms against the Sikhs and against our
interests.

The Sardar Mehardil Khan, one of the brother
chiefs of Qandhar, advised by the Shah of Persia
and by Count Simonich, arrived at Kabul with
the avowed purpose of frustrating the designs of
the British envoy, and inducing the Amir to give
him his dismissal and to settle his affairs with the
Russian agents. He and the Amir now began to
talk thus, that they really want a written engagement
from the British government, not only to protect
them against Mohammed Shah, but also pledging
its influence, money, and arms to force Ranjit Singh,
a faithful ally of the English, to give up all the
Afghan territory, which, on the other hand, the
Russians and Persians have offered to recover for
them.

The winter was now past, and still the Amir did
not dismiss the Russian agent from his court, as he
had promised in his intercourse with Sir Alexander,

and had written in his letter to Count Simonich.
On the contrary, he entered more and more into
close intimacy and conversation in public with him,
and invited him openly to pass evenings and have
dinners in the palace with him. Now it became
evident that the Amir of Kabul was unfeignedly
attaching himself to the Russian government, and
that the further stay of Sir Alexander Burnes was
not honourable to the name and credit of his government. He made his last report, therefore, of the
steps which the Russian agent had taken, and of the
throwing off of the mask which the Amir had
hitherto assumed and worn to deceive us, stating
circumstantially the proofs that he and his minister
had become colder in their manners towards us, and
warmer in their intercourse with Captain Vikovich.
At last the letter of the Governor-General arrived
for the Amir, stating that if he was inclined to
attach himself to the other powers, he had better
give leave for departure to Sir Alexander Burnes,
which alternative was readily accepted. Our failure
in the negotiations soon became public, and the
people, especially the traders, feared to deal with the
mission. The bankers would not lend the money

necessary for our journey, and the muleteers refused
to supply conveyances unless permitted by the Amir.
Two or three days passed without any progress in
the preparations for the return of the mission to
Peshavar, and at length I waited upon the Amir
with a note from Sir Alexander Burnes.   After I
had dined with him I delivered it into his hands,
and Sardar Mehardil Khan read it before him.
The tone and the words of the letter were written
strong, but just, and worthy of the British envoy.
This naturally roused the mind of the Amir and of
his party, and after assuring me of orders to supply
us with everything the mission wanted, the only
word I heard him saying to his adherents and to the
Qandhar chief was that he had not anticipated that
matters would go so far, nor that the Russian government would come so openly forward to further
his ends in spite of the English.   He continued,
smilingly, that as the British envoy was offended, he
should not lose time to stir up Vikovich to inform
his government of the state of affairs at Kabul.

Moreover I am astonished to read in Mr. Masson's
work that the Amir Dost Mohammed was exalted
at the submissive humility of Sir Alexander Burnes,

who always addressed and answered him with his
hands closed and the word of "Gharibnavaz," and
that he (Masson) had never given information of
Vikovich having letters for the Lahaur chief. I
had more opportunities than Mr. Masson to be present when Sir Alexander Burnes had interviews
with the Amir and with many other independent
rulers of Asia, but I never heard him accosting any
of them in the humble manner described by this
worthy gentleman. His tone of voice with the Amir
of Kabul and with the chiefs of other places was
conspicuous, and bore the accents of dignity worthy
of his government and rank; and I have heard the
chiefs myself saying that his "Guftar va Kirdar"
(meaning his sayings and doings) bespeak of his
talent and his high notions. With regard to his
misrepresenting the information which Mr. Masson
gave him, I can only say that no British officer
charged with such high functions of his government,
and entrusted with the welfare of his country, as Sir
Alexander Burnes was, would commit such a gross
act as to misrepresent the information in order to
support his own views. Every line of the four
volumes of the valuable work of Mr. Masson speaks

of the author's sound judgment and independent
character, it cannot be denied; but not one human
being on the face of the earth will impartially admit
that his opinions did always stand firmer and wiser
than those of the other men who at that time conducted their arduous duties honourably, and who are
now no more to defend themselves. I rejoice to see
the independence of Mr. Masson duly estimated;
but if that independence were accompanied by the
least shadow of that gratitude which he owed for the
patronage he received from Sir John Macneil, Sir
Alexander Burnes, Sir Claude Wade, Sir William
Macnaghten, and other functionaries, it would have
reflected a laudable credit upon him. But alas, they
are now of no use to him, and the work is published.
In broad words, if an obliged Englishman were to
make such return to his obliging and national friends
as Mr. Masson has made, what then can be expected
from an Asiatic like myself? I have great regard
for the person, talent, and character of Mr. Masson,
but I beg to say that I do not like his principles as
displayed in throwing loads of disparagement on the
memory of those who lost their lives in the service
of their country, and are not now able to answer the

remarks of Mr. Masson or of any one besides. He
quotes some lines of the various notes from Sir
Alexander Burnes, Sir William Macnaghten, and
the then chairman of the India House, &c., to prove
the authenticity of his opinions; but unfortunately
they are not alive to give publicity to the notes which
Mr. Masson wrote to them at that time. They are
dead, and the valuable work comes out. May success attend the sale, and the second edition appear
with alterations!

Captain Vikovich made a very long and interesting report of his negotiations with the chiefs of
Qandhar and the Amir of Kabul, and despatched it
for his Excellency Count Simonich, the Russian
ambassador with the Shah of Persia. Our agent,
however, found means to obtain a copy of that
interesting document before it reached its destina-
tion.

*The Russian Ambassador at Tehran, to Amir Dost Mo-
hammed Khan, of Kabul.*

(After compliments.)

" IN these happy days the respectable
Haji Ibrahim Khan, one of your people, arrived at the door of
His Majesty the Shah. He has now got leave to return to

you, and I embrace the opportunity to write to you, being induced to do so by the praises which I am always hearing concerning you, and the friendly conversation which has passed between your man and myself. Through him, therefore, I send this friendly letter, and hope that you in future will keep up a correspondence with me.

" Considering me your friend, I trust that you will strengthen the bonds of friendship by writing to me, and freely commanding my services, as I shall be happy to do anything for you.

" Look upon me as your servant, and let me hear from you.

(Sealed)   " GRAF. IWAN SIMONICH,
Minister Plenipotentiary of the Russian government."

Letter to the Amir of Kabul, forwarding the preceding from Haji Ibrahim, his Agent at Tehran.

(After compliments.)

" I REACHED the camp of the Shah in the month of Jamadi-ul-aval. When His Majesty learned the contents of your letter he was happy and kind to me; at that time the Shah was at Chashma Ali, seven marches from Tehran, near Dam Ghan; he stated that on arriving at Khalpush he would discharge me with some messages for you. On his reaching Khalpush he went to punish the Turkmans, and I accompanied His Majesty as desired. When we returned to Sharood the winter set in, and the Shàh, by the advice of his counsellors, left his artillery there, abandoned the intentions of going to Hirat this year, and returned to Tehran. He ordered his nobles to get ready by Nauroz, for an expedition to Hirat.

" The Shah directed me to inform you that he will shortly send an Elchi, who, after meeting you, will proceed to Ranjit Singh to explain to him, on the part of the Shah, that if he (Ranjit Singh) will not restore all the Afghan countries to you, the Amir, he must be prepared to receive the Persian army. When the Shah takes Hirat he has promised to send you money and any troops you may want.

" The Russian ambassador, who is always with the Shah, has sent you a letter, which I enclose. The substance of his verbal messages to you is, that if the Shah does everything you want, so much the better; and if not, the Russian government will furnish you (the Amir) with every thing wanting.

" The object of the Russian Elchi, by this message, is to have a road to the English in India; and for this they are very anxious. He is waiting for your answer, and I am sure he will serve you. The letter you sent by Agha Mohammed Kashi pleased the Shah very much, and he (Mohammed Husain) will soon return to you.

" The Asef-ul-Daulah, the ruler of Khorasan, has written to the Shah that he saw Yar Mohammed Khan on this side of Farah; he says he has not power to oppose the

Shah, but he will not serve him until the Shah gives him money to take Qandhar and Kabul.

" I send you the letter (Firman) of the Shah, which will, I trust, meet your approbation."

Major Mackeson, British Agent, Camp Shekwan, to Sir Claude Wade, political Agent, Lodiana.

" THE Russian envoy at Kabul gave out that he intended to visit Lahaur, in order to have some friendly conversation with Maharajah Ranjit Singh, and to send an account of his Highness's military power and resources to the Emperor."

Major Mackeson to Sir Claude Wade.

Camp Khanpur, 12th Feb., 1838.

" HIS Highness next adverted to a letter he had received from Peshavar, mentioning that the Russian envoy intended to come on to Lahaur."

Sir Alexander Burnes to Sir William Macnaghten.

Kabul, 4th March, 1838.

" I HAVE the honour to report, for the information of the Right Honourable the Governor-General of India, that I have more grounds for believing that Captain Vikovich, the Russian agent at Kabul, is charged with letters from his government to the Maharajah Ranjit Singh. I observe that

Colonel Stoddart mentions this as a surmise to Sir John Macneil ; and a few days ago Mr. A. Ward wrote to me from Peshavar, to know if the ' on dit' of M. Vikovich's going to the Panjab were true.

" I have made every inquiry on this subject, and in the course of yesterday Mr. Masson was informed that the Russian agent had letters for the Maharajah, and that the purport of them was to the effect, that if his Highness did not withdraw from Peshavar, the Russian government would compel him."

Sir Claude Wade to Sir W. H. Macnaghten.

21st March, 1838.

" I HAVE the honour to transmit an open letter to your address from Sir A. Burnes, dated the 4th instant, repeating, from Kabul, the report which had formerly reached Peshavar, that the mission of Captain Vikovich would extend to Lahaur."

Sir Alexander Burnes to the Earl of Auckland.

Kabul, 3rd *Dec.,* 1837.

" IN the despatches, which I forward by this opportunity to Sir W. Macnaghten, your Lordship will find a report of the extraordinary circumstance of an agent having arrived at this capital direct from St. Petersburgh, with a letter from the Shah of Persia and from the Count Simonich, the Russian ambassador at Tehran.

" Before I enter upon the messages delivered by the

agent to the Ameer, it is proper to state the information which has reached me regarding what has passed at Qandhar. In my official communication of the 9th September last, your Lordship will remember that I reported the departure of one Haji Mobin on a mission to Persia; and, as it was believed, in pursuance of the advice of the Russian ambassador. That individual accompanied Mohammed Shah to Khorasan, and was requested by His Majesty to await the arrival of Captain Vikovich, and to proceed with him to Qandhar. The connexion between Russia and Persia in this part of the transaction leaves little doubt of the whole being a concerted plan between these powers. The statement made by the emissary to the Sardars of Qandhar was to the effect that Russia had full influence in Persia: and that they should assist the Shah, and draw on him for money, and if their drafts were not paid, that the Russian government would be responsible for their discharge; but that they should follow the wishes of Mohammed Shah, if they sought the Emperor's good offices, and on no account ally themselves with the English nation. This declaration, if true, is certainly most explicit; but though it has been communicated to me by a man whose other reports entirely tally with all that is passing in Qandhar, and who is the individual that made known to me five months ago the then inexplicable nature of Haji Mobin's mission, I should not wish your Lordship to give to it that confidence which I seek to place on the report of events that have transpired at Kabul.

Y

"On the evening of the 20th inst. the Amir received the Russian messenger. On the agent's producing Mohammed Shah's raqam, the Amir felt a degree of irritation which he could hardly control, and said, in Afghani, that it was an insult to him, and a proof of Mohammed Shah's being guided by advisers; for his master, the Emperor, wrote him a letter, and the subservient Shah of Persia arrogated to himself the right of sending him a raqam, or order, with his seal in the face of the document. The agent was then dismissed, and invited to the Bala Hisar on the following day.

"The communications which passed on this second occasion have also been made known to me, and are of a startling nature. M. Vikovich informed Dost Mohammed Khan that the Russian government had desired him to state its sincere sympathy with the difficulties under which he laboured; and that it would afford it great pleasure to assist him in repelling the attacks of Ranjit on his dominions; that it was ready to furnish him with a sum of money for the purpose, and to continue the supply annually, expecting, in return, the Amir's good offices. That it was in its power to forward the pecuniary assistance as far as Bokhara, with which state it had friendly and commercial relations; but that the Amir must arrange for its being forwarded on to Kabul. The agent stated that this was the principal object of his mission; but that there were other matters which he would state by-and-by; that he hoped the Amir would give him a speedy answer to despatch to St. Petersburgh, and that with reference to himself, he would go, if dismissed, along with it, though he gave the Amir to understand (and under which impression he still continues) that it was his wish to remain, at least for a time, in Kabul. The report of this interview has been communicated to me from two sources, and they both agree in the substance of what passed.

" Having thus laid before your lordship these strong demonstrations on the part of Russia to interest herself in the affairs of this country, it will not, I feel satisfied, be presumptuous to state my most deliberate conviction that more vigorous proceedings than the government might wish or contemplate than have been hitherto exhibited are necessary to counteract Russian or Persian intrigue in this quarter.

"By one class of politicians everything regarding the designs of Russia in this quarter has been disbelieved. By another, the little which has transpired has excited immediate, and, in consequence, what may be termed groundless alarm. For the last six or seven years I have had my attention directed to these countries, and I profess myself to be one of those who do believe that Russia entertains the design of extending her influence to the eastward, between her dominions and India. With her commercial operations, she has invariably spread the report that her designs were ulterior ; and the language of her agents has lately been, that as the affairs of Turkey and Persia are adjusted, she sought an extension of her influence in Turkistan and Kabul.

Such reports would deserve little credence if unsupported by facts ; but assisted by them, they gather higher import- ance, and exhibit views which, but for the greatest vigilance, might have eluded notice for years to come.

"There being, therefore, facts before us in the transac- tions passing at Kabul, it seems impossible, with any regard to our safety, to look on 'any longer in silence. If Russia does not entertain inimical feelings directly to the British in India, she avows that she wishes for the friendly offices of the chiefs on our frontier, and promises them her own in return ; so that it is useless to conceal from ourselves that evil must flow from such connexions, for this is, indeed, casting before us a challenge. It is a true maxim that prevention is better than cure, and now we have both in our hands. We might certainly wish to delay a while longer before acting ; but it is now in our power, by the extended and immediate exercise of our already established influence, to counteract every design injurious to us.

"I trust that the free expression of my sentiments will not prove displeasing to your Lordship : I am emboldened by the confidence which has placed me here to speak accord- ing to my conviction."

Sir W. H. Macnaghten to Sir Alexander Burnes.

20th January, 1838.

"His Lordship attaches little immediate importance to this mission of the Russian agent, although he will bring all the circumstances connected with it to the notice of the home authorities, as it undoubtedly marks a desire, which has long been known to exist on the part of the Russian government, to push at least the influence of their name to our Indian frontier; and the proceedings, especially of the Russian envoy at Tehran, in regard to it, are open to much observation.

" His Lordship is much gratified at the deference to our views shown by Dost Mohammed Khan, in requesting your advice as to the reception of this agent; and he entirely approves your having sanctioned his being admitted to the presence of the Amir, and treated with becoming civility. If he be not already gone from Kabul, you will suggest to the Amir that he be dismissed with courtesy, with a letter of compliments and thanks to the Emperor of Russia for his proffered kindness to the Kabul traders. His mission should be assumed to have been, as represented, entirely for commercial objects, and no notice need be taken of the messages with which he may profess to have been charged.

" This of course will be recommended by you, in the event of the Amir being firmly disposed to abide by our good offices. If he should, on the other hand, seek to retain the agent, and to enter into any description of political intercourse with him, you will give him distinctly to understand that your mission will retire; that our good offices with the Sikhs on his behalf will wholly cease; and that, indeed, the act will be considered a direct breach of friendship with the British government. It has been before at different times stated to you, that the continuance of our good offices must be entirely dependant on the relinquishment by the Amir of alliances with any power to the westward."

From the Amir Dost Mohammed Khan of Kabul to His Excellency Count Simonich.

"Your friendly letter was delivered to me by the respectable Captain Vikovich, and I was delighted to read this your second epistle.

"If I were to offer full thanks for such kindness, it would be as impossible as to confine the river in a small vessel, or to weigh its water with stones.

"I fully understand the messages which you had sent to me through Captain Vikovich, and confidently expect that your imperial government will support and defend my honour, and by doing so, it will be easy to win the hearts of friends.

"I thank you for the offer you made to arrange my affairs, and further for your informing me that you do not merely tell me so ; but that you will fulfil your promise. I expect much more from your friendly government, and my hopes have been increased. Though the distance between us is great, it does not prevent our approach in heart. My mind is put in peace by your friendly messages, and I hope it will continue so.

"Before the arrival of the agent of your government

(Captain Vikovich), the English government had deputed Sir Alexander Burnes, who is now with me in Kabul. That officer is sowing the seeds of friendship between Ranjit Singh and myself; nothing is yet settled, however, but let us wait the result.

" On the winter ceasing, and the roads opening, I will despatch Captain Vikovich by any road he prefers. At present, on account of the snow, I have postponed his departure.

" I hope you may continue to enjoy happy days."

From Captain Vikovich to Count Simonich.

" HAVING departed from Qandhar 2nd (or may be the 27th) November, of the past year, 1837, I arrived at Kabul on the 8th of December. The reception of Dost Mohammed Khan, and his condescension towards me, were sufficiently marked—polite as kind.

" I was lodged in the house of the first minister, Mirza Abdulemi (probably Abdul or Abdallah) Khan, and after three days' (waiting), I demanded an audience, when I delivered the imperial credentials [literally the most high letter] and the letter of your Lordship; and to that I added verbally, that the object of my coming was to evince to him, and to the rulers of Qandhar, the very gracious wishes (or inclinations) of the Emperor; and to declare that His Majesty the Emperor was pleased to return a gracious reply to the letter of Dost Mohammed Khan, and vouch-

safed to him protection and friendly alliance; that the
rulers of Afghanistan having made up or reconciled their
differences among themselves [this passage is rather guessed
at, being unintelligible] should acknowledge or place themselves under the dominion of Persia, with whom Russia is
connected by truly friendly relations.

"The Amir (Prince), in showing his satisfaction at the
imperial letters (credentials), gave me to understand that a
friendly treaty (on the part) of the Afghans with the Persians could not be (subsist), because an English envoy, Sir
A. Burnes, now here, has concluded (or was concluding) a
mutual treaty. That Dost Mohammed Khan having collected as large an Afghan army as possible (should go, or
was to go) to the assistance of Kam Ran against the Persians
besieging Hirat; and by that treaty the English bound
themselves to give (supply) to the Afghans twenty thousand
muskets [I cannot exactly make out the word thousand; but
suppose it. Some words here about the Russian alliance
not legible]; and to make over to the possession of the
Afghans, Peshavar, and the other conquests of Ranjit, on
the right bank of the Indus; and that the treaty was despatched to Calcutta, for the information of the Governor-
General of India, Lord Auckland. Thus terminated my
first interview with the Amir Dost Mohammed Khan, but
his vizier Mirza Abdool (Husain) Khan almost daily comes
to me, and makes various inquiries regarding the power of
Russia and of the other European governments. In the
meantime Sir A. Burnes departed (went) for Qandhar, ac-

companied by the lieutenant of artillery, Leech, in order to (induce) the Qandhar rulers (to enter into) a treaty, and (to withdraw themselves) from friendly relations with the Shah. The English have established between Kabul and Qandhar a kind of (letter-post); and they have written (or it has been written) that the Persians are defeated, have retreated to Meshid, and have suffered extremely from hunger (want of provisions). All this has occasioned Dost Mohammed Khan to conduct himself very coldly towards me; and then, as he daily (converses) with Burnes, from my arrival here to the 20th February, I have hardly (or two or) three times been in his presence. Having discovered (or learnt) from Mirza Abdul Khan that he [I do not make out whether Abdul Khan is here meant, or Dost Mohammed] had a secret distrust of (or dislike to) English influence (or connexion), I endeavoured, as much as possible, to strengthen it, and succeeded in shaking his previous (or at a former time) confidence in and friendship towards them.

"In the meantime, on the 21st February was received from Lord Auckland a reply distinctly (decidedly) to cancel (refuse) all that Burnes had negotiated (or agreed upon); but in his letter (not clearly made out) he does not advise (dissuades) the rulers of Afghanistan to enter upon any alliance with Persia or with other powers; that the Afghans were in a great measure indebted for their independence to the support of the English, who restrained Ranjit Singh from conquest.

" The true cause (reason) for such proceeding of Lord

Auckland, as Burnes declares, is the following:—Ranjit
having received from the Company a proposal to give the
Afghans Peshavar, and other conquests, that he would
willingly comply with the wishes of the Company upon receiving intimation to that effect [some reference here to the
territories between the Indus and Kashmir, and securing
the succession to his heirs, but I cannot make connected
sense of it]. On receiving such proposition from Ranjit,
Lord Auckland replied, that in consequence of (or on the
occasion) the approach of the Persian Shah to Hirat, he
decidedly (objects) and advises Ranjit to retain Peshavar,
and to oppose himself to the movements of the Shah, who,
as reported, is resolved to extend his march (or conquest)
on the borders of India.   Dost Mohammed Khan abandon-
ing his hopes of assistance (not clearly made out) on the
part of the English, has sent to Qandhar (the purport) of
the letter received from Lord Auckland, and requested for
consultation and co-operation one of the Sardars of that
place; Sir A. Burnes, on his part, has written to Lieut.
Leech (being) at Qandhar, that he should by all means
endeavour to dissuade the Sardars from going to Kabul,
and with Dost Mohammed Khan.   But the ill-conducted
intrigues of Leech have been disclosed, and roused the
Sardar Kohen Khan, and led the Afghans to adopt the
contrary course—to join Dost Mohammed Khan, and break
off all connexion with them (the English), and place themselves under the sway of Persia, with the guarantee of Russia;
that the Shah should supply (one hundred thousand) mus-

kets for the equipment of Kabul and Qandhar army, and
that after taking Hirat, the Shah himself with his troops
should advance into Afghanistan, for the recovery of the
provinces conquered by Ranjit. In demonstration of the
sincerity of this proposal, the Amir Dost Mohammed Khan,
and the Sardar Kohen Khan,—as one of their proceedings.
Mirza Abdul Khan, who not only possesses the entire confidence of Dost Mohammed Khan, but influences all affairs
in Afghanistan particularly,—and the Sardar Mehir Khan.
They request me to set out (in the course of a month) to
forward (or obtain from your Lordship) the guarantee—
that the Persians shall fulfil the conditions upon which the
Afghans agree to submit themselves to the sway of Persia;
and for that purpose I intend leaving Kabul on the 26th or
27th April. Sir Alexander Burnes has frequently demanded
of Dost Mohammed Khan, that I should be immediately
dismissed, and that the rulers of Afghanistan should engage
not to enter into any negotiations (or relations) with Persia
and Russia; but seeing that now affairs have taken entirely
another turn, he does not wait for the arrival of his companions, who, last autumn, went into Turkistan, and having
instructed Lieutenant Leech to proceed from Qandhar to
Shikarpoor and Hydrabad, (where he probably) suspects
that the ruler of Sindh may enter into the confederation
forming between Persia and Afghanistan, he left Kabul on
the 19th (or may be 17th) instant (April); and went
through Peshavar to Lahaur. I have the honour to present
for the favourable consideration of your Lordship, a brief

description of Afghanistan. I venture to infer (conclude) that with some pains and discretion the Russian government (administration) — here — as well as in commercial, as political relations. The geographical position of Afghanistan makes it the only — through which a conqueror can — from Qandhar to the very shores of the ocean; — barren desert, which can never be passable by any kind of military force (or detachments); on the north and north-west the road (way) from Turkistan is bounded (closed) by the strong pass of Hindu Kush, which has only two roads hardly passable for the space of four (I cannot make out whether the next word is months, or some term implying distance, I think the former), (several words here not legible)—for military stores, or supplies of an army. The people of Afghanistan are warlike, and if the mutual animosities existing between the several authorities (ruling powers) were reconciled, they could oppose the united forces of all India. Being a place where it is difficult (as it is in all such places) to display (or enforce) the maritime power of Russia; it nevertheless participates (lends its aid) in the reliance and influence which your Lordship has ably succeeded in diffusing throughout Persia. In these countries your ———, which extends as far as the exploits of the Persian armies, accompanies the name of your Lordship, and no one of the inhabitants of Kabul, nor of Qandhar, doubts that the Shah, when leaving Tehran, gave over to your Lordship the reins of government—for my part, I do not doubt, that, by the aid of this, something permanent may be done (established here); the

English have appreciated the full importance of this country in a political point of view (bearing), and they have spared neither trouble nor expense to gain a footing (or to instal themselves) in Afghanistan, as, without doubt, is known to your Lordship. Their successes, in respect to the defence of Hirat, and this mission of Sir Alexander Burnes, as it appears (to have been), cost him (or them), as far as I can ascertain, three hundred rupees, he (or they), during eight years residence here, (or possibly it may be ' when here eight years ago '), made purchases to the extent of one hundred and fifty rupees. From the year 1832 there has been here an established English agent, receiving a salary of one thousand rupees. ·He left Kabul, together with Sir Alexander Burnes. On my arrival at Tehran, I shall have the honour more particularly to lay before your Lordship the affairs of Afghanistan. At present I venture to beg most humbly that the desired guarantee (by the Afghans) should be acknowledged by your verbal condescension in the camp of the Shah.

      (Signed)   " VIKOVICH, Lieutenant."

CHAPTER XII.

The British Mission leaves Kabul—Iniquitous counsels given to the Amir respecting it—He rejects them—The Amir attaches himself wholly to Russia—Departure of Captain Vikovich—Honours paid him—Affairs of Sindh—Opinions current in Hindustan relative to Russia—The Asiatics anticipate reverses for the British power in the East—Correspondence, and other Documents—Reasons for the advance of the Army of the Indus—Negotiations set on foot by the British Government.

HAVING delivered the last letter of the Governor General to the Amir Dost Mohammed Khan, and had an audience of leave with him, the British Mission quitted Kabul on the 26th of April, 1838, and his son Gholam Haidar Khan escorted us to a distance of four miles from the city. The minister Mirza Sami Khan came to Butkhak, and presented Sir Alexander Burnes and myself with three horses in a most miserable condition. He remained and dined with me, and during the night we had a long conversation with that officer. He stated that Captain Vikovich has promised positively the pecuniary aid of Russia and the military assistance of Persia

for furthering the objects of the Amir; and the
minister then trying to make us believe his regret at
our departure, and his neutrality of feeling in regard
to the success of the Russians at the court of Kabul,
said to Sir Alexander Burnes that all this was
brought about by the Sardar Mehardil Khan of
Qandhar. When it was pointed out to him that
wisdom cannot permit one to place much credence
in the extravagant proposals made by distant powers
to the Amir, the minister replied that it is not
Persia that we rely upon, but Captain Vikovich in
Kabul, and Count Simonich in the Persian camp,
who is a legally authorised representative of the
Emperor of Russia. These he said have become
guarantees, and have made agreement to support the
Amir in recovering the Afghan territory from the
Sikhs. Since Russia is one of the greatest powers
of Europe, and her representative with the Shah of
Persia is reckoned to be an Emperor, and that this
race of men is celebrated for adhering to their word,
as is well known in Khorasan, all this leaves little
room to doubt that the Russian ambassador could
have proposed and agreed to anything which was not
authorised by his government, and that the cabinet

of St. Petersburgh will not act accordingly. He
says that the letter of the Amir to the address of the
Governor-General will follow us, and shortly afterwards we bade adieu to the minister and came to
Tezin.   The Mission was escorted to Jelalabad
safely by Nazir Ali Mohammed, and yet various
reports were privately received from Kabul that
some of the chiefs, as Mohamud Khan Bayat. and
Agha Husain, were advising the Amir to massacre
the Mission, or at least to detain it till a large sum
of money is paid by the English government for its
ransom, which will furnish him with the means of
defence against his impending danger.   The Amir
wisely paid no attention to such rash counsels of his
friends; and Dr. Lord and Mr. Wood, who were
invited by Mir Mohammed Morad Beg of Qunduz,
returned to Kabul after the Mission had departed
from that city.   They suffered no molestation, but
being received coldly by the Amir Dost Mohammed
Khan, they were sent away safely to Jelalabad, and
thence followed us by the Kabul river to Peshavar.
Lieut. Wood had also heard from authentic sources,
and observed on his way through Kabul, that the
Amir and Captain Vikovich had grown very familiar

with each other, and that the former had attached himself without reserve to Russia.

There is no doubt that although the Mission of Sir Alexander Burnes proved to be unsuccessful in its chief purpose, yet it afforded ample information at the time of the proceedings and the steps which the Russian government had openly taken into the politics of Afghanistan. The Sardar Mehardil Khan and the Amir addressed letters respectively to Mohammed Shah, King of Persia, stating all the circumstances of the negotiations, and of the failure and departure of the British envoy. Captain Viko- vich told the Amir that he will transmit a sum of fourteen lakhs of rupees to him ; and the Russian ambassador in Persia requested the Shah to accede to all the terms of the chiefs of Qandhar and of the Amir of Kabul, since they had entered into alliance and friendship with Russia.

The Amir at length dismissed Captain Vikovich with all honour; and appointing Habbu Khan an agent on his part to go with him, he desired Mehar- dil Khan to take them safe to Qandhar. Here, on this occasion, the Russian agent was treated with much more distinction than he was on his way to

z

Kabul. The chiefs, at his request, unanimously
wrote letters and treaties for the satisfaction of the
Russian ambassador at the Persian court, who had
made himself guarantee on the part of his government that he will not only make these chiefs masters
of Hirat, but will cause Mohammed Shah to give
Ghuryan also to them; and they on their part sent
Mohammed Omar Khan with about two hundred
and fifty horse to wait upon the Shah and Count
Simonich. The Amir also, though becoming much
more unpopular by his alliance with Persia and with
Russia, was engaged in repairing the Bala Hisar of
Kabul and the fort of Ghazni, and in urging the
Shah and Count Simonich to subdue Hirat and to
push on to Kabul. The arrival of Mohammed Omar
Khan, the son of Kohandil Khan, the principal
chief of Qandhar, in the Persian camp, and the
seizure of Frah by Mohammed Saddiq, another son
of the chief, gave no proof of want of vigour nor any
encouragement to the Afghans in their hopes of now
defending Hirat; and many were desirous to desert,
and even to surrender it to the Qandhar party in the
Persian camp, if any one would venture to make
such a communication to them. Captain Vikovich

returned again from Hirat to Qandhar, and supplied
the chiefs with ten thousand Russian ducats, which
Kohandil Khan distributed amongst his troops. He
also informed him that Mohammed Shah had given
permission to Count Simonich to bring Russian
forces to reduce Hirat and to send money to the
chiefs in Afghanistan; and that, according to the
European law, his presence in Qandhar will prevent
the Governor-General of India and its allies from
taking any hostile attitude towards that city. That
officer wrote also to the Amirs of Sindh to keep
themselves easy, and promised that he, with the
Sardars, will in three months hence be on the banks
of the Indus with them. Such communications undoubtedly would not be favourable to the cause of
the British in Sindh; and moreover the chiefs of
Qandhar publicly declared that they are paid and
requested by the Shah and by Russia to proceed
against the territory of Hirat, and that if Qandhar
during their absence was attacked by any inimical
power, the Russian government, acting on its agreement and guarantee, will supply them with money
to recover it from the enemy. When the chief
started on his march towards Hirat, Captain Viko-

vich supplied him with grain brought from the villages under the authority of Persia; and he had
cunningly spread a report that he was acting under
the authority of Count Simonich and of the Shah of
Persia, who is the ally of his master the Emperor.
He accordingly accompanied the camp of the Sardar,
and the Shah of Persia promised to send Agha
Sayad Mohammed with money to the Amir of
Kabul, and the Russian ambassador sent at this time
some presents to the Amir (perhaps those left behind
by Captain Vikovich). The intelligence of this
despatching of the letter of the Russian agent to the
Sindhians was found by Sir Henry Pottinger to be
true, and there was no doubt that the Russian name
and influence was materially injurious to British
interests even as far as to the eastern side of the
Indus. The rumours of the power and bravery
of the Russians, exaggerated by distance and talked
of in Oriental style as it passed from one person to
another, had given ample reasons for restlessness in
the minds of the discontented chiefs of India. This
was indeed not limited to Mahomedans only, but
extended to the Rajput chiefs also of that country;
and every one of them was looking forward with

anxiety for the expected reverses of the English. Tired of tranquillity, and aspiring and longing for that pomp which all Asiatics enjoy during public confusion, they were whispering their wishes and preparing themselves to be ready at a moment's call, and to throw off the mask of quiet discontent against the rule of the British government.

Lord Auckland to Amir Dost Mohammed Khan.

Simla, 27th April 1838.

(After compliments.)

"I HAVE received your letter, and fully comprehend its contents.

"It has been a source of much regret to find that your views of what is most for your advantage have led you to decline the good offices which I have tendered, for the purpose of effecting a reconciliation between you and Maharajah Ranjit Singh, on the only terms on which I could, consistently with what has appeared to me just, engage to exercise my mediation for the settlement of the unhappy differences existing between you.

"With the explanation, however, of your sentiments which you have now afforded to me, my further interposition in this affair could not lead to beneficial results; and as, in so unsettled a condition of things, the continuance of Sir A. Burnes, and of the officers under his orders in Afghanistan,

would not be conducive to the good ends which I had hoped
to accomplish by their deputation, 1 have now issued orders
to them to return to India ; and they will accordingly set
out, on receiving from you their dismissal, for which their
immediate application will be made to you.

" I have to express to you my acknowledgments for your
attention and kindness to these officers while residing in
your dominions.

" (Signed)   AUCKLAND."

———

Sir Alexander Burnes.

" ON the night of the 25th April, I had the honour to
report for the information of the Right Hon. the Governor
General, that I had had my audience of leave with the
Amir of Kabul ; and I quitted the city on the following
day (the 26th), being escorted about two miles from its
gates by three of the Amir's sons ; and also accompanied to
the first halting-place, Butkhak, by Mirza Sami Khan. It
is now my purpose to lay before his Lordship such additional particulars as illustrate the opinions of Dost Mohammed Khan, and the views which it seems he has in
contemplation, and which, since we can no longer act with
him, will, as it appears to me, require counteraction. I
inquired into the truth of these reports in circulation
regarding the Amir having actually gone over to Persia,
and sought the security of Russia. The reply was, that
they were too true. I asked what had really occurred, and

learned that some of the Amir's family, or that of his brothers at Qandhar, were to be sent with letters to the Shah ;
that Captain Vikovich had promised to get the guarantee
of Russia to all their arrangements; and that when Hirat
fell, either to send part of the Persian force through the
Hazarahjat to Kabul, or furnish the Amir with money to
expel the Sikhs from Peshavar, which, he had said, was the
more easily to be exacted from the Shah, who was a large
debtor to Russia.

" It will be remembered that the Amir, in my last interview with him, offered no palliation of the intercourse
which he had had within the last few days with Captain
Vikovich.

" I have had intelligence of it that leaves little or no
doubt on the subject.

" Captain Vikovich has already asked leave to set out
forthwith to Hirat.

" Whatever are the plans of Persia and Russia, it will
now be no fault of the chief of Kabul if they come not to
maturity. He still gives out that he would not trust
Persia alone, but seconded M. Goutte and Captain Vikovich, he considers the Russian guarantee will gain for him
all his ends, and, besides being able successfully to contend
with the Sikhs, as certain of ministering to his ambition, and
fixing his supremacy."

Amir Dost Mohammed Khan to Lord Auckland.

(After compliments.)

"ALL the conversation which has passed between Sir A. Burnes and myself from the day of his arrival is well known to your Lordship, and consequently it is needless to repeat it.

" I also wrote a second time respecting the determination of the King of Persia, and the expectations of this friendly nation (Afghans) for the protection and enlargement of their possessions, which it had hoped from the British Government for a long time.

" It is well known to your Lordship that the Afghans expected very much from the English, from the day the Honourable Mountstuart Elphinstone came to Afghanistan, for that gentleman made a treaty with the Afghans of an offensive and defensive nature :

" Since Sir A. Burnes discovered that the Afghans were quite disappointed, and he has no powers from your Lordship to satisfy this nation, he is now returning to India with my permission.

" When Sir A. Burnes reaches India he will minutely speak to your Lordship on all the circumstances of this place.   There are many individuals who have enjoyed the favour of the British; but our disappointment is to be attributed to our misfortune, and not to the want of the British Government."

From Lieutenant Wood.

" The non-arrival of our baggage detained us a few days
in Kabul, during which we had an ample opportunity of
observing how far recent events had influenced the public
mind.   The Qizalbash or Persian parties, numbering
many of the most respectable citizens of Kabul, rejoiced at
what had occurred; but the mass of people, Afghan and
Tajik, were at no pains to conceal their discontent.

" Dost Mohammed Khan was engaged at chess when we
entered the apartment; and while the interview lasted, he
affected to be more intent on his chess-board than on the
political game which we well knew was the uppermost in
his mind.   His manner was at first cold."

Sir Alexander Burnes.

" With reference to Russia, her proceedings are open to
so much remark, after Count Nesselrode's disavowals, that,
I presume she must either disavow Captain Vikovich and
M. Goutte as her emissaries, or be made responsible for
their proceedings.   I have only again to repeat my most deliberate conviction, founded on much reflection regarding the
passing events in Central Asia, that consequences of a most
serious nature must, in the end, flow from them, unless the
British Government applies a prompt, active, and decided
counteraction.   I do not offer these as my opinions, founded
on the periodical publications of all Europe (though the

coincidence of sentiment in all parties does not want in weight), but as formed on the scene of their intrigues; and it is my duty, as a public servant, earnestly to state them to my superiors.

" As I am despatching this commission from Jelalabad, half way to Peshavar, I have received good information that the Amir has been constantly with Captain Vikovich since I left, and that officer has earnestly solicited permission to proceed to Hirat by the direct road of Hazarajat, and offered the solemn pledges to do all which the Amir wishes, under a month. He has also bound himself to address Maharajah Ranjit Singh, after retiring from Peshavar; and when Dost Mohammed Khan asked if he had authority to do so, he replied that he had a letter to that potentate which would soon set matters right.

" Explaining further the plans of the chiefs of Kabul and Qandhar, consequent on their new alliance with Persia and Russia.

" The day after you left Kabul the Amir had a private meeting with the Sardar Mehardil Khan, Reshid Akhund-zadah, and Mirza Sami Khan. They have settled that Mo-hammed Azim Khan (the Amir's son), and Mirza Sami Khan, should leave Kabul, and having joined Mohammed Omar Khan and Mulla Reshid, at Qandhar, proceed to Hirat, and wait upon Mohammed Shah on the part of the Kabul and Qandhar chiefs.

" Sardar Mahardil Khan has addressed a letter to Mo-hammed Shah, which, after being sealed by his brothers at

Qandhar, will be sent by express. The contents of the letter are as follows:—

" ' On the arrival of Qambar Ali Khan, your Majesty's agent, at Qandhar, it was resolved that Mohammed Omar Khan should wait upon the Shah on the part of the Qandhar chiefs. Meanwhile, Sir Alexander Burnes reached Kabul, as an agent of the British Government, on which our elder brother Dost Mohammed Khan sent a letter, preventing us sending Mohammed Omar Khan to his Majesty on the following grounds: the British Government and Ranjit Singh are very near the Afghans, and Mohammed Shah is a distance of three months' journey; and that Amir feared these two powers may be offended, and endeavour to ruin him, which his Majesty could not prevent. Regarding the superiority of our brother (the Amir), and seeing the good of the governments, we recalled Mohammed Omar Khan from Giriskh, on account of the confusion; when we received authentic information of his Majesty's arrival at Hirat, I left Qandhar, and came to Kabul, and brought about the dismissal of Sir A. Burnes, and induced the Amir to send his minister Mirza Sami Khan to his Majesty, and from Qandhar Mohammed Omar Khan, and Mulla Reshid, to wait upon his Majesty.'

" The contents of the Amir's letter to Mohammed Shah are as follows:—

" ' When Qambar Ali Khan reached Qandhar, Sir A. Burnes also came to Kabul, on the part of the English Government. He prevented my entering into an alliance

with your Majesty. As the Shah was at a distance I kept
Sir A. Burnes in evasive discourse, and having the sure
information of your Majesty's arrival at Hirat, I dismissed
him instantly. I have now appointed my son Mohammed
Azam Khan to wait upon your Majesty. I will obey the
orders (amar) of his Majesty in future.'

" The chappar has been despatched with the above letter
to Hirat.

" This proposal of the Mirza to the Amir originates in
his sagacity, for he has settled every thing with Captain
Vikovich, who has promised that on reaching the camp of
Mohammed Shah he will send the Amir the sum of forty
lakhs of rupees. The above officer is boasting very much
what he will do to protect and exalt the Amir, but it is
needless to mention those affairs minutely.

" After your departure from this place, the Amir sends
for Captain Vikovich daily to his court, and makes arrangements with him which are as yet not written.

" On Tuesday evening a man by the name of Bahar, in
the service of Kohandil Khan, came to Kabul with letters
from the Russian agent with Mohammed Shah to Captain
Vikovich. Alladad, who had accompanied Qambar Ali
Khan, has also returned to Qandhar, with other letters from
Mohammed Shah and the Russian agent, to the address of
the Qandhar chiefs.

" His Excellency has instructed the Shah to satisfy the
chiefs of Qandhar, and the Amir of Kabul, at any rate, and
give whatever they want, since they have written to him (the

ambassador) through Captain Vikovich, and accepted the friendship of Russia.

" The Amir has dismissed Captain Vikovich with all honour and respect; and that officer has proceeded to Qandhar, along with Sardar Mehardil Khan, accompanied on the part of Dost Mohammed Khan by Hubu Khan Barakzai, enjoying the Amir's confidence.

" The Qandhar family will wait on the Shah without delay, and be introduced through Captain Vikovich; and it is understood at Kabul, that the Amir will send his own subsequent messengers direct to Hirat by the Hazarah road.

" (Signed)   A. BURNES."

" After perusing the treaty the Russian envoy took it to Mohammed Shah, who agreed to every article of it. The envoy made himself guarantee for the fulfilment of its articles, and sent it back to the Sardars, along with his own letter, the contents of which are as follows :—

" ' Mohammed Shah has promised to give you the possession of Hirat, and I sincerely tell you that you will also get Ghoryan, on my account, from the Shah. It is, therefore, advisable that you send your son Mohammed Omar Khan to Hirat, where you must also afterwards come.

" ' When Mohammed Omar Khan arrives here I will ask the Shah to quit Hirat, and send your son along with his Majesty to Tehran; I (the Russian envoy) will remain here with twelve thousand troops; and when you join, we will take Hirat, which will be afterwards delivered to you!'

" On the arrival of this letter the Sardar had no bounds to his joy, and sent it to Kabul. The report was, that it did not please the Amir at all.

"Sardar Mehardil Khan has returned to Qandhar. The Russian Agent (Vikovich), who accompanied him from Kabul to this place, was received here with honour, since the Russian Envoy at Hirat had written strongly to the Sardars, that they must treat Vikovich with all sorts of consideration; and believe his tongue, oath, and words, as if they were from him (Russian Envoy).

*　　*　　*　　*　　*　　*

" The Sardars have sent Mohammed Omar with two hundred and fifty horsemen to Hirat, to wait upon Mohammed Shah, and have sent an elephant for His Majesty, and some shawls for the Russian Envoy.

" The Sardars have sent one hundred and fourteen letters, &c., ordering the heads of Sistan, Farah, Sabzvar, and other Afghans, to join their son Mohammed Saddiq Khan at Farah. They have also informed them that the Russian Envoy has made them the 'Mir Afghan,' and has promised to give them possession of Hirat, when, if any of them will not obey our (Sardars') orders, he will be banished from the country for ever.

" You must also know that the days in which you saw

Dost Mohammed Khan are departed. He is no longer popular. His joining the Russians has utterly ruined him in the eyes of all Mahomedans. ‐

"This has quickened Dost Mohammed Khan's plans; he has set out about repairing the Bala Hisar of Kabul, and the fort of Ghazni; he has also increased his taxes in the Kohistan; and, as you know, this only increases his difficulties. He now sends messenger after messenger to the Russian Ambassador and the Shah, urging them to settle affairs at Hirat, and come on to Kabul, when the country will be theirs.

"You take no notice of the fire which has been kindled in Khorasan and Afghanistan. You will see how far it extends in the course of six months.

"Mohammed Shah has written a letter to the Sardars of Qandhar. The contents of the letter were much; but tell you the result of it.

"Since the arrival of Mohammed Omar Khan, His Majesty has become sure of the attachment of the Sardars at Qandhar, to Persia, and that they should be at ease on account of their son, Mohammed Omar Khan; after taking Hirat, His Majesty will send Vikovich to them, and the Amir Dost Mohammed Khan, with the amount of nine lakhs of rupees, and then they must hold themselves ready to receive the orders of the Shah.

"This letter was sealed by the Shah, his Minister Mirza Haji Aghasi, and the Russian Ambassador.

"Mohammed Omar Khan was received by ten thousand

Persian cavalry, and presented with four guns and five pairs of dresses of honour. The Shah has given him a place near his own tent, and his Agent, Alladad Khan, lives with the Russian Ambassador. Mohammed Omar Khan gets two hundred ducats every day for his expenses; and the Shah has told him that he will do much more for the Sardars than he told them in his letters.

"This intelligence was sent by Mohammed Omar Khan to his father Kohandil Khan, through Khodadad Khan, chappar (courier), who arrived here in eleven days from Hirat.

"Two days after the arrival of Mohammed Omar Khan, the Persians made an assault on Hirat, and lost four hundred people, besides two hundred or three hundred wounded. Borowski and Samsan have been dreadfully wounded, and the former nearly killed. The head of one of the Russian officers was cut off and taken into the city by the Afghans. After this engagement both parties returned to their own quarters.

"The arrival of Mohammed Omar Khan at the Persian camp has deeply disheartened the Afghans at Hirat. Many of them have turned against each other, and if the Sardars at Qandhar write to Mohammed Omar Khan, he would easily take Hirat, for the Afghans would likely surrender it to him.

"Mohammed Sadiq Khan, the eldest son of Kohandil Khan, has possessed Farah, and is repairing it.

"On the 18th October, I wrote to Captain Leech about

Captain Vikovich, the agent of the Russian Ambassador, on which you are also informed.

"On the 26th of the above month, Captain Vikovich reached Qandhar, having left Mohammed Shah at Kosan, on the other side of Ghoryan. Sirdar Kohandil Khan wanted to send his son Mohammed Omar Khan, and three hundred horsemen for his reception, but Captain Vikovich prevented the Sardar doing so. He entered the city alone, and put up in the house of Mirza Yaha.

"Captain Vikovich told the Sardars that he was the bearer of sixty thousand ducats. Out of the above sum he has a bill for forty thousand ducats on the treasury of Kirman, and that money will be paid in three months hence to Dost Mohammed Khan; ten thousand ducats he has in cash for the Sardars, who will get ten thousand more from Qayn, when they go with their army of Hirat.

"After a long discussion on both sides, the Sardars took the ten thousand ducats from Captain Vikovich, and divided them. Kohandil Khan has pitched one coss from the city on his way to Hirat, and troops are daily assembling to join him.

"The Russian Ambassador then asked the Shah his opinion of taking measures about Hirat: he told him to send money to the Afghan chiefs. The Shah said, 'When the Afghans come against Hirat, I will also order my forces in Khorasan to join them in attacking that city.' On this the Ambassador told the Shah if the city of Hirat was not even taken by the combined arms of the Afghans and Khorasan, what then was the mode to reduce it; the Shah pointed out to the Ambassador that it was not according to Treaty, that Russian forces should pass through Persia, but now His Majesty would make no objection if that Government should send their army through it to reduce any country they liked. This permission from the Shah was received by the Ambassador with great thanks and pleasure. The Ambassador has gone with the Shah.

"The Sardars told Captain Vikovich that they were now quite satisfied about Hirat, but they feared for Qandhar, which may be taken by the English. He answered then, that it was not the law among Europeans that one nation should dare to conquer a foreign land in the presence of an officer from another, and therefore his (Vikovich's) presence will prevent the English coming. These words have made the Sardars totally fearless of any ill luck.

"On this the Sardars and also Captain Vikovich wrote separate letters to the Mirs of Sindh, saying that they should remain quiet for three months, and the Mirs will soon see them on the Indus with their army.

"The proceedings of Captain Vikovich at Qandhar are matters of notoriety here, and may have a prejudicial effect at Hyderabad. I also find that the Russians have sent presents to Ali Khan, the Bilochi chief of Sistan. I keep Colonel Pottinger informed on these matters, and indeed on all that is going on."

To Major R. Leech.

"I YESTERDAY asked Kohandil Khan what he meant by proceeding towards Hirat in the present crisis of affairs, and what was to be done with the English? He said that if the English were encamped on the plains of Qandhar, he could not help going as far as Farah. He said his only plan was to remain at Farah, as the Persians and Russians had told him; and if Qandhar in the interim should be taken or besieged, the Russians would have the blame; that the Russians would give money and troops to them, that they might come back and fight at Qandhar; and that if they did not find the English there, they might employ the resources put at their disposal to subdue Hirat.

"Sardar Kohandil Khan has left Qandhar, having distributed ducats to his army; he expected to arrive at Farah on the 9th of November.

"Captain Vikovich has brought one thousand kharvars of grain for the Sardar, that was in the fort of Shamshuddin Khan.

"Aladad Khan and Captain Vikovich arrived at Qandhar on the 17th October, bringing with them ten thousand ducats, which Kohandil Khan immediately applied for. The Russians answered, that it rested with Aladad Khan, to give the money as soon as the Sardars should start.

"On the 21st October, the Sardars pitched their pesh khanah (advanced tents), and received the ten thousand ducats. Sardar Kohandil Khan took for his share two thousand seven hundred ducats; Sardar Rahamdil and Mehardil Khans took the same; Mir Afzal Khan received nine hundred and fifty ducats; and Mohammed Sadiq Khan the same sum.

"On the 22nd October, four messengers arrived from Amir Dost Mohammed Khan, saying that Sir A. Burnes and Lieutenant Wood had arrived at Peshavar with thirty regiments; that the Sikhs had retired from Peshavar, and urging the Sardars not to quit Qandhar.

" Sardar Kohandil Khan showed the letter to Captain Vikovich, who said that they were at liberty to act as they pleased. The Sardars said they would start in four days."

Sir Alexander Burnes.

" THIS agent does not wish to figure as a Russian, but as a Persian; he gives out that his proceedings are guided by Mohammed Shah's orders, whose ally and friend is his master the Emperor.

" Sardar Mehardil Khan has pitched at Vashien, Sardar Kohandil Khan (in company with Captain Vikovich) at Kishknakhued; and Sardar Rahamdil Khan, near the Hauz Madad, twelve coss from the city. All the troops are preparing to follow and join them.

" Abdul Saheb Khan, the servant of the Russian ambassador, passed through Qandhar on his way to Kabul, in charge of the dress of honour for Dost Mohammed Khan.

" Our intelligence from Qandhar has been all along accurate, and you will see that the letters sent from Qandhar to Hyderabad, under Captain Vikovich's instigation (if not by himself), have at last come to light, as stated in the sixth paragraph of Colonel Pottinger's letter of the 23rd instant (November, 1838), now forwarded. It now turns out that the chiefs of Qandhar have offered a portion of their Russian bribe to the chief of Kelat, and such is the unhappy fatality hanging over these disunited chiefs ; which throws considerable light on the intrigues of Russia in that quarter, and in which Captain Vikovich is represented to have taken a prominent part.

" Captain Vikovich has given ten thousand ducats to the Sardars of Qandhar, and promised them ten thousand more when they arrive at Farah, and the same number again on reaching one march on this side of Hirat, and twenty thousand ducats on besieging that city. The Sardars have consequently left Qandhar, and arrived at Farah. Mehardil Khan has been sent back to Qandhar ; for he was afraid of the Ghilzais making an insurrection, because the heads of that tribe, Abdulrahman Khan, and Sultan Mohammed Khan, the sons of Shahabuddin Khan, and Gul Mohammed Khan, the son of Khan, had received letters from Shah Shuja ; and because in the city there were Haji Khan, Sohbat Khan, and Mama, in whom the Sardars had but little confidence.

" The Russian agent, who lately came to Dost Mohammed Khan, presented six hundred yards of long cloth and a few pieces of broad cloth. He has put up at Mirza Sami Khán's.

"On the 11th December Sardar Mehardil Khan invited Captain Vikovich to a party at his house, where there were present Mulla Nasu, Nazar Mohammed Khan, and Haji Husain Alli Khan, the Persian ambassador. The Sardar told Captain Vikovich that he (the Captain) had told them (the Sardars) that on that side of the Indus was the British government, and on this side that of Mohammed Shah, who owes allegiance to Russia; that since they had also submitted themselves to Russian allegiance, it behoved him to assist them against the English, who are now going to invade Afghanistan. Captain Vikovich answered that they were not in allegiance of Russia, because though he had given them ten thousand ducats to set out for Hirat, they had not yet travelled twenty-five cosses during fifty days, and that when they arrived at Hirat he could assist them against any enemy. He also added that he was deputed to Amir Dost Mohammed Khan, and that the Amir had sent his letter to Russia by his man Habbu Khan, declaring himself a servant of the Russian government, and given an unsealed copy of it to himself; that the man had come as far as Qandhar, and then disappeared; that he sent the copy of the letter to his government, and received a letter for the Amir to the effect that he (the Amir) was not a servant but a friend; that if he wanted the Russian friendship he should write so, and it would send to him four lakhs of ducats and four officers skilled in artillery and infantry exercise; and that he was waiting for an answer to that letter from the Amir, after the receipt of which he would return to Russia.

" He also stated that the Russian government had more reliance on Dost Mohammed Khan's intellect and power than on the chiefs of Qandhar, because he, notwithstanding his poverty, and being without means, is fighting against the Sikhs who are provided with everything."

CHAPTER XIII.

Reluctance of the Indian Government to interfere with Captain Vikovich—Proceedings of Count Simonich—Sir A. Burnes and Sir J. Macneil urge the necessity of vigorous measures—The north-western Frontier—Lord Wellesley's opinion—Policy of the British government—Shah Shuja—Correspondence, and extracts from various sources illustrative of British policy in Afghanistan—The British government resolve to restore Shah Shuja—Mission to Ranjit Singh—Tripartite Treaty—Preparations—Declaration of the Governor-General —Letter to the Shah of Persia.

IT has been well known to all, and published in various papers, and in the government despatches, that the Earl of Auckland, then the Governor-General of India, did not attach much importance to the mission of Captain Vikovich and the Russian intrigues in Afghanistan; and judiciously considered that the whole matter should be decided by the authorities of England in Europe. But yet the circumstances, which were daily assuming more and more and now wearing constantly an unfavourable aspect, would neither dictate nor approve the policy of his Lordship to treat always a subject of such magnitude thus slightingly. His Excellency Count Simonich, the Russian ambassador, with his other colleagues, was not only superintending and planning the assault upon Hirat, against the advice of the British minister, but was actually deputing agent after agent, and sending money and grain to the Amir of Kabul and the chiefs of Qandhar. Sir John Macneil was in the meantime dismissed by the King of Persia, and Sir Alexander Burnes by the Amir of Kabul. Both of these functionaries, well versed and experienced in the politics of the East, and noted for their knowledge of the feelings of that country, well proved also in their anxiety for the welfare of British India, and in their zeal to preserve the national honour, urged upon the Governor-General the consideration of the necessity so apparent for taking immediate steps to counteract the openly united intrigues and encroachments of the Russian ambassador and of the Shah of Persia, which had most effectually made their way into Sindh and the interior of India. It is unnecessary for me to beg the readers to trace their way back in the histories of former times, and in the records and

publications which are so numerous, and which all
bear a prompt witness that whenever any rumours of
invasion from the west of the Indus have been afloat
they have always excited very much the people of
India.   Even Zaman Shah contemplated at one
time the plan of an expedition to proceed towards
Lahaur, with the view to cross the Sutlej, and his
correspondence with the Tipu Sultan were topics of
great deliberation and interest to the British authorities of that day.   Notwithstanding that barrier of
British India was admitted by Lord Wellesley to be
the territory of Ranjit Singh, yet his Lordship, in
consideration for the safety of the English possessions, made a capital remark, regardless of all ties of
friendship which might be in existence with the
rulers of that country: "I consider that we have
nothing more between us and the most desirable
frontier everywhere but the territory of Ranjit.   If
we were threatened on the north-west, for example,
by an invasion of the Russians, we should, in self-
defence, be obliged to take possession of the country
to the foot of the hills, as we could not leave an
intermediate space in which the enemy might establish themselves."   The Earl of Auckland was also

informed that the letters of Sir John Macneil, despatched to Sir A. Burnes through the Bombay government, "proved all previous conjectures to be well founded, and that M. Vikovich was what he had given himself out, an agent from the Emperor of Russia." Meanwhile the reports of the unpopularity and the internal dissensions of the government of the Amir Dost Mohammed Khan had frequently reached the ears of our government. Taking all these points into one deliberate view, it became necessary that a friendly government should be established in Afghanistan, and the Barakzai chiefs, who are inimically disposed towards the British, must be removed from the usurped authority of Afghanistan.

It is well known that the British government in India, alarmed at the startling advance of Napoleon, had deputed the Honourable Mountstuart Elphinstone for this purpose, and had entered into alliance with Shah Shuja-ul-mulk, who, by adverse circumstances, was since obliged to leave his dominions, and to take refuge in Lodianah. He had tried several times to accomplish the recovery of his throne, but through want of resolution had repeatedly failed in his attempt. All the princes of India, and particularly those of Central Asia, nay, even some of the Barak-zai, I have heard saying that Shah Shuja was driven away by his own servants, and sought refuge among, and the protection of, the English. They added, that these, by the rules of honour and as a powerful nation, were bound to replace him on the throne; that they would have done in this no more than was done by a former king of Persia, in the case of Dara Shikoh, when he fled through the fear of Au-rangzeb. Though Shah Shuja, by his long inactive life and private residence at Lodianah, had lost the abilities of a sovereign, yet his name and person, and the hereditary right, were not only considered by the Governor-General to constitute him the best instru-ment for gaining the end in view, but were also recommended as such by the best authorities and of the largest experience. Sir Alexander Burnes, after his departure from Kabul; writes to the Earl of Auckland in these terms:—*

June 3, 1838.

" It is clear that the British government cannot, with any credit or justice to itself, permit the present state of

---

* Sir John Hobhouse's Speech, page 33.

affairs at Kabul to continue. If this be left undone, they
will succumb to Persia and Russia, and become the instruments for whatever those powers desire. I therefore distinctly state that the evil lies beyond Afghanistan itself, and
must be dealt with accordingly.

"If it is the object of government to destroy the power of
the present chief of Kabul, that may be effected by the
agency of his brother, Sultan Mohammed Khan, or of Shah
Shuja-ul-mulk; but to ensure complete success in the plan,
the British government must appear directly in it, that is, it
must not be left to the Sikhs themselves.

"Of Sultan Mohammed Khan, the first instrument at
command, you will remember that his brother, Dost Mohammed, plainly confessed his dread of him if aided by
Sikh gold, and with such aid the ruler of Kabul may be
readily destroyed; but Sultan Mohammed has not the
ability to rule Kabul: he is a very good man, but incapable
of acting for himself; and, though fit as an instrument for
getting rid of a present evil, he would still leave affairs as
unsettled as ever when fixed in Kabul; and he is consequently a very questionable agent to be used at all.

"As for Shuja-ul-mulk personally, the British government have only to send him to Peshavar with an agent, and
one or two of its own regiments as an honorary escort, and
an avowal to the Afghans that we have taken up his cause,
to ensure his being fixed for ever on his throne."

The opinions of Sir John Macneil with regard to

the right of the Sadozai family, or of Shah Shuja, are expressed in this manner :*—

" Though the sovereignty of the Afghans has passed out of the hands of Ahmed Shah's descendants, the Durrani tribe, it appears, maintain an undoubted ascendancy in the nation. The Barakzais have usurped the greater portion of the power of the Sadozais ; but the latter family still maintains itself in Hirat, and has a strong hold on the prejudices, if not on the affections, of a large portion of the Durranis.

" That the Barakzais, holding Kabul and Qandhar in independence, would not appear to have conciliated the attachment of the Durranis, who depend in a great measure for their power on influences foreign to their tribe. To force their rule therefore on the people would not only be a difficult operation in itself, but, if sought to be effected through the mediation of the British government, would require a degree of support from us which we cannot, in my opinion, afford to give to the present possessors of power in Afghanistan, or rather to the ruler of Kabul, without bringing new elements of discord into action, productive of more evil to the peace of Afghanistan, and of the whole country, than the preservation of the sovereignty of the Afghans in the Sadozai family would be worth."

Sir Claude Wade, the political agent at Lodianah, having continued a rapid communication and inter-

* Correspondence relating to Afghanistan, No. 5, page 20.

course with all the chiefs of Afghanistan, and by this means possessing a full knowledge of the feelings of the inhabitants, who frequently visited Shah Shuja,* preferred that His Majesty should be placed on the throne in the room of the Amir Dost Mohammed Khan.

" In this letter Sir Claude Wade endeavoured to impress upon Lord Auckland the opinion that Shah Shuja-ul-Mulk ought to be preferred to Dost Mohammed,—and stated why he differed from Sir Alexander Burnes on that point. Gentlemen would do well to peruse that important document, the facts stated in which, and the inferences drawn from them, are directly at variance with what was said by that Honourable Gentleman on the opposite side. In one place Sir Claude Wade says, ' My own sources of information, which have been repeatedly authenticated both by natives and Europeans, who have visited Kabul, lead me to believe that the authority of the Amir (Dost Mohammed) is by no means popular with his subjects, and many instances in confirmation of the fact might be adduced from the reports of Mr. Masson, even when that individual has been willing to render every justice to Dost Mohammed Khan's abilities."

As quoted by Sir Claude Wade,† who sums up his advice by these words :—

" I submit my opinions with every deference to the

---

* Sir John Hobhouse's Speech, p. 37.   † Ibid., p. 39.

wisdom of his Lordship's decision; but it occurs to me that less violence would be done to the prejudices of the people, and to the safety and well-being of our relations with other powers, by facilitating the restoration of Shah Shuja, rather than by forcing the Afghans to submit to the sovereignty of the Amir."

Above all the authority of Mr. Masson, from his long intercourse with the Afghans, and from being the news-writer of the Indian government, will undoubtedly appear a predominant feature in the evidences already quoted.*

" The British government," said one of those on whose information that government acted (Mr. Masson), " could employ interference without offending half-a-dozen individuals. Shah Shuja, under their auspices, would not even encounter opposition; and the Amir (Dost Mohammed Khan) and his friends, if he has any, must yield to his troops or become fugitives. Another presumed recommendation of Shah Shuja was this—pointed out by the same authority. No slight advantage, were Shah Shuja at the head of government (in Afghanistan), would be that, from his residence among Europeans, he would view their intercourse in these countries without jealousy, which cannot be expected from the present rulers, but after a long period, and until better acquaintance may remove their distrust."†

---

* Thornton's History of British India, vol. vi. p. 150.
† Correspondence relating to Afghanistan, No. 5, p. 20.

" The failure of Shah Shuja is now most sincerely lamented by all reflecting minds : I myself, however, rejoiced at it at the time, but the course of events seems to prove that his success would have been felicitous to the country, and the wishes of all classes even now turn to his restoration.

" I must confess," writes Mr. Masson to Sir Claude Wade,* "I am not very sanguine as to any very favourable result from negotiations with the Barakzais (that is Dost Mohammed and his brothers). They are chiefly indeed their own enemies ; but their eternal and unholy dissensions and enmities have brought them to be considered as pests to the country, and the likelihood is that affairs will become worse rather than better while they remain."

Mr. Lord and Lieutenant Wood, on their return from Qandarz, secured the unanimous voice of the population in Kabul against the Amir, and in favour of the Shah ; the latter of whom thus expresses his own opinion :—

" Annoyed at Dost Mohammed's reception of Vikovich, the Russian emissary, and disquieted by the departure of the British agent, they looked to the Amir as the sole cause of their troubles, and thought of Shah Shuja and redress."

On these various and unquestionable evidences, given by the authorities well versed in the politics

* Sir John Hobhouse's Speech, p. 38.

2 B

of that quarter, where the danger was impending, the Earl of Auckland resolved to establish Shah Shuja on the throne, and thus to extinguish the flame of the united intrigues of Russia and of Persia on the west side of the Indus, before it extended to the eastern bank of that river. It was considered desirable, previous to forming an expedition for that purpose, to make the Maharajah Ranjit Singh, the ruler of the Panjab, a party in this important undertaking. Shah Shuja, who was watching with extreme anxiety the proceedings of Sir Alexander Burnes's late mission in Kabul, and, as he said himself, praying for its failure, was now informed that the British government were to restore him to his dominions, using both their money and their arms in his favour.

The Governor-General of India deputed Sir William Macnaghten, Bart., on a mission to the Court of Lahaur; and Sir Claude Wade and Sir Alexander Burnes were also directed to co-operate with him. The mission was favourably received by the Maharajah,* and the negotiations commenced with good designs, and ended successfully. The

* See ' Ranjit's Court,' by the Hon. Captain Osborn.

THE LATE MAHARAJAH RUNJEET SINGH

form of the agreement was in great portion the copy of that into which the ruler of the Panjab and the Shah had entered in 1833-4, with the exception of the third party—the British—which had now become an accomplice in the affair, and which agreed that while the Sikh and English troops engaged and encamped together to promote the cause of the Shah, the slaughter of the kine should not be permitted, as being against the religion of the Sikhs. The following is the copy of this tri-partite treaty, which must be borne in mind, and referred to on the release and departure of the Amir Dost Mohammed Khan from the British territory, through the Panjab, escorted by Captain Nicolson.

Treaty between the British Government, Ranjit Singh, and Shah Shuja-ul-Mulk, concluded at Lahore on the 26th June, 1838.

" WHEREAS a treaty was formerly concluded between the Maharajah Ranjit Singh and Shah Shuja-ul-Mulk, consisting of fourteen articles, exclusive of the preamble and conclusion : and whereas the execution of the provisions of the said treaty was suspended for certain reasons : and whereas at this time Sir William H. Macnaghten having been de-

2 B 2

puted by the Right Honourable George Lord Auckland, G.C.B., Governor-General of India, to the presence of the Maharajah Ranjit Singh, and vested with full powers to form a treaty in a manner consistent with the friendly engagements subsisting between the two states, the treaty aforesaid is revived and concluded, with certain modifications; and four new articles have been added thereto, with the approbation and in concert with the British government, the provisions whereof, as contained in the following eighteen articles, will be duly and faithfully observed.

" 1. Shah Shuja-ul-Mulk disclaims all title on the part of himself, his heirs and successors, to all the territories lying on either bank of the river Indus that may be possessed by the Maharajah, viz., Kashmir, including its limits E. W. N. S., together with the fort of Attak, Chach, Hazara, Khebel, Aub, and its dependencies, on the left bank of the aforesaid river, and on the right bank Peshavar, with the Usafzai territory, Khataks, Hasht Nagar, Michni, Kohat, Hangu, and all the places dependant of Peshavar, as far as the Khaibar Pass; Bannu, the Vazivi territory, Daur, Tank Gorak Kalabagh, and Khushalgar, with their dependant districts, Dera Ismail Khan and its dependencies, together with Dera Ghazi Khan, Kot Mittan, Omar Kot, and their dependant territory, Sanghur, Harand, Dajal, Hajipur Rajanpur, and the three Kachis, as well as Munkera, with its district, and the province of Multan, situated on the left bank. These countries and places are considered to be the property, and to form the estate of the Maharajah; and the Shah neither has, nor will have, any concern with them; they belong to the Maharajah and his posterity, from generation to generation.

" 2. The people of the country on the other side of Khaibar will not be suffered to commit robberies and aggressions, or any disturbances, on this side. If any defaulter on either state, who has embezzled the revenue, take refuge in the territory of the other, each party engages to surrender him; and no person shall obstruct the passage of the stream which issues out of the Khaibar defile, and supplies the fort of Fatahghar with water, according to ancient usage.

" 3. As, agreeably to the Treaty established between the British Government and the Maharajah, no one can cross from the left to the right bank of the Satlej without a passport from the Maharajah, the same rule shall be observed regarding the passage of the Indus, whose waters join the Satlej, and no one shall be allowed to cross the Indus without the Maharajah's permission.

" 4. Regarding Shikarpur and the territory of Sindh, lying on the right bank of the Indus, the Shah will agree to abide by whatever may be settled as right and proper, in conformity with the happy relations of friendship subsisting with the Maharajah through Sir C. Wade.

" 5. When the Shah shall have established his authority in Kabul and Qandhar, he will annually send the Maharajah the following articles, viz. fifty-five high-bred horses, of approved colour and pleasant paces, eleven Persian scymitars, seven Persian poniards, twenty-five good mules, fruits of various kinds, both dry and fresh, and Sirdas or musk melons, of a sweet and delicate flavour (to be sent throughout the year), by way of Kabul river and Peshavar; grapes, pomegranates, apples, almonds, raisins, pistahs or chesnuts, an abundant supply of each; as well as a piece of satin of every colour; choghas of fir, kim khabs wrought with gold and silver, and Persian carpet, altogether to the number of one hundred and one pieces; all these articles the Shah will continue to send to the Maharajah every year.

" 6. Each party shall address the other on terms of equality.

" 7. Merchants of Afghanistan who may be desirous of trading to Lahaur, Amratsar, or any other parts of the Maharajah's possessions, shall not be stopped or molested on their way; on the contrary, strict orders shall be issued to facilitate their intercourse, and the Maharajah engages to observe the same line of conduct on his part with respect to Afghanistan.

" 8. The Maharajah will yearly send to the Shah the following articles, in the way of friendship—fifty-five pieces of shawls, twenty-five pieces of muslin, eleven dupatahs, five pieces of kim khab, five scarfs, five turbans, fifty-five loads of barah rice (peculiar to Peshavar).

" 9. Any of the Maharajah's officers who may be deputed to Afghanistan to purchase horses, or on any other business, as well as those who may be sent by the Shah into the Panjab for the purpose of purchasing piece goods or shawls, &c. to the amount of eleven thousand rupees, will be treated by both sides with due attention, and every facility will be afforded to them in the execution of their commissions.

"10. Whenever the armies of the two states may happen to be assembled at the same place, on no account shall the slaughter of kine be permitted to take place.

"11. In the event of the Shah receiving an auxiliary force from the Maharajah, whatever booty may be acquired from the Barakzais in jewels, horses, arms great and small, shall be equally divided between the two contracting parties. If the Shah should succeed in obtaining possession of such property without the assistance of the Maharajah's troops, the Shah agrees to send a portion of it to the Maharajah by way of friendship.

"12. An exchange of missions charged with letters and presents shall constantly take place between the two parties.

"13. Should the Maharajah require the aid of any of the Shah's troops, in furtherance of the objects contemplated by this Treaty, the Shah engages to send a force, commanded by one of his principal officers. In like manner the Maharajah will furnish the Shah, when required, with an auxiliary force, composed of Mahomedans, and commanded by one of his principal officers, as far as Kabul, in furtherance of the objects contemplated by this Treaty. When the Maharajah may go to Peshavar the Shah will depute a Shahzada to visit him, on which occasion the Maharajah will receive and dismiss him with the honour and consideration due to his rank and dignity.

" 14. The friends and enemies of each of the three high powers, that is to say, the British and Sikh Governments and that of Shuja-ul-Mulk, shall be the friends and enemies to all and to each of them.

" 15. Shah Shuja-ul-Mulk engages, after the attainment of his object, to pay without fail to the Maharajah the sum of two lakhs of rupees, of the Nanak, Shahv, or Kaldar currency, calculating from the date on which the Sikh troops may be despatched for the purpose of reinstating His Majesty in Kabul, in consideration of the Maharajah stationing a force of not less than five thousand men, cavalry and infantry, of the Mahomedan persuasion, within the limits of the Peshavar territory, for the support of the Shah, and to be sent to the aid of His Majesty whenever the British Government, in concert and counsel with the Maharajah, shall deem their aid necessary ; and when any matter of great importance may arise in the westward, such measures will be adopted with regard to it as may seem expedient and proper at the time to the British and Sikh Governments. In the event of the Maharajah requiring the aid of any of the Shah's troops, a deduction will be made in the subsidy, proportioned to the period for which such aid may be afforded ; and the British Government holds itself responsible for the punctual payment of the above sum annually to the Maharajah so long as the provisions of this Treaty are duly observed.

" 16. Shah Shuja-ul-Mulk agrees to relinquish, for himself, his heirs, and successors, all claims of supremacy and

arrears of tribute over the territories now held by the Mirs
of Sindh (which will continue to belong to the Mirs and
their successors in perpetuity), on condition of the payment
to him by the Mirs of such a sum as may be determined,
under the mediation of the British Government, one million
five hundred thousand of rupees, and of such payment being
made over by him to the Maharajah Ranjit Singh on these
payments being completed. Article 4, of 12th March,
1833, will be considered cancelled, and the customary
interchange of letters and suitable presents between the
Maharajah and the Mirs of Sindh shall be maintained as
heretofore.

" 17. When Shah Shuja-ul-Mulk shall have succeeded in
establishing his authority in Afghanistan, he shall not attack
nor molest his nephew the ruler of Hirat, in the possession
of the territories subject to his government.

" 18. Shah Shuja-ul-Mulk binds himself, his heirs, and
successors, to refrain from entering into negotiations with
any foreign state without the knowledge and consent of the
British and Sikh Governments, and to oppose any power
having the desire to invade the Sikh or British territories
by force of arms, to the utmost of his ability.

" The three powers, parties in this Treaty, viz. the British
Government, the Maharajah Ranjit Singh, and Shah Shuja-
ul-Mulk, cordially agree to the foregoing articles. There
shall be no deviation from them in any way whatever, and
in that case the present Treaty shall be considered binding
for ever, and this Treaty shall come into operation from and

after the date on which the seals and signatures of the three contracting parties shall have been affixed.

" Done at Lahaur, this 26th day of June, in the year of our Lord 1838, corresponding with the 15th of the mouth of Asarh, 1895, æra Bikarmajit.

(Signed) " AUCKLAND,

" RANJIT SINGH,

" SHAH SHUJAH-UL-MULK."

While the Governor-General was ratifying the above-mentioned treaty with the Maharajah, and with Qazi Mohammed Husain, on the part of Shah Shuja-ul-Mulk, and was framing the plan of the projected expedition, the arrival of advices from England, " characterized doubtless by Lord Palmerston's usual vigour,* led to the renewed considera-

* I forgot to mention in the preceding and proper place, when I was invited by the minister of the Amir of Kabul, in the presence of M. Vikovich, the conversation turned on the composition, taste, and love of poetry. The Russian agent said to the minister that Europeans consider the taste for poetry a sign of lazy habits, but the scientific inventions productive of wealth ; and the tact of the principal leaders of the politics of the states are the national amusement and talk of the day. The Mirza replied that if that was the case, no nation in Europe can boast of excelling in science more than the English; and their successful career in India, China, and Barmis says much for the excellence of their politics. Here M. Vikovich hesitatingly replied that Russia has now roused from slumber, and her mi-

OUAZI MAHOMED HUSSAN KHAN.

tion of the plan for establishing a British influence at Kabul, by the restoration of Shah Shuja," strengthened and confirmed the determination of the Earl of Auckland, and thus the expedition of Afghanistan was resolved on.

On the return of Sir William Macnaghten from the Court of Lahaur, preparations were made to put the contemplated schemes of policy into immediate execution, and the declaration of war was proclaimed and circulated in all parts of India and Afghanistan.

Declaration on the part of the Right Honourable the Governor-General of India.

Simla, 1st October, 1838.

" THE Right Honourable the Governor-General of India having, with the concurrence of the Supreme Council, directed the assemblage of a British force for service across the Indus, his Lordship deems it proper to publish the

---

nister Count Nesselrode is considered at the present age to be matchless in politics, and would shake the whole of Europe if there was not one rival for him, " Vazir i daval i Kharajah Inglisyah (the English minister for the foreign affairs), Lord Palmerston." He also added that Louis Philippe, King of the French, is the wisest sovereign, but fears Count Nesselrode, who has not yet acknowledged him as King of that nation.

following exposition of the reasons which have led to this important measure.

"It is a matter of notoriety that the treaties entered into by the British government in the year 1832 with the Mirs of Sindh, the Navab of Bahavalpur, and the Maharajah Ranjit Singh, had for their object, by opening the navigation of the Indus, to facilitate the extension of commerce, and to gain for the British nation in Central Asia that legitimate influence which an interchange of benefits would naturally produce.

"With a view to invite the aid of the *de facto* rulers of Afghanistan in the measures necessary for giving full effect to those treaties, Sir Alexander Burnes was deputed, towards the close of the year 1836, on a mission to Dost Mohammed Khan, the chief of Kabul. The original subjects of that officer's mission were purely of a commercial nature. Whilst Sir Alexander Burnes, however, was on his journey to Kabul, information was received by the Governor-General that the troops of Dost Mohammed Khan had made a sudden and unprovoked attack on those of our ancient ally the Maharajah Ranjit Singh. It was naturally to be apprehended that His Highness the Maharajah would not be slow to avenge the aggression; and it was to be feared that the flames of war being once kindled in the very regions into which we were endeavouring to extend our commerce, the peaceful and beneficial purposes of the British government would be altogether frustrated. In order to avert a result so calamitous, the Governor

General resolved on authorising Sir Alexander Burnes to intimate to Dost Mohammed Khan that if he should evince a disposition to come to just and reasonable terms with the Maharajah, his Lordship would exert his good offices with his Highness for the restoration of an amicable understanding between the two powers. The Maharajah, with the characteristic confidence which he had uniformly placed in the faith and friendship of the British, at once assented to the proposition of the Governor-General, to the effect that, in the meantime, hostilities on his part should be suspended.

" It subsequently came to the knowledge of the Governor-General that a Persian army was besieging Hirat; that intrigues were actively prosecuted throughout Afghanistan, for the purpose of extending Persian influence and authority to the banks of, and even beyond, the Indus; and that the court of Persia had not only commenced a course of injury and insult to the officers of Her Majesty's mission in the Persian territory, but had afforded evidence of being engaged in designs wholly at variance with the principles and objects of its alliance with Great Britain.

"After much time spent by Sir A. Burnes in fruitless negotiation at Kabul, it appeared that Dost Mohammed Khan, chiefly in consequence of his reliance upon Persian encouragement and assistance, persisted, as respected his misunderstanding with the Sikhs, in urging the most unreasonable pretensions, such as the Governor-General could not, consistently with justice and his regard for the friendship of Maharajah Ranjit Singh, be the channel of submitting to the consideration of his Highness; that he avowed schemes of aggrandizement and ambition injurious to the security and peace of the frontiers of India; and that he openly threatened, in furtherance of those schemes, to call in every foreign aid which he could command. Ultimately, he gave his undisguised support to the Persian designs in Afghanistan, of the unfriendly and injurious character of which, as concerned the British character in India, he was well apprized, and by his utter disregard of the views and interests of the British government, compelled Sir A. Burnes to leave Kabul without having effected any of the objects of his mission.

"It was now evident that no further interference could be exercised by the British government to bring about a good understanding between the Sikh ruler and Dost Mohammed Khan, and the hostile policy of the latter chief showed too plainly that, so long as Kabul remained under his government, we could never hope that tranquillity of our neighbourhood would be secured, or that the interests of our Indian empire would be preserved inviolate.

"The Governor-General deems it in this place necessary to revert to the siege of Hirat and the conduct of the Persian nation. The siege of that city has now been carried on by the Persian army for many months. The attack upon it was an unjustifiable and cruel aggression, perpetrated and continued notwithstanding the solemn and repeated remonstrances of the English envoy at the court of Persia, and after every just and becoming offer had been made and re-

jected. The besieged have behaved with a gallantry and
fortitude worthy of the justice of their cause; and the
Governor-General would yet indulge the hope that their
heroism may enable them to maintain a successful defence
until succours shall reach them from British India. In the
meantime the ulterior designs of Persia, affecting the interests of the British government, have been, by a succession
of events, more and more openly manifested. The Governor-
General has recently ascertained by an official despatch from
Sir J. Macneil, Her Majesty's envoy, that His Excellency
has been compelled, by a refusal of his just demands, by a
systematic course of disrespect adopted towards him by the
Persian government, to quit the court of the Shah, and to
make a public declaration of the cessation of all intercourse
between the two governments. The necessity under which
Great Britain is placed of regarding the present advance of
the Persian army into Afghanistan as an act of hostility
towards herself, has also been officially communicated to the
Shah, under the express of Her Majesty's Government.

"The chiefs of Qandhar (brothers of Dost Mohammed
Khan of Kabul) have avowed their adherence to the Persian policy, with the same full knowledge of its opposition
to the rights and interests of the British nation in India,
and have been openly assisting in the operations against
Hirat.

"In the crisis of affairs consequent upon the retirement
of our envoy from Kabul, the Governor-General felt the
importance of taking immediate measures for arresting the

rapid progress of foreign intrigue and aggression towards
our territories.

" His attention was naturally drawn at this conjuncture
to the position and claims of Shah Shuja-ul-Mulk, a monarch who, when in power, had cordially acceded to the
measures of united resistance to external enmity, which
were at that time judged necessary by the British government, and who, on his empire being usurped by its present
rulers, had found an honourable asylum in the British
dominions.

" It had been clearly ascertained, from the information
furnished by the various officers who have visited Afghanistan, that the Barakzai chiefs, from their disunion and
unpopularity, are ill-fitted, under any circumstances, to be
useful allies to the British government, and to aid us in our
just and necessary measures of national defence. Yet so
long as they refrained from proceedings injurious to our
interests and security, the British Government acknowledged
and respected their authority ; but a different policy appeared to be now more than justified by the conduct of
those chiefs, and to be indispensable to our own safety.
The welfare of our possessions in the East requires that we
should have on our western frontier an ally who is interested
in resisting aggression and establishing tranquillity, in the
place of chiefs ranging themselves in subservience to a
hostile power, and seeking to promote schemes of conquest
and aggrandizement.

" After serious and mature deliberation, the Governor-

General was satisfied that a pressing necessity, as well as every consideration of policy and justice, warranted us in espousing the cause of Shah Shuja-ul-Mulk, whose popularity throughout Afghanistan had been proved to his Lordship by the strong and unanimous testimony of the best authorities. Having arrived at this determination, the Governor-General was further of opinion that it was just and proper no less from the position of Maharajah Ranjit Singh, than from his undeviating friendship towards the British Government, that his Highness should have the offer of becoming a party to the contemplated operations.

"Sir William H. Macnaghten was accordingly deputed in June last to the court of his Highness, and the result of his mission has been the conclusion of a tripartite treaty by the British Government, the Maharajah, and Shah Shuja-ul-Mulk, whereby his Highness is guaranteed in his present possessions, and has bound himself to co-operate for the restoration of the Shah to the throne of his ancestors. The friends and enemies of any one of the contracting parties have been declared to be the friends and enemies of all.

"Various points had been adjusted which had been the subjects of discussion between the British Government and his Highness the Maharajah, the identity of whose interests with those of the Honourable Company has now been made apparent to all the surrounding states. A guaranteed independence will, upon favourable conditions, be tendered to the Mirs of Sindh, and the integrity of Hirat, in the possession of its present ruler, will be fully respected; while

2 c

by the measures completed or in progress, it may reasonably
be hoped that the general freedom and security of commerce
will be promoted; that the name and just influence of the
British government will gain their proper footing among the
nations of Central Asia; that tranquillity will be established
upon the most important frontier of India; and that a lasting barrier will be raised against hostile intrigue and en-
croachment.

"His Majesty Shah Shuja-ul-Mulk will enter Afghanistan, surrounded by his own troops, and will be supported
against foreign interference and factious opposition by a
British army. The Governor-General confidently hopes
that the Shah will be speedily replaced on the throne by
his own subjects and adherents; and when once he shall be
secured in power, and the independence and integrity of
Afghanistan established, the British army will be with-
drawn. The Governor-General has been led to these
measures by the duty which is imposed on him of providing
for the security of the possessions of the British crown; but
he rejoices that, in the discharge of his duty, he will be
enabled to assist in restoring the union and prosperity of
the Afghan people. Throughout the approaching operations, British influence will be sedulously employed to further every measure of general benefit, to reconcile differences,
to secure oblivion of injuries, and to put an end to the dis-
tractions by which, for so many years, the welfare and happiness of the Afghans have been impaired. Even to the
chiefs, whose hostile proceedings have given just cause of

offence to the British Government, it will seek to secure liberal and honourable treatment, on their tendering early submission, and ceasing from opposition to that course of measures which may be judged the most suitable for the general advantage of their country.

" By order of the Right Honourable the Governor-General of India.

(Signed)   " W. H. MACNAGHTEN,

" *Secretary to the Government of India,*

"*with the Governor-General.*"

Immediately after this a few men of war were ordered through the Bombay government to land troops in the Persian island named Kharak; and having taken possession of the place, waited there for further advice. It was also suggested that a large number of British forces should be collected at Firozpur, and proceeding thence in company with the Shah Shuja, should march upon Kabul, passing through Sindh, the Bolan Pass, Qandhar, and Ghazni; and that the Shah Zadah Taimur, with the Sikh contingent, should shape his course within the Panjab, so as to divert the attention of the Kabul chief from the Khaibar side. The rendezvous of the troops, now nominated the army of the Indus, was appointed

2 c 2

to be at Firozpur, where the Governor-General had an interview with the Maharajah Ranjit Singh.

Let us turn back to the affairs in Persia. Sir John Macneil, who was compelled to leave the Persian camp, and who was on his way back to the Turkish frontier, was now apprised of the arrival of the man of war, and wrote immediately to Colonel Stoddart, still in the Persian camp, to inform the Shah of the proceedings undertaken by the British government, and if his Majesty were not to relinquish the siege of Hirat, the army now landed in the island of Kharak will be directed to march through Persia. The gallant colonel submitted the following proposal to the Shah, which perplexed and brought His Majesty to his senses, and the bugle of retreat was sounded, and the siege of Hirat raised.

"I AM directed by Her Britannic Majesty's Minister Plenipotentiary to state that he has been entrusted by Her Majesty's Ministers to inform your Majesty that the British Government look upon this enterprise in which your Majesty is engaged against the Afghans as being undertaken in a spirit of hostility towards British India, and as being totally incompatible with the spirit and intention of the alliance

which has been established between Great Britain and
Persia. That consequently, if this project is persevered in,
the friendly relations which up to this time have so happily
subsisted between Great Britain and Persia must necessarily
cease, and that Great Britain must take such steps as she
may think best calculated to provide for the security of the
possessions of the British crown.

"I am further directed to inform your Majesty, that if
Hirat should have surrendered to your Majesty, the British
Government will consider your Majesty's continuing to
occupy that, or any other portion of Afghanistan, as a
hostile demonstration against England.

" Her Majesty's Minister Plenipotentiary anxiously hopes
that, by speedily withdrawing the Persian army into your
Majesty's own dominions, your Majesty will avert the in-
evitable consequences of persevering in a course of hostility
to England.

"The British government also demands reparation for
the violence offered to its messenger, which is a matter quite
distinct from the question of Hirat. Her Britannic Majesty's
Minister Plenipotentiary trusts your Majesty will grant that
reparation in the manner which he pointed out, and thus relieve the British Government from the necessity of having
recourse to other measures to exact it.

" Your Majesty is no doubt informed by the government
of Fars that a body of British troops, and a naval armament
consisting of five ships of war, have already arrived in the
Persian Gulf, and that for the present the troops have landed

on the island of Kharak. The measures your Majesty may adopt in consequence of this representation will decide the future movements and proceedings of that armament; but your Majesty must perceive, from the view which Her Majesty's Government has taken of the present state of affairs, and from the effect which must have been produced in the minds of Her Majesty's Ministers and the British authorities in India by the subsequent proceedings of the Persian Government, with which they were not then acquainted, that nothing but the immediate adoption of measures to comply with the demands of the British Government can induce the authorities acting under the order of that Government to suspend the measures which are in progress for the defence of British interests, and the vindication of British honour.

"In the meantime Her Britannic Majesty's Minister Plenipotentiary will pursue his journey to the Turkish frontier, and will remove all the English from the Persian territory; but he trusts that the bad counsel of the ill-disposed persons who have induced your Majesty to persevere in a course which has placed affairs in this position will no longer influence your Majesty; and that, guided by your own wisdom and by a regard to the true interests of Persia, your Majesty will adopt such measures as will enable Her Britannic Majesty's Minister Plenipotentiary to return to your Majesty's Court, and restore to its former footing of cordiality the alliance between the two governments. Your Majesty has seen that all Her Britannic Majesty's Minister Plenipotentiary has stated to your Majesty in regard to these matters, has been dictated by sincerity and truth, and by an anxious desire to avert the evils which it was obvious must result from a perseverance in the course which the Persian Government was pursuing; and he again assures your Majesty that nothing but immediate danger and injury to Persia can result from rejecting the demands of the British Government.

"That God may guide your Majesty to a wise decision, and that he may forgive those whose evil counsels have led to such a state of things, is the earnest prayer of an old and faithful servant, who has ever been a sincere well-wisher of the Shah and the Persian Government."

Many people, who pretended to be well informed in the affairs of Afghanistan, said, on the arrival of the dispatch of Colonel Stoddart, stating that the Persians had raised the siege of Hirat, that now there was no necessity any longer for the government of India to persevere in crossing the English army beyond the Indus into those distant regions. This circumstance, indeed, altered the disposition of the campaign in respect to the number of the troops, but it did not change the measures of the Governor-General; and in a political point of view his Lordship justly felt it incumbent upon himself to remember that there were many reasons in existence of great weight and importance which require the completion of his contemplated objects.

Firstly: Though the Persians had raised the siege of Hirat on the 9th of September, 1838, yet the forts and districts of Ghuryan, Kurukh, Sabzvar, and Farah, at two marches beyond the boundary of Qandhar, were still occupied by the Persian authorities; and from the following letters it will appear that the British officer at the court of Persia was urging upon the Persian government to give up the possession of those places to the Afghans, and that on the 29th of November, 1838, he had not succeeded in his negotiation; and I may safely state that the fort and district of Ghuryan were not restored by the Persians to the Hirat government till more than a year after the British had occupied Afghanistan, or long after the departure and failure of the mission of Major Todd from Hirat.

From Lieutenant-Colonel Sheil to His Excellency Mirza Masud, the Minister for Foreign Affairs.

Tehran, Nov. 22, 1838.

" In the communication which Colonel Stoddart conveyed to His Majesty the Shah, from his Excellency the British minister, subsequent to his departure from the Royal camp, his Excellency Sir John Macneil announced to His Majesty that if His Majesty should retain any portion of the Afghan territory, the British government will consider such a proceeding as a hostile proceeding against itself. Her Britannic Majesty's envoy extraordinary has now learnt that the troops which occupied Ghuryan, and also those which took possession of Farah, Sabzvar, and Khurrukh, in the name of the Shah of Persia, continue to hold those places in the name of His Persian Majesty.

" Agreeably to the instructions I have received from Sir John Macneil, I have the honour to request that your Excellency will furnish me with information on this subject, and I request you to state whether or not the troops which have occupied Ghuryan, Farrah, Sabzvar, and Khurrukh, hold these places for the Shah of Persia, or are subject to His Majesty's orders."

Tehran, Nov. 29, 1838.

" I HAVE the honour to acknowledge the receipt of your Excellency's letter of the 10th Ramadan (28th November), in reply to the communication which I addressed to you regarding the continued occupation by the Persian government of Ghuryan, Farah, Sabzvar, and Khurrukh.

" Your Excellency having given no reply sufficient to convey the information I sought, whether the above places were garrisoned by Persian troops, or were held by troops in the name of His Persian Majesty, I am obliged to conclude from your silence that the intelligence which had been received by His Excellency Sir John Macneil, on this subject, is correct, and that the above places are held by troops in the name of His Majesty the Shah, and are under His Majesty's orders.

" I am instructed by Her Britannic Majesty's minister plenipotentiary to intimate to His Persian Majesty's ministers, that he feels it to be his duty to protest against the continued occupation of Ghuryan by Persian troops being regarded as constituting any right on the part of Persia to retain permanent possession of that fortress or district.

" With regard to Farah, Sabzvar, and Khurrukh, I am directed by his Excellency Sir John Macneil to call on the Persian government to fulfil the engagement into which His Majesty the Shah entered at Hirat, of complying with the whole of the demands of the British government, and to issue the necessary orders for immediate evacuation of these places, furnishing me at the same time with an authentic copy of that order, for the information of the British government."

Secondly: If the army had not moved, the occupation of those places would not, in consequence of any negotiation, be abandoned by the Persians; and if they were allowed to keep it, the results were apparent, and are well described in a letter from Sir John Macneil to Lord Palmerston.

" If the Shah should effect the subjugation of any portion of Afghanistan, he will employ the influence of the chiefs who may have submitted to him to disturb the power and the quiet of those who have not ; and when he has been elated with success, and has secured a footing in that country, from which it may be difficult to drive him, I fear that apprehension of a rupture with England would no longer deter him from prosecuting his conquests ; and though he might hesitate to seek foreign aid for the purpose of getting possession of Hirat, he might not improbably be induced to have recourse to it for the purpose of enabling him to retain a conquest which he had already made."

Thirdly : M. Vikovich was even then distributing money to the chiefs of Qandhar, who, in adherence to the treaty concluded between them and Persia, and guaranteed by the Count Simonich, were acting inimically towards Hirat under the influence of the personal presence and guidance of Captain Vikovich.

Fourthly : If the Governor-General were to leave the chiefs of Qandhar and the Amir of Kabul to pursue their own plans, the result would be that Persian agents, superintended and directed by Russian officers, would be placed in the court of the above chieftains ; and intrigues would have been conducted and extended by them even to the very heart of India; for branch missions of the united states of Persia and Russia had already been passing through Sindh, &c.

Fifthly: By the Tripartite treaty, which was already ratified, the British government and the Lahaur Court were bound to replace Shah Shuja, who at the time was earnestly sought by the Afghans, and in whose person the English found the means of holding a friendly relation with the kingdom of Afghanistan.

Under all the preceding grave and urgent considerations the Governor-General ordered the march of the army of the Indus; and it left Ferozpor on the 10th of December, 1838. The whole number of the force available for employment in the Afghanistan expedition, according to Major Hough's account, was as follows:—

	Men.
1st. The army of the Indus (from Bengal) under Major-General Sir Willoughby Cotton .	9,500
2nd. Major-General Duncan's reserve division, at Ferozpor, &c.	4,250
3rd. Shah Shuja's contingent	6,000
4th. The Bombay force under His Excellency Lieutenant-General Sir John (afterwards Lord) Keane	5,600

Men.

5th. The Bombay reserve or Sindh force . . . 3,000

      Total number to act in Sindh and

        Afghanistan 28,350

Previous to the opening of the campaign I was attached to the Mission, and the Governor-General, after a long conference with me on the various points connected with the progress of the army, and the advancement of the views of the government in Afghanistan, made me the bearer of his letters to the address of the bankers at Multan and to the Lohani merchants at Darahband, for the purpose of raising money, collecting supplies, and employing carriages for the use of the army. Sir Alexander Burnes was directed to go ahead of the army and negotiate an offensive and defensive treaty with the Mirs of Khairpur in the Upper Sindh; and Sir Henry Pottinger to form the same with the Mirs of Haidarabad in the Lower Sindh; while Major Mackison had to negotiate with the Navab of Bahavalpur, or the Daudpotra chief, to facilitate the progress of the army in his territory, and to supply Shah Shuja with certain equipage.

The bankers in Multan and the Lohanis in the

Derahbad were highly flattered with the contents of the letters from the Earl of Auckland. The former sent boats down the Chenab and the Indus, loaded with money and grain, to meet the wants of the army on its arrival at Shikarpur; and in addition to this they lent their personal assistance to Major Thompson and others, the commissariat officers who followed me into that city. The latter also collected a considerable number of camels, and brought provisions after the army to Qandhar.

The judicious proceedings and negotiations of Major Mackison with the Daudpotra chief gave ample comforts and easy means to get supplies to the army of the Indus; and I myself heard Sir Willoughby Cotton saying that every one in his camp seemed well satisfied while passing through the Bahavalpur territory.

As to the progress and results of the negotiations committed to Sir Alexander Burnes and to Sir Henry Pottinger in Sindh, I have only this remark to make in this place: that after a very short period of successful negotiations by those functionaries, and a short time of their absence from that country, the fate of that dominion has been finally doomed, and it is now connected to and joined with the British empire of India; wherefore I deem it desirable to reserve my saying on such grave subject, will put the whole matter briefly into one view in a separate chapter. It will prove amusing to the readers to find from what I have quoted, the highest and un-questionable authorities on this point, that how justly and how far back the Mirs of Sindh had discovered our ambitious designs for the conquest of their coun-try; and how prudently they suspected our travellers and even myself, who went to examine their country; and how far they were right in their anticipations is now clearly understood, since we have become the masters of their country, and they are banished.

END OF VOL. I.

London: Printed by WILLIAM CLOWES and SONS, Stamford Street.

LaVergne, TN USA
27 January 2010
171332LV00004B/74/P